*On Deconstructing Life-Worlds*
Buddhism, Christianity, Culture

# AAR

## American Academy of Religion
## Cultural Criticism Series

Cleo McNelly Kearns
Editor

Number 3

*ON DECONSTRUCTING LIFE-WORLDS*
BUDDHISM, CHRISTIANITY, CULTURE

by
Robert Magliola

# ON DECONSTRUCTING LIFE-WORLDS

## BUDDHISM, CHRISTIANITY, CULTURE

by
Robert Magliola

Scholars Press
Atlanta, Georgia

# ON DECONSTRUCTING LIFE-WORLDS
## BUDDHISM, CHRISTIANITY, CULTURE

by

## Robert Magliola

With some significant differences Part Two, section (iv), and parts of Part Two, section (iii) of the present work appeared earlier in the present author's "In No Wise is Healing Holistic," in David Loy, ed., *Healing Deconstruction: Postmodern Thought in Buddhism and Christianity,* also published by Scholars Press (1996).

Grateful acknowledgement of permission to cite is made to the following copyright holders:

HarperCollins Publishers Ltd., London, U.K., for passages from Tom Riseman's translation of and commentary on the *I Ching* and in his *Introduction to the* I Ching (1980)

Bantam Books, New York City, for Roger Shattuck's English translation of Guillaume Apollinaire's "Le Paon" in *Modern European Poetry* edited by William Barnstone et al. (1966)

Felix Stefanile, for 14 lines of the poem "The Day We Danced the Saint" in A.L. Lazarus, Barriss Mills, Felix Stefanile, Bruce Woodford, *A Suit of Four,* Purdue University Press, West Lafayette (1973)

**Library of Congress Cataloging in Publication Data**
Magliola, Robert R.
    On deconstructing life-worlds : Buddhism, Christianity, Culture
/ by Robert Magliola.
        p.     cm. — (American Academy of Religion cultural criticism
series ; no. 3)
    ISBN 0-7885-0295-6 (cloth : alk. paper). — ISBN 0-7885-0296-4
(paper : alk. paper)
    1. Philosophy and religion.  2. Magliola, Robert R.  3. Derrida,
Jacques.  4. Prāsaṅgika.  5. Buddhism—Relations—Christianity.
6. Christianity and other religions—Buddhism.    I. Title.
II. Series.
BL51.M247  1996
291.1'75—dc20                                                    96-27889
                                                                 CIP

Printed in the United States of America
on acid-free paper

# DEDICATION

*Flori Carmeli oblatus,*
  this book is dedicated

-to my beloved three children, Lorinda-marie, Jon-carlo, Clara-marie;
-to the dear Chinese People, and some Saffron Robes;
-to Jacques Derrida, the Black Robe of Braille;
-to Karl Rahner, S.J., blackrobe;
-to David *Tracy*.

The term *mantra* "signifies a 'crossing over', through thought (Skt. root *man*, 'to think', and *tr*, 'to cross over') . . . ."
> —Aurobindo, *The Secret of the Veda* (cited in H. Coward, *Derrida and Indian Philosophy*, p. 64)

mais...

"Mais si *tr* est chaque fois altéré, transformé, déplacé, par ce qui paraît le compléter, il garde une sorte de suffisance, non pas une identité à soi, sens ou corps propre, mais une étrange et altière indépendance. Il ne la tient pas du noyau sémantique *trans* ou *tra*.
  Ni un tout ni un morceau, ni métaphore ni métonymie..."
> —Jacques Derrida, *La Vérité en Peinture*, p. 196

-to dear Flannery O'Connor, here below the Robes so she can better deconstruct them.

# FOUR-Corner Table of CONTENTS

— *CATUṢKOṬIKĀ* (SKT.): CALLED NAGARJUNA'S "FOUR-CORNERED LOGIC"

—"...THE ENSIGN, SAYS THE LORD, WHOSE FIRE IS IN ZION, AND HIS
FURNACE IN JERUSALEM." —Isaiah 31:9

PREFACE

by

Edith Wyschogrod


Robert Magliola has written a highly unusual book. To identify its
genre would already be to misread it. Perhaps the best way to enter
it, is to consider it as a meditation upon the mark of crosshatching,
i.e., the X. For Magliola this X displays the space of his life, the
vectors of Christianity and Buddhist meditative practice. The work
elucidates both the writer's life and the non-space (as it were) between
these religions.

Magliola's previous book published in the West on religious
thought, *Derrida on the Mend*, shows how Derrida's writings and the
thought of Nagarjuna, the great Madhyamika or Emptiness School
theoretician, intersect, already prefiguring the crosshatching explicated
in the present book. In the earlier work, he analyzes the reductio ad
absurdum arguments of the Madhyamika which, he shows, operate in
the manner of Derrida's deconstruction of entitative formulae. But in
*Derrida on the Mend*, the crosshatching is itself crosshatched in that
Christianity is to enter into itself, into what for Magliola is its inmost
core, the doctrine of the trinity, and rethink itself in the light of a
deconstructive/differential practice. In my view this book was not only
a rich and original reading of deconstruction, but a groundbreaking work
of Catholic theologizing. Only a very few Catholic thinkers—Jean-Luc
Marion is another—are both schooled in classical and medieval
metaphysics and have developed startlingly original positions. Magliola,
whose work is not only difficult but whose imbrication in Buddhism
increases its complexity, deserves the full attention of those interested
in doctrinal issues and in inter-religious conversation. What distinguishes Magliola's writings is the control of the tradition he is
deconstructing, of Buddhist texts and Chinese culture (nine years of
teaching and research in Taiwan) and of French, English, German and
Latin literary and philosophical texts (he has a Princeton doctorate in
comparative literature with a concentration in phenomenology/
hermeneutics).

The crosshatching of the present book works along multiple axes: the X is Christianity's cross turning on its side as well as the striking through of a word to show that an essentialist concept or reading is to be ontologically reconfigured (Heidegger) or semantically disseminated (Derrida). But this work is not *about* technical issues; it is *about* Magliola's life, a life whose atomic simples, what he calls psycho-bio-graphemes, are exposed in all their nudity in juxtaposition with citations from Chinese texts and Western poetry. Magliola's erudition allows him to breathe easily in the discursive space of deconstruction, a space that reminds the reader of the poetry of John Ashbery in its movement from one conscious state to another. And like Derrida, who "invokes and mimes" his own terminology, so too Magliola invokes and mimes his own life.

Magliola recounts the crosshatching that constitutes the double-binds of his life: his Italian-American childhood (not at all the garden variety immigrant story); his several years in a Jesuit seminary with its pre-Vatican II regimen; his unhappy marriage; his struggles with the American academic establishment, both in Ivy League and State universities; his emigration to Taiwan. The first half of the work is a *cri de coeur*, impassioned and poetic. Here is an example: "What could have been the dear sweet Rose's gloriole years, and my years of strapping *virilità*, were irrevocably past. Her springtide and mine unspent... 'Reason enough to cry'. *O Sancta Mater Ecclesia*, you should have given us more options, somehow. Somehow." Part One concludes with a brief but wonderfully insightful reading of a passage about divine androgyny from Flannery O'Connor's "A Temple of the Holy Ghost."

The work's second half engages other issues: his consternation at those misreadings of Madhyamika Buddhism which give to the notion of emptiness a Yogacara or idealist reading, thus undermining Madhyamika's deconstructive power. This is not an issue of Buddhist scholasticism but one that relates to the crosshatched practices of meditation (described in various contexts by Magliola) as well as to Derrida's notion of *dénégation*, a negation that endlessly undoes itself. Thus Magliola writes: "Derridean trace, mark, etc., is perhaps the closest a Western reader has yet come to the Buddhist notion of *tattva*—thisness, thatness—the intersection of spontaneity (i.e., pure impermanence) and Buddhist relationality (i.e., pure dependency)." These notions when cited out of context may appear somewhat obscure, but along with such important conceptual matters as the doctrine of the two truths and the logic of the tetralemma, are meticulously analyzed.

The biographical segments of this memoir are not recollections in the manner of Proust's symbolic madeleine cakes and the theme of Vinteuil's sonata, post hoc creations of presence, but rather bring to the fore transitoriness and becoming in their very passage, the ungroundedness of things. For Magliola this ungroundedness implies a hope expressed in the concluding passage that the "samenesses" opened by a crosshatched differing/intersecting of Buddhism and Christianity, and Judaism, and other religions, "can help to heal the world."

# CROSSHATCHING THE BUDDHA, a Prolusion

> "Prolusion: n. [L. *prolusio*, prelude, fr. L. *proludere*, to
> play or practice beforehand, . . . .]
> 1. . . . . . . . . . . . . . . . . . . . . . . . . . . . . . .
> 2. An introductory and often tentative discourse."
> —*Webster's 3rd New International Dictionary*,
> excerpted

"To crosshatch: v.t. & i. To mark with series of parallel lines that cross,
especially obliquely."

"To hatch: v.t. 1. To produce (young) from an egg or eggs by incubation,
natural or artificial; to produce (young) from (eggs). 2. To originate;
concoct; contrive.
      v.i. 1. To produce young. [M.E. *hacchen*]"

"To hatch: v.t. 1. To mark with hatching. 2. To inlay in fine lines.
[F. *hacher*, to chop, hack. See 'hash']"
> —*Webster's New Collegiate Dictionary*,
> excerpted

> The "'criss-cross' [hatched] sayings of the old monks
> all over the country."
> — Zen/Ch'an idiom[1]

In "Mémoires d'aveugle: l'autoportrait et autre ruines," the exhibition
on blindness and art organized by Jacques Derrida at the Louvre in
1991,[2] blindness mimes its own inevitabilities,—black herbages of its
own dead sense, yes, but further flowerings too, of acuity, of vivification,
of fragrant scents. Incense. ("Can one sign with a perfume?"[3]) There is a
contemporary truism, and true enough, that self-portraiture, like
autobiography, is from the start purblind-to-itself. "L'ouvre où ne pas
voir," Derrida's computer filename for his Louvre essays,[4] puns in
quite other directions:—L'ouvre (Louvre) où/ou ne pas voir. 'The opening/

---

[1] See K'uan Yü Lu [Charles Luk], *Ch'an and Zen Teaching*, Second Series
(London: Rider and Co., 1961), p. 185 and ftnote 7.
[2] The exhibition assembled 60 works, most of them drawings, with Derrida's
annotating essays posted next to them.
[3] Derrida, "Ulysses Gramophone," in his *Acts of Literature*, ed. Derek Attridge
(London and N.Y.: Routledge, 1991), p. 297.
[4] See endnote 1 of M. R. Rubinstein's "Report from Paris: Sight Unseen," in *Art in
America* (April 1991), p. 53.

xiv *Crosshatching*

opener where one can't see'. Or, 'The opening/opener or not to see.'[5] With a touch (even to the computer), not-to-see can open up Writing. So self-portraiture and autobiography go on: go on in their other truths.

Part One of this book is so-called 'autobiography', postmodern autobiography because it knows that the most it can Write is other truths, truths to which it is blind/purblind (depending). Being that these truths are neither subjective nor objective, the irony is that they can only be generated if the author aims to be as true-to-memory as possible: this is to say, these other truths differ from but require the (author's) 'honest intent' to report his/her life—be it his/her so-called interior life or his/her public life—'as it really transpired'. It is precisely this 'honest intent' which forces reflexivity, and it is precisely to this reflexivity that postmoderners are so sensitive. Postmoderners realize autobiographies are willy-nilly *about* autobiographers-writing-autobiographies. And they realize the memories to which they aim to remain faithful are necessarily *displacements* from the start: indeed, 'honest efforts' serve to reiterate displacements and to deviate further. Nor is capitulation, a surrender to 'fictive intent', to so-called *subjectivity*, any sort of solution. Autobiography, after all, is about how one thinks to construct, interpret his/her life, and one doesn't 'perceive' his/her life as fiction. Thus, instead, the style of postmodern autobiography panto*mimes* its topic: its style acts out, and acts out flamboyantly, the life-story it is telling/making. It can be even said, in fact, that the aforesaid 'one' is verily two (or a doubled two, and more).

> Through the opening of the fourth surface or through the empty box in
> the center of the four squares, you shall have been swept off
> [*entraînés*], overcast [*surjetés*] in a still unended, unending
> labor [*travail*]. The square or, as you wish, the cube, will not
> close itself up.
> —Derrida, "Les greffes, retour au surjet"[6]

The word *mujo* [J.] means "without top" or
"has no top." There is nothing above
or outside this Buddha way.
> —Daido Loori, Sensei[7]

---

[5] There are other possibilities too, of course, quite a few of them. Derrida even makes mention of Venetian blinds,—the moveable slats, the alternating blind-spots, of a louver.

[6] In his *La dissémination* (Paris: Seuil, 1972), p. 398. My translation.

[7] In *The Ten Directions*, Vol. X, No. 1.

Part One aims to show how the philosophies/religions which it sets out in its last section (entitled "Crosshatch"), and the Quad*rature* it proposes, came about. How the Quadrature was *eked out* of my own life-experience—its rations, for better or worse, of happiness and deprivations. For I maintain that all philosophers, even the most 'rationalist', 'impersonal', and 'objective', write from and are written by their life-events, the theater of their lives, no matter from how deeply below the surface such psychic stage-machinery may happen to pull its strings, work its levers. A philosophical autobiography, instead, aims to *show* the strings and levers. *Afortiori*, perhaps, postmodern ones even *mimic* such a show (which is not to say either that they are *un*true, you understand).

A prophet 'speaks in front of, before'. Part One writes some prophetic lines, I think, underneath and between and before. About the Christianities. About the Catholic Church into which I was born. About the United States. About the American academic establishment. When one (two²) has traveled/lived in as many countries as I have, there are many chances to witness American arrogance around the world: the evidence just keeps on capitalizing. A witness can become quite red-tempered. Incensed. But the United States of America does not take criticism well. It is said prophets are hated: Shelved. And their writings unshelved. The compensation is that some prophets can wait and wait,—they have, it seems, a very long shelf-life. Part One's lines are compromised, of course. As Derrida's texts like to remind us, the etymology here is still from L. *compromittere*, 'to promise mutually': *com-*, 'mutually' + *promittere*, 'promise'. The truths of lines are clinched only as their readers are signatory to them. Are signatory to them.

With—
head: askant,
glance: patronizing,
lips: pursed,
gesture: dismissive,

more than one of my more casual acquaintances— usually a professor of literary criticism—has reproved my continuing interest in Jacques Derrida. Their unsolicited advice?— "That's dead already. Get with it, will you? And diversify! Cite a lot of different thinkers." Ah!—the patter of little criticism. (Christopher Frye's old riposte.) In fact, I dare say that I know many philosophers well, and that I do keep abreast of the 'latest developments'. My position, and it is a respectable one, is that the history of philosophy has been an ongoing iteration/reiteration of several so-called *moments*, though no doubt the West has privileged 'constructions' and the East has often privileged what can be called 'dissolutions'. What came to be named, in recent European philosophy, 'deconstruction' (a term more often evoked in English-language cultures and in disciplines other than philosophy) is really a reinscription-with-a-difference of one (or more) of these moments. Deconstruction reinscribes-with-a-difference all those moments in European philosophy which demonstrate that the principles of identity and self- identity, and all holisms no matter how cleverly displaced, are radically defective.

Jacques Derrida, the old (essence and) substance-abuser, enables me to work-out, *in contemporary discourse*, what I find to be re/peatedly the case in my own life-events, namely,—that things do not 'properly' assemble themselves into unities, into wholes. I would think that in every historical period there have been at least some thinkers whose primary attention has been upon dissolution in this sense. Unabashedly I believe[8] that the contribution of my ongoing work has been (1) to intersect Derridean and Madhyamikan Buddhist deconstructions; (2) to appropriate Derridean traces in terms that cut-across Buddhist ones (e.g., Derrida's *tout autre / la même*, and Nagarjuna's 'two truths'); (3) to appropriate (other) Derridean traces that enable some points of Christian theology to be differently re-thought. Is it not conspicuous, at least for those who know Derrida well, that I write/am-written by a script deviating considerably from his?

In his many pages on alchemical symbolism, Carl Jung several times remarks the (hidden) sameness of the chemical retort and its contents: or, otherwise put, the complicity of the container and the contained. Especially in the Part One which follows below, the style is contrived to enact this figure in elaborate ways, for all the while I was writing I knew that the momentum of the Writing—of Writing's secret shifts and shunts and checks—would work at counter-purposes to my 'stylistic' intentions. Derrida, for his part, again and again points to (what is *stricto sensu*) a logical fallacy,—the reinscription of a particular in/as its own universal: a member of a set is treated simultaneously as the definition of the whole set. In the interests of a sort of postmodern pedagogy (and its parody), I have introduced a kind

---

[8] Believing involves performatives, of course. Performatives, with all the liabilities thereof.

of *décalage* in the titles and subtitles of this book, and staggered other elements as well. There are asymmetries and loops and rifts. There are graphic traits that may drift or free-float. Some emblematic images may rear and collapse, sometimes in (possible) jest of their very pretension, and sometimes not. The ludic thread displays, I hope, some stitches popularized by Nabokov,—logogriphs, for example (but misaligned). And there are allusions to heraldry and the like, for the dear Gaels and Brits. At the same time, I have aimed to write the density, the Opaqueness of life. Because in some instances I have held back the specifics involved (and this to spare the privacy of individuals), my emotional measure—the index of my Rage, if you will—may sometimes seem, given the paucity of factual context, very *excessive*. To write these cases of traumata, lesser and greater, I have evoked the style of 19th and early 20th century chronicles of *la vie intérieure*: descriptions of 'states-of-soul' (but askew), and so-called 'objective correlatives' (but fractured). (For what it is worth to the reader: be advised that, three months ago 'as of this writing', a Zen Master with full and 'authentic' transmission in the Sanbo Kyodan line, who is also a Roman Catholic priest 'in good standing', advised me—"Ride your Rage, ride it all the way to liberation.")

This book's proportions are out of whack. Besides, each time I supplemented and supplemented, I summoned forth the manuscript again: most of it was composed in the early 1990's, but I have kept needling it with nonces and pertinences all the way into 1996. And the text transgresses topic-categories and genre-boundaries. Because Part Two follows logocentric conventions, and Part One does not, this book swings, perhaps, on refractory hinges. Like life's text. And like life's text (don't be fooled), the *soi-disant* 'autobiography' does *not* come full circle.

This book's text has *rip-stitches*, no doubt many sorts of them, which enable a devoiding of its logocentric assertions (as does life's text). Which is not to say the logocentrisms (must) lack validity (L. 'strong', 'effective', 'healthy'), since—as Madhyamika Buddhism explains very adequately—*saṃvṛti* can have a kind of validity (see Part Two). In Part One, many of the rip-stitches are intended (though 'silent' and very easily missed), so readers may collaborate, if they wish, in the author's version of how life's text can build and de-void. In the moments of cutting (intending/deconstructing), the etcher cannot see the point of contact between stylus and plate.[9] No doubt the (decon-structive) reader will pull stitches on me, on my intentions, even on my deconstructive rip-stitches, and no doubt the text, the Writing,—with its relentless crossing of diagram and program, repetition and change,[10]—will devoid both of us and itself. As will others/Other. While all the while, the strings of holisms at once (re)constitute. If Madhyamika Buddhism's 'two truths' can teach westerners anything (and Madhyamika Buddhism, like all the Buddhisms, surely can), it is this constitution/devoidness, constitution/devoidness, constitution/devoid-ness, ... , so serviceable both to secular deconstructionists and religious theologians, as well as so many others (see Part Two).

While I do maintain that the religions of Buddhism and Christianity make their contributions precisely by way of their *differing* from each other, it does *not* follow that European Christianity cannot *also* learn something from Asia,—from Hindus and Buddhists in particular. Nagarjuna's 'two truths' can provide Christianity an effective way of talking about constitution/devoidness in its *own* Christian tradition (see Part Two), a constitution/devoidness which has always been there but which Christian theology has not much addressed, simply because Greco-Roman thought does not serve the 'two truths' well, can't formulate them well. Indeed, how unlike its present form Christian theology would be today if Christianity and its Scriptures would have moved primarily Eastwards instead of West, away from Hellenic and Roman essentialism instead of into it.

> A brother went to Abbot Theodore and began to question him and to ask about things which he had not yet experienced or put into practice himself. The elder said to him, 'As yet you have not found a boat, and you have not put your luggage aboard, and you have not yet begun to cross the sea. How can you speak as if you had already arrived at the place you are planning to go to? When you have put into practice the things you talk about so well, then you will be able to speak...'.
>
> —*Sayings of the Desert Fathers (Verba Seniorum)*[11]

---

[9] As draftsmen cannot see the exact point where their instrument is touching paper, as Derrida pointed out (thus) in his exhibition at the Louvre.
[10] Please consult the epigram at the very beginning of Part Two.
[11] In A. Placa and B. Riordan, *Desert Silence: A Way of Prayer for an Unquiet Age* (Locust Valley, N.Y.: Living Flame Press, 1977), p. 89.

This book *On Deconstructing Life-Worlds* may render some readers
impatient: Buddhist readers because the 'autobiographical' Part One
does not deliver Buddhist doctrine complete and intact[12]; Christian
readers because Part One does not expound on the sublime raptures of
a Teresa of Avila or John of the Cross, for example. Let these readers
be assured that I know the Christian mystical tradition well, and I
have likewise studied Buddhism a long time.[13] But this book is not
written by the arrived for the arrived. This book heeds the warning of
Abbot Theodore: it writes/is-written-from the cross-hatch of world,
Other/others, and multiple-self which is called 'my' experience and
practice, and bears 'my' signature. I *intend* (sic) to write only what I
have lived and practiced.

I have found the boat, two boats,—a leaky fishing boat and a
*yāna* that some sutras say does not have to cross[14]; and I'm out on the
water in both of them. In the sweet darkness, the fragrant breeze
touches me sometimes, for minutes or hours. Jesus said to Peter, "I
tell you the truth: when you were young, you used to bind yourself and
go where you wanted; but when you are older, you will stretch out
your hands and another will bind them and take you where you don't
want to go" (John 21:18). Which may or may not happen to you too.
But 'crosshatching', the work of this book, is especially for those who,

---

[12] Here are some examples. (1) Ch'an/Zen Buddhism does not look *behind* or
*below* things for their 'meaning', whereas it could be said that in some ways (not
essentialist) I do. (2) Theravada and Mahayana come to terms with evil in
differing ways from mine. Thich Nhat Hanh in one of his poems says "I am the
child in Uganda, all skin and bones,/ My legs as thin as bamboo sticks,/ And I am
the arms merchant,/ Selling deadly weapons to Uganda." What the great
Vietnamese monk means is that our Compassion should flow from perfect
empathy. This understanding of Compassion/Empathy may remind one of
Catholicism's 'Mystical Body of Christ', but is universal not conditional. (3)
Within the frame called 'history' I cannot affirm Karma except in the broadest
sense, i.e., that sooner or later good or bad deeds will have good or bad effects in
history.
[13] Part Two demonstrates some of this, I think.
[14] "'O Distinguished ones, where are you going and from where have you come?'
'Venerable Subhuti, the Blessed One has taught the doctrine in order [to show
that] there is no going to anywhere and no coming from anywhere'" (—The *Pile of
Jewels Sutra*). Quoted in Candrakirti's *Analysis of Going and Coming*, trans.
Jeffrey Hopkins (Dharmasala: Library of Tibetan Works and Archives, 1974; 76),
p. 23. Readers may want on their own to compare this work, which is chapter two
of Candrakirti's commentary on Nagarjuna's *Mūlamādhyamakakārikās*, with
Derrida's treatment of 'going', 'crossing', and 'arriving': I discuss the latter in Part
Two, ahead, at the beginning of section iv. The comparison earns remarkable
returns.

perhaps Prometheus-bound,[15] '*double-bind* themselves and do not go
where they want to go'. And the work, God-willing, leads to where
'Another will double-bind them and take them where they shall *want*
to go'. To the liberating Neither-Nor which is interminable (and
sacred) Double-Bind(s).

If not 'arrived', why do 'I' bother to write this book at all?
Because I am on the water, not at sea. That is, I dare think 'my' crosshatched experience can really help others. My readers. Writers. Co-
signatories. And this 'heap of five piles' is happy.

A Chinese reading this book may be disconcerted by my
deployment, in the 'autobiography', of several hexagrams from the *I
Ching*. These hexagrams mark several points in the text but are
rarely commented on in the overt narration: this does not mean that
they have been scattered into the text by a dilettante. In all the books
I've read on the *I Ching*, it is the philosophical assumptions, so
different from the common Occidental ones, which so impress me. For
example,—(1) that change is incessant; (2) that change is ongoing
transformation; (3) that transformation follows subtle codes; (4) that
these codes, based on 'timeliness' as they are, often privilege latency,
passivity; (5) that all change is cyclical, traversing sooner or later both
poles of an opposition; and (6) that all change is concrete and subtle
(thus the stunning poetic phraseology of the *I Ching*). A Westerner
would be very wrong to think that the *I Ching* must be used
'superstitiously'. Carl Jung's remarks on the *I Ching* are very much to
the point, and have influenced my 'usages' in Part One. Deconstructive
readers know of course that the term 'usage' is moot, afortiori in a
postmodern text. Besides, the *I Ching* is a principal text of the Taoists
(and in a way, the Confucianists), not the Buddhists.

Part Two is a so-called formal disquisition on the philosophies/
religions which are both assumed and produced in Part One. Part
Two, by comparing the Prasangika-Madhyamika Buddhist tradition
and Derridean deconstruction (section i), extends and finesses the
comparison of Nagarjuna and Derrida which occupied much of my
*Derrida on the Mend* (1984;86). This same Part crosshatches Derridean
'double-bind' and Christian theology (section iv), examining in particular
the so-called late-phase Derrida of "Comment ne pas parler—

---

[15] Or even on a chain-to-Evil. In the Christian tradition, for example, one reads of
those who are 'on-the-chain' to Satan, who is himself—for the time being—
'bound-up'.

Dénégations" (section ii). Involved as I am in what is called 'Buddhist-Christian Dialogue', the strategies of this chiasmic encounter receive special attention (section iii). I argue that there should be inaugurated at least a second track that proceeds by *negative* imbrications rather than a presumed 'ground-in-common' and other holisms.

> Remarque: [Engraving] A mark made in the margin of
> a plate to indicate its stage of development
> prior to completion.

Closing remarks.
—The term "crosshatching" works in this text and on itself at least according to all the differing *senses* of the word's/words' etymology, though the dominant *meaning* may be 'placement *sous rature* (under erasure)', a titular emblem for deconstruction. This book constitutes 'samenesses' by way of differences.
— "Il y a là cendre," most literally "There is THERE cinder," and/or "Ago THERE cinder," is a catch-phrase which Jacques Derrida—by reiterating it in his work over many years—has rendered quite noticeable.[16] Near the beginning of Part One I deploy it in order to further philosophy/religion in saltire. So does life comport. Both connections and garbles, punctuated as they may otherwise be by chance and blindness and dissociated effects, are carefully researched. (If interested, see in particular *The Soncino Books of the Bible* [which has Hebrew text and verse by verse commentary], the *Dizionario Etimologico Italiano* [Florence, 1950], the *Französisches Etymologisches Wörterbuch* [W. Wartburg, 1928], plus Du Cange, Littré, and the O.E.D.)
—The etchings cannot be completed until readers have signed. Perhaps, sometimes, readers begin to sign Part One by breaking it down to deconstructive conditions called 'psycho-bio-graphemes'. Whence the Part's subtitles. (There is more to deconstruction than this, of course.)
—After my dear Brown-robed Patroness and my children, this book is offered (as indicated) to/for the Chinese people, whose culture is traditionally said to have been hatched from the cracks in Turtle Shells (turtle: F. *tortue*), cracks induced by overheating and then construed in augury. And whose very writing, it is sometimes said, evolved from these cracks. If things Chinese are not much in this

---

[16] Not the least in his *Feu la cendre / ciò che resta del fuoco* (Florence: Sansoni, 1984; Paris: Editions des femmes, 1987).

preface, it is only because they are so much in the text's body which follows (and precedes).

—Written last but posed
as almost first, this 'preface'
is affixed during the month
of August in Krung Thep, formerly
known (before 1782) as
'Place of Olives',[17]
      —In Thailand,
      in the Church of Santa Cruz,
      near Phra Phuttha Yot Fa bridge,


......Where the writer,
Christ-in-Mary in his belly,
pauses to begin yet another crossing
to yet another Buddhism.

---

[17] See J. Cummings, *Bangkok* (Hawthorn, Australia: 1992), p. 10.

# ACKNOWLEDGMENTS

Thank you to Professor Kuang-ming Wu for reviewing my past work in Chinese *kung-an*, work which constituted the preparation and backdrop for several sequences in this 'cape and sword drama'. Thank you to Professor Mordechai Aviam for consulting with me on Hebrew-language references. My special gratitude to Ru-ying (Vinia) Huang and Shu-chen Chiang, former graduate students of mine who are now themselves professors: Ru-ying Huang provided for the Chinese graphics in my manuscript, cross-checked the accuracy of Chinese translations, and researched many sources for me; Shu-chen Chiang made sure my facts and figures apropos of contemporary history, Mainland Chinese and Taiwanese, are as correct as can be. My appreciation also to the Tibetan Buddhist Group at Rice University, Texas, scholars who in the spring of 1994 managed to give me needed guidance even in our short time together.

*Toutes mes reconnaissances* to my Scholars Press academic editor, Cleo McNelly Kearns, and the highly efficient Scholars Press staff, Dennis Ford (Associate Director), Kathie Klein (Assistant Manager for Publications), and Leigh Andersen (Publications Coordinator).

My deepest gratitude to my dear son Jon-carlo, a graphics designer by profession, who co-produced with Scholars Press the bookcover design; and to my dear daughters, Lorinda-marie and Clara-marie, professionals in their own right, who together with their brother co-produce so much of the joy in my life.

A special thank you to Ramón García and his company, CDS, Toms River, N.J., for the help given me in the preparation of this manuscript, its atypical format and diagrams and so on (I recommend his services to scholars whose computer-savvy is, like mine, only half-way hatched).

# PART ONE

# CURRICULA VITAE

## Section One

### Curriculum Vitae:
### Psycho-bio-graphemes in Saltire

Hai!—Swoosh!

<u>*STROKE*</u>
of the two-edged (GK *distomos,* 'two-mouthed')
sword (Rev. 1:16)

> "saltire: ... an X-shaped cross; esp. St.
> Andrew's Cross; ...
>
> "in saltire: ... one bendwise and the
> other bendwise sinister so as to cross
> each other..."        [*Heraldry*]
> —Webster's New College Dictionary

"Once the Blessed One was dwelling in Rajagrha at Vulture Peak
mountain, together with a great gathering of the sangha of monks...,
and at the same time noble Avalokitesvara, the bodhisattva mahasattva,
while practicing the profound prajnaparamita, saw in this way: he saw
the five skandhas to be empty of nature."
        —*The Sutra of the Heart of Transcendent Knowledge* [1]

> "Where the Body (Gk. *sōma*) is, there also the eagles/vultures
> (Gk. *aetoi*) will be gathered together."
>                         —Luke 17:18

---

[1] Trans. into English from Tibetan, with reference to several Sanskrit editions,
by Nalanda Trans. Committee (Boulder, Colorado: shrineroom manual, prv. circ.,
Karma Dzong).

"For as the lightning comes from the East and shines as far as the West, so will the *par/ousia* of the Son of man. Wherever may be the Dead Body (Gk. *ptōma*), there the eagles/vultures (Gk. *aetoi*) will be gathered together."

—Matt. 24:27,28.

"The Christ-like figure again, of the 'who?' ['qui?'], of the X. of *L' arrêt de mort,* over whom 'it's about time we raised a cross', says the doctor who condemns him. The translators will have to refer here to what is said about chiasmus, about Χ (*chi*) and the *ichthus* in 'R+ (par dessus le *marché* ,)' (in reference to Adami)..."

—Jacques Derrida, "LIVING ON: *Border Lines*"[2]

"Ars longa vita brevis. The Est—?"

—E.E. Cummings, *HIM* [3]

"'...vers l'Est? Les ponts sont *coupés?*'"

—Derrida citing Sollers, *La dissémination* [4]

"To say that the Divine was Creation divided by Destruction was as close as one could come to a definition."

—Tom Robbins, *skinny legs and all* [5]

Determinacies connect, slip, slide, garble
always already... So many signatories already...
 disseminating already——
 Blind-spots recurring (arhythmically) already——

 .

 .

 .

 .

Celia                                                                          cinder
"s'il y a ...     "                                                         sender (post.)
 "il y a là cendre"[6]: Elijah (H. *Eli-yāh* = 'God [is] Yahweh') there Sender

[2] Trans. James Hulbert, in H. Bloom et al., *Deconstruction and Criticism* (N.Y.: Continuum, 1984), p. 165.

[3] N.Y.: Liveright Pub., 1927; rpt. 1955, p. 22.

[4] Derrida, *La dissémination* (Paris: Seuil, 1972), p. 386.

[5] N.Y.: Bantam, pbk., 1991, p. 462.

[6] Derrida, *La carte postale* (Paris: Flammarion, 1980), p. 7; Engl. trans. A. Bass, *The Post Card* (Chicago: Univ. of Chicago Press, 1987), p. 3; and passim in his

*ascendre* (M.F.): 'to go up' (v. Merkabah mysticism)
ilia (anat.) cf. Ezekiel 3:3;... 'iliac passion' (path.)

Sacroiliac

Ilya (R.)
 Leah (Bib.)
.        "Over Mary's crown is the fiery sword of Elijah, signifying a spirit of zeal
.        for the Lord. The coat of arms of the Dis*cal*ced Carmelite Order is similar,
.        except for the fact that the mountain evolves into a cross at its tip."
.                              —Description of Coat of Arms, Order
.                                   of the Blessed Virgin Mary of Mt. Carmel[7]
.

 Sandra
 Alessandra
"il y a là cendre"[8]: *El y Alá senda* (Sp.) = [Jewish God] El and [Moslem God]
                                       Allah + 'path' (Sp. *senda*)
 d' encre     *El y Alá cendra* (Sp.) = El and Allah + 'bone-ash' (Sp. *cendra**)
(cf.Numbers 5:22-24)
Ilia (L.) = Ilia-Rhea, Roman Goddess, Mother of R. & R.
.                                   **cendra*: the bone-ash used to make
.                                       refractory furnaces that separate
.                                       precious and base metal.
.

'Herb Alexander' (*Paris quadrifolia*, bot.) = 'Herb Paris' (M.L.'herb of a couple'):
                                       pharm. herb, curative/toxic
          Alexander (=Paris, Homeric hero)
          Alexander (356-323 B.C.), conjoiner of West-East (Greece-Orient):Alexandrine
                                       School, Library, Style
Ilia (Gk.& L., adj.): 'of Troy'; *Troia* (It.): 'whore'; *tròia* (It.): 'macchina bellica' (cf.
                                       ballistae, mangonels)
"Il y a là cendre"[9]: Ili/A/lysaunder
          *Alexandre (Légende de l')*...Alixandre (M.F.)...Alysaunder (M.E.) ...
                                       ...Chrétien de Troyes

'An Alexander and Ilya Salkind* Production, Copyright (C) 1982': *Superman III***
                                       (cinema)
          **Sal*(L.)/*Kind*(G.), etc.   Eo.loc. Krypton and Kryptonite
                    cf. *kryptos* (Gk.): 'hidden, covered, concealed, secret—see more at
                                       "crypt'"
          **Cf. Nietzsche's *Übermensch*

---

work. Henceforth, when referring to Derrida's writings, wherever I supply dual
references (to the French, and a published English trans.), the French precedes
the semicolon and the English follows it.
[7]*Carmel's Call: Manual for Members of the Lay Carmelite Order* (Darien: The
Carmelite Press, New Aylesford, 1991), p. 124.
[8] Derrida, "Comment ne pas parler—Dénégations," in his *Psyché: Inventions de
l'autre* (Paris: Galilée, 1987), p. 561; Engl. trans. Ken Frieden, "How to Avoid
Speaking—Denials," in S. Budick and W. Iser, eds., *Languages of the Unsayable*
(New York: Columbia University Press, 1989), p. 29. Henceforth called
"Dénégations."
[9] *La dissémination*, p. 408.

.

'*La ilâha illâ Allâh*' (A.): 'There is no God but Allah'.

> "... I have never yet been able to speak of what my birth,
> as one says [comme on dit], should have [aurait dû] made
> closest to me: the Jew, the Arab."

> —Derrida, "Comment ne pas parler: Dénégations"[10]

xxxxxxxxxxxxxxxxxxxxxxxxxxxxxxxxxxxxxxxxxxxxxxxxxxxxxxxxxxx

"Mais *gl*? Son *gl*? le son *gl*, le *gl* d'angle, son *gl*?"

> —Derrida, *La Vérité en Peinture* [11]

*Maglio*: It., n.m. Mallet, hammer.
*Maglia*, It., n.f. Stitch, mesh, knot, knitted garment, vest, network.
*-ola*, It., augmentative suffix.

Magliola, Roberto Rino.

(On the brim of World War II—)
—Born at: Christ Hospital, close to New York City, in New Jersey.
Name of Father: Ugo Bruno Francesco Magliola. Maiden name of
Mother: Florinda Antonietta Meroni.

—According to the Rite of the Roman Catholic Church, baptized:
'Robertus' (Roberto Rino). At the Church of the Epiphany.

Born by Caesarian Rupture, on October 7th, the Feast of the
Holy Rosary—"What a blessed day to be born—it *augurs* so well!,"
Monsignor Capoano would later say ('born of a rupture', did that
augur too?). The only child of middle-aged parents who loved each
other and me deeply-totally-tenderly-noisily in the age-old Italian
manner. My mother and father, naturalized citizens, perforce
measured everyday their own kind of rupture, cross-wise between
themselves and others and vertically between and inside themselves—
old Italian world and new American one, two halves that did not quite
fit. My mother, Lombard, from a family poorer than my father's but
just as goodly, 'floor lady' in a sweat shop in her twenties and already

---

[10] "Dénégations," 562; 66.
[11] Paris: Flammarion, 1978.

a designer of fashion neckware in her thirties. Devout Catholic. "Patriotic American."[12] My father, Piedmontese, graduate of the Art Institute of Torino, Italian army *alpino* in World War One, specialist in Period Furniture with a French firm, draftsman, and later a designer for an American architectural firm ("church trusses," and specialized "sliding doors" which he invented on 'company time' and his employer patented). Political radical, but via *rhetorica sola*.

> The day we danced the Saint our shoulders worked
> beneath the logs, to the music of a march,
> and rowdy with religion we cut loose
> to try a jig with that long weight on us,
> left flank together, then to the right, then left,
> running a little, then stopping dead:
> the young girls screamed to watch our statue leap
> out of its chocks, it seemed, and lean at them,
> his fresh paint flashing in the sun like fire.
> ...while up ahead fat Father Ferdinand
> swung with the weight, the Pope's own pachyderm,
> '*Laetantur coeli!*' roaring, to our jibes.
> 'Don't get to heaven too soon!' Rodolfo cried,
> and the logs rumbled, but our Saint stayed put."
> —Felix Stefanile, "The Day
> We Danced the Saint"[13]

Northern and Southern Italians did not get along well in America back then, and we didn't "dance the Saint" as Neopolitans do (though we did equivalent things, especially when we made the round of seven churches on Holy Thursday), but for me North and South are 'closed into a single party', and my Italian-American childhood resonates better to this poem—emblematically and otherwise—than to any other.

Punctuating my childhood, at the head of long banquet tables I remember my *nonno*, my paternal grandfather, man-who-had-lost-his-country auspex flushed with wine, standing tall to summon rows and

---

[12] All countries of the New World have equal right to the noun and adjective 'American', of course. The citizens of the United States have by and large appropriated the term for the United States exclusively, since, for them (the majority of them), other parts of the Americas don't really count. Here and hereinafter I (for the most part) regretfully comply, because the noun and adjective 'United Statesian', while in the dictionary, is simply too harsh-sounding for words.

[13] In A. L. Lazarus, et al., *A Suit of Four* (W. Lafayette: Purdue Univ. Studies, 1973), p. 49.

rows of gathered relatives to attention. Latter-day Ghibelline, he reduced them to silence by reciting Charles Martel[14] according to Dante:

> .........."Tutti sem presti
> al tuo piacer, perché de noi ti gioi.
> Noi ci volgiam coi principi celesti
>   d'un giro e d'un girare e d'una sete,
>   ai quali tu del mondo già dicesti:
> 'Voi che 'ntendendo il terzo ciel movete';
>   e sem sì pien d'amor, che, per piacerti,
>   non fia men dolce un poco di quiete."
> —*Paradiso*, Canto viii, 32- 39

And I remember nonna Adelina, my maternal grandmother, early each morning unpleating long scroll-length sheets of paper which she otherwise kept folded in her prayerbook. On the pages were the death dates of all her deceased relatives and friends, her "dead," her *morti*, each of whom she prayed for (and to, conditionally[15]) on the proper calendar day, their 'heavenly birthday'. I remember the Umbrian-style church the Italian parish had meticulously reconstructed; its larger than life Crucifix, accessible to the homage and embrace of all; the swarms of Italian women (and some men, and some children—little Roberto included) covering the gored and bloodied feet of the Christus with kisses. And the hushed adoration of the Eucharist, the all-night Vigils when the church—except for the candles and golden rays—was dark and womb-like (a wet and moist building, a yin building, my Chinese colleague Professor X would have said, not too approvingly, if he had seen it back then—but we loved it...I would still love it as much, if the same nine-foot Crucified One had been allowed to stay).

> I call it consolation when the soul is aroused by an interior
> movement which causes it to be inflamed with love for its Creator
> and Lord, and consequently can love no created thing on the face of

---

[14] Dante's speaker is Charles Martel ('martel' means 'hammer'), the young Angevin prince whom he met in 1294. But this Charles' name and lineage no doubt reminded Dante of the first Charles Martel (688-741), grandfather of Charlemagne. The Carolingian balance between Church and State was one Dante admired, and intended to invoke against the Church's excessive political involvement throughout the 13th century.

[15] Prayed *to*, because Catholic teaching holds that souls in heaven or purgatory can intercede for others. If so many of these relatives, when still in this life, made it their custom to pray for others, why would they want to stop in the next life?

the earth for its own sake but only in the creator of all things. It is
likewise consolation when one sheds tears inspired by love of the
Lord...

—St. Ignatius of Loyola, *The Spiritual Exercises* [16]

By the time I had reached the age of seven, religion occupied the
intima of my life. Only child that I was, and of introspective temperament, a psychologist—no doubt—would have no trouble glossing my
condition. In the Catholic tradition, *consolationes* (a term not well
served by the treacly English 'consolations') are 'interior joys', 'affective'
in nature, which are 'sent' by God. Holy blandishments of sorts, from
which God weans the soul as it becomes more mature. What I to this
day 'remember' so vividly—and can *existentially* testify to—is a quantum
jump in 'my' religious experience that began at the age of ten and continued for seven years. Heretofore my psyche had been a *sensorium*,
perceiving and actively interacting with (what I named as) God's
'consolations'. Now for sustained intervals (one or two hours) I would
experience loss of all active control of my affective life. It was as if God
for lengths of time was expropriating my (in the technical sense)
*affective intentionality*. God was animating the *noēsis* and the *noēma*
of it. Comparatists of world religion and psychiatrists, both, have long
since established—of course—that the 'phenomenology' of this
experience is shared, or so it seems, by many adherents of diverse
religions, especially in prepubescence and adolescence.

Attempting to enumerate what characterized the *sursum cordas*
'sent' me, I can attest that about half were utterly tranquil, gentle,
accompanied by no fanfaronade whatsoever, and the others were
power-spikes of fervor, but of a fervor differing distinctly from
emotions of any kind. The uptakes were not (at least consciously)
sought after; in fact, they often 'came' unexpectedly. They were
neither trance-like nor analogous to intoxication, since the intellect
and will—while trained on 'God'—remained keenly aware of their
surroundings, and capable of external action if necessary. The
experiences were not at all orgiastic, corybantic: they were always felt
in the solar plexus, not in erogenous zones; in fact, there was a
marked allayment, even suspension, of normal emotion and of sexual
sensation. (Of course, it can be argued—and has been—that this
suspension is precisely symptomatic of sublimation: *tout court*, that

[16] Trans. A. Mottola, introd. by R. Gleason (Garden City, N.Y.: Image, 1964),
p. 129.

the mechanics of sublimation work this way.) Both Tibetan Buddhists and the Christian mystical tradition, here San Juan de la Cruz being a good case in point, have supplied elaborate and refined descriptions of the *phaseologies* of the 'vita affectiva' (in these schemes, I'd barely begun to scale the scarp: my youthful consolations, while so precious to me, qualified only as a beginner's piddling). Carl Jung began the reformulation of this tradition in purely psychological terms. I am convinced he shows at least that the Unconscious can work to mature and heal the psyche via 'meditative absorption', etc., and that this process is long and complicated (also, Jung says, it can be deceptive and destructive,—a Banyan-root tangle, this). Umberto Eco, in his enormous best-seller *Il nome della Rosa* has further popularized the notion that sexual *jouissance* and religious bliss 'feel' the same. As a not unmarried man (to invoke Chinese litotic form) I have the where-withal to say now that at least in my case the two *experiences* belong to very differentiated orders (we are talking here of *phenomenology*, not etiology nor a possible hidden reciprocity). For those who have not had 'religious' experience, a caution: 'If you haven't had it, don't deride it'. I shall be broaching, ahead, a 'working attitude of mind' toward meditative phenomena in general, but for me the status of my youthful girandoles of soul remains Undecidable. More was involved, I think, than mere glandular juice, and/or Freud's auto-suggestion, and/or Jung's 'autonomous' mechanism.

From the age of eight(!) I had determined to become a Catholic priest. In my prayer-life I repeatedly did generous but apparently reckless things. At the age of fifteen I recall how captivated I became with the *Spiritual Exercises*, and specifically its Third Mode of Humility,—when "I choose reproaches with Christ thus suffering rather than honor, and when I am willing to be considered as worthless and a fool for Christ Who suffered such treatment before me, rather than to be esteemed as wise and prudent in the world."[17] In the blundering enthusiasm of youth, 'I' ignored the all-important provision St. Ignatius attaches, that the Third Mode is for the 'advanced',—"the first and second forms [of humility] already possessed and the praise and glory of the Divine Majesty being equally served..." Breathless, 'I'—not knowing it was 'I'—promised Christ that for Him I would even make the sacrifice of giving up my priestly vocation. He could prevent my vocation, I told Him, if He so willed,—

---

[17] Ignatius of Loyola, *The Spiritual Exercises*, p. 82.

so that I could suffer 'reproach' and give the suffering to Him out of love. Such jejuneness my confessor laughed off, of course, and I assume 'God' did too, but—by chance, or some ineluctable determinisms, or Divine Providence, or Sartrean fate, or all of these or some or none of these (more of this theme anon), my vocation was not to bear fruit.

Non

Non
une cloche
au fond de moi-même
a vibré
entre une quadruple
paroi

—Paul Claudel[18]

Hexagram 36: Darkening of the Light

---

[18] From his *Cent phrases pour Eventails*, collected in the *Oeuvre Poétique* (Paris: Gallimard, 1967), p. 741. Each of Claudel's poems is juxtaposed with the Chinese calligraphy of a Japanese ornamental fan. But, see Derrida on *quadrature, quadrangle, quadrant, quadrat,* and so on, in *La dissémination,* pp. 386-7, et seq., and in *La vérité en peinture,* '+R', et seq., and passim in his work.

("Here the trigrams' position is the opposite of Chin. Here K'un, the earth, is above Li, the sun or light. Hence the image of approaching nightfall, or the darkening of the light.")

The Lines: Six at the Top—No light, but obscurity.
          First he ascended to heaven; then he descends
          to the bottom of the earth.

                              —*I Ching (Book of Changes)*[19]

I went to public schools in my earlier years, and then to a private Catholic preparatory school, the latter involving a long commute (two hours going in the morning, three hours returning each evening: each direction, two buses, two subway trains). Throughout, I earned straight A's, no doubt more because I was bookish and less because I was bright. Then, when seventeen years old, the Jesuit Seminary, Platts-burgh, New York (high in blue-green Adirondack Mountains, on the verge of Lake Champlain). The Society of Jesus, called the Church's 'militia'. And in those days, prior to Vatican Council II, keeping a quite severe regimen still. For the first two years (novitiate), we lived six days out of seven in 'holy silence' (Thursdays were holidays, but— naive overreacher that I was, mornings I stayed in my *cellula* instead, reading, studying).

    Anamnesis: Images—Summers, early morning meditation outside (5:30 a.m.)... the tall grass giving up its mist... my brother Jesuits, opaque shadows scattered in the fog, pausing for the tolling of the Angelus-bell, and then slowly gathering from out of the silver vapor

---

[19] Hexagram 36, *I Ching*, as translated in Tom Riseman's *Introduction to the I Ching* (Wellingborough, Northamptonshire: Aquarian, 1980), p. 56. History has transmitted to us an *I Ching* with 64 Hexagrams, each accompanied by a Judgement, an Image, and Annotations tied to its six lines (usually my citations here are just excerpts from a Hexagram's pertaining text). I use the Riseman *translation* and commentaries because in my life-events it has been precisely the rhetoric of this *translation* which has tolled, 'con-signed and counter- signed' (compare Derrida, *Glas*, p. 225) my own affectivities. Though I know well how to 'cast the yarrows-stalks', personally I have *never* treated the *I Ching* as my 'arbiter' per se: rather, it has (seemingly) interacted with me in much the same way T.S. Eliot says his 'objective correlatives' work. For those who do not read Chinese but who wish to study more scholarly translations, two recent works are: T. Cleary's *I Ching* (Shambala, 1992) and M. Secter's *I Ching Clarified: A Practical Guide* (Tuttle, 1993).

for outdoor Mass. Winters, evenings... black sky, gold stars... in clusters of three, chanting the rosary in guttural Latin, chugging ourselves through knee-deep snow...around and around we go, shivering in temperatures of 5 below zero. Afternoons, all year... our black cassocks flapping, pausing one by one at the bulletin board, reading the day's Requests for Prayer from people in need... then keeping those 'special intentions' in prayer the whole day through. Three days a week, during the penitential seasons... lined up in the hallways, each whipping his own bare back with the rope *flagellum*, "taking care to avoid the spine and renal areas"... and two days a week, each wrapping the barbed *catena* around his own left thigh, taking care that the little coltrops sting "but do not puncture and cause infection."

Anamnesis: Affectivity—Slow murrain, slow slow murrain, then thanatosis, then death. After I had been a novice for one month, the wellspring of ten years dried up—all consolations abruptly stopped. Which is to say, in my case—all affective life stopped. Those waters were not to return again for a long, long time, and back then it seemed as if they were never never to return.—"I cast for comfort I can no more get...than blind / Eyes in their dark can day or thirst can find / Thirst's all-in-all in all a world of wet."[20] Slowly, relentlessly, the resultant insensibility ceded to black depression. I lost over fifty-five pounds of weight, dropping down to ninety-five pounds. (My parents— we were only allowed to see *externi* once a year—were, you can well imagine, devastated.) Without the underpinning of affection, my emotions began—slowly, inexorably—to choke to death. Without the competence, yet, to interpret the whys and wherefores of my deep despondency, I refused to even consider the likelihood I should not take vows (the phase of Denial, I would tag it now.) Besides, had not the Tradition supplied precious instructions just for a 'trial' like this?—

> In Albula I learned to know a certain saint who lived as it is fitting for a saint. After she had given away all for the sake of the Lord, she had left a cover to protect her from the cold, and this she gave also. Soon after this, God afflicted her with the greatest inner pain and a feeling of loneliness. Whereat she complained and said to Him: 'Is this meet, dear Lord? You have taken all from me, and now You Yourself forsake me too!'

---

[20] From Gerard Manley Hopkins, S.J., "My own heart let me more have pity on," collected in C. Phillips, ed., *Gerard Manley Hopkins* (Oxford: N.Y., 1986).

> Here, then, God repaid—by means of sorrow—the great services
> performed for Him. And there can, indeed, be no better payment, for
> the true meaning of it is that one is paid with the [hidden] love of God.
> Do not let your heart cling to inner solace. For that is in the
> manner of common soldiers: they demand their daily wages at once.
> Give your service as the noblest officers serve their king—for nothing!
>           —St. Teresa of Avila[21]

In the United States there's a Puritan ethic and a mythology of success. He
who is [financially/politically] successful is [considered] good. In Latin
countries, in Catholic countries, a successful person is [considered] a
sinner. In Puritan countries, success shows God's benevolence. In Catholic
countries, you're sure God loves you only when you've suffered.
          —Umberto Eco[22]

I was not a saint, however, and I was psychologically immature and a
spiritual neophyte. St. Teresa's story for many reasons was inappli-
cable to my case, but I had no way of knowing.

So firm was my *ideational* enthusiasm, my conceptual commitment to the 'idea' of the Religious Life, that it carried me forward
anyway. The novice master, jovial Irishman that he was, saw my
intense faith, my steely will, my devotional imagination—novices each
in turn routinely practiced the giving of sermons before the whole
community, and the giving of *puncta* for daily meditation: mine were
'inspired', and unusually well-received. Throughout the two years, I
had reported my ongoing despondency to the master, of course, but he
apparently decided that it was surmountable. When the time came,
he approved my taking of vows. We progressed to the next stage of
Jesuit training, the intense classical study outlined in the *Ratio
Studiorum*.

Before two more years had expired, or four years from my initial
arrival, I had plummeted into full nervous breakdown. The vows could
be dispensed, that was no problem, but—as long as I possibly could—I
resisted, resisted, resisted, blind in the Certainty that God would not
'reject' me, and that the 'dark night' would be lifted in due time. How,
I reasoned, could the Christ have fed me priestly aspirations all my
youth, and now, 'reverse Himself' by reversing me?

---

[21] Trans. in H. A. Reinhold, ed., *The Soul Afire: Revelations of the Mystics* (N.Y.:
Doubleday, Image pbk., 1973), p. 317.
[22] "That is why he [Eco] wears his fame uneasily," the *New York Times* reporter
adds, in this interview quoted from the New York Times Service by a Taiwanese
wire service, 1988 (no more precise date supplied).

A not admitting of the wound
Until it grew so wide
That all my life had entered it
And there were troughs beside.[23]

At the end, I remember such atony of soul that I was almost comatose. At last I gave it up, and signed the Request for Release from Vows.

Hai!—Swoosh! $\overline{STROKE}$ of the two-edged sword. . . . . . .
                                The last night before the arrival of my dispensation from Rome, I remember sitting alone, in the dark, in the back of the chapel, and hurling towards the Tabernacle the bitter heart-cry of a jilted lover. "How could you? How could you! Swoosh your cleaver, You crosshatcher of hearts!" I felt my skull and its brains melt down and blot out,—high high overhead the pot of boiling oil had tilted and let fall. (When this God reigns, it pours.)

    Returned to the parental hearth, I regained enough warmth at the fire to try Religious Life one more time—this time in an Italian order (I have always learned my lessons hard). Within a year I became so unstable that I had to leave before vow-taking. The Divine *ignis* seemed an *ignis fatuus*, indeed. Now, thirty-five years or so later, I can look back at this seminary life with that insight which comes, I think, from so-called success in the 'secular' non-Catholic (and often anti-Catholic) world, and from broad and long international experience, and—perhaps most of all—from a more normal socializing with women. Self-critique of course plays a crucial role in this, and I undertake it ahead, but at this point let me winnow out some more general observations about Roman Catholic seminary life. If we assume the changes effected by Vatican Council II (1962-1965), and if—for the purposes of the present discussion—we limit ourselves to the doctrinal parameters of Roman Catholicism, what would I answer to the question—(1) Should celibate seminary life be continued? What would I answer to the question—(2) Should monastic life be continued? (Monastics stay in monasteries, take vows, and need not be ordained; seminarians, when diocesan, usually go on to life in parishes.[24])

---

[23] Emily Dickinson, *The Poems of Emily Dickinson*, 3 vols,, ed. T. Johnson (Cambridge: Harvard Univ. Press, 1958), poem #1123.
[24] I am simplifying. The definitions are more complicated. Briefly put, a 'Religious' takes vows, and may or may not go on to priestly ordination (Sisters and Brothers do not). Some 'Religious' are 'monastics'. Others—like the Jesuits,

To the first question I would answer by applauding a post-Council change in seminary admission policy: now, in most of western Europe and in the United States, the more general practice is for diocesan and Religious seminaries to receive candidates only after they've graduated from co-educational colleges or universities. I have seen all too many priests—say 15 or 20%—of my (quite large) circle of clerical acquaintances who have, perhaps, doctorates, but who emotionally are still adolescents: stunted by abnormal formation in their teenage years, they've never really grown up.[25] I was personally surprised—as well as appalled, of course—by the recent exposés of Catholic clergy, homosexual or not, who have molested children. Personally I have not known any priests who have done this, but it is also true that most of the priests I know either work in universities or are monastics: their apostolates do not involve children. However, given what I have said above about the general immaturity of Catholic clergy in the United States, perhaps the recent revelations should not have surprised me: such widespread 'underdevelopment' was bound to generate extreme cases, cases of sickening misdevelopment. As to the question of homosexuality, how it computes into the unhappiness of the celibate life I do not know. Personally I have not met a statistically meaningful number of priests who show signs of latent homosexuality. Among my priest-acquaintances, I have not known of any practicing homosexuals. It would seem 'prima facie' that—for a homosexual male—life in a community of celibate males is analogous to what life would be for a heterosexual male in a community of celibate women. That is, the life would seem calculated to enhance enticement and frustration. However, I am no expert in these matters. Nor do they pertain—thank God—to this my own 'life-account'. What I *can* affirm is that Catholic seminary-life must attend much more to

---

Vincentians, etc.—do not recite the Liturgical Hours in-common, and have an apostolate in the midst of the secular world. Diocesan priests are not vowed, but take promises of celibacy, and obedience to their Bishop.

[25] Apropos, for professional corroboration, see "A Deeper Clerical Problem than Sex," in the *National Catholic Reporter* (April 16, 1993), p. 17, which in turn cites Eugene Kennedy and Victor Heckler, *The Catholic Priest in the United States: Psychological Investigations* (U.S. Catholic Conference, 1972): "Kennedy and Heckler contend that the priesthood is tailor-made for the underdeveloped personality. The underdeveloped priests, they say, can maintain positions of prestige and security and can protect their powers from being tested by the competition of the world. 'The priesthood for many of these underdeveloped men is a vocational choice that allows them to continue in life without really needing to develop. It offers them a setting in which they can survive without growing' (p. 12)."

deep meditation (what was called *contemplatio* in the old western tradition), and to the role of the body in 'contemplative' life. (More about this topic, momentarily...)

The larger percentage of priests with whom I'm well-acquainted—say 50–60%—are emotionally mature, but they suffer the celibate life as a painful deprivation of intimacy (not so much of sex as of intimacy). For this reason, among others, I personally think that the Roman Church would be well-advised to allow married candidates access to priestly ordination,—as was its early practice, and is the continuing practice of Catholicism's eastern rites and of the Eastern Orthodox Churches. What I have said thus far may have some relevance for the life-style of Religious Sisters, but as a male I am qualified to make neither the judgments nor the applications.

The problematic of psyche-body-spirit is one of those many about which the Roman Church should be humble enough to learn from the Orient, and in this case specifically from Hinduism, a religion which knows well to celebrate both the natural and the mystical. Hinduism says that a Brahmin's life has four phases:—when single, under the parents' and teacher's roof; when married, under one's own roof; after the children have grown and left home, under a forest roof (as a meditating hermit); and then lastly, under no roof at all (as an enlightened mendicant).[26] That is, the *natural phaseology* of the human being is such that—when physical virility has run its course and the middle-aged phase begins—the psyche, replete with experience, is finally *ripe and ready* for the demands of religious surrender. In the spirit, if not the letter of this practice, the Roman Church should at least evolve institutional structures which welcome and indeed encourage widowers into the priesthood, and especially, widows, widowers, and the legally 'separated' into Religious Life (contemplative communities in particular).[27] Protestant Christians and others may find what I've said so far confirms their own opposition to institutionalized celibacy, and they may even suspect that, knowing its dangers firsthand, I

---

[26] For the historical relationship of the Brahmin's life-style to Zen, see R. H. Blyth, *Zen and Zen Classics* (Tokyo: Hokuseido, 1960), Vol. I, p. 29.

[27] Some of this is permitted now, but rarely. It surely is not promoted and encouraged as the 'wave of the future' (which I think should be done). These late entrants may require medical care or retirement after relatively short periods of service, but normally I think they could be expected to bring funds with them upon entry, funds the interest off which could yield a monthly income (the equivalent of the dowry expected of incoming cloistered religious in the old days).

oppose such an institutionalized life-style. Actually, I think Protestants are very wrong to foreclose celibate monasticism, but I also think it is unwise for the Roman Church to foreclose priesthood to the married. In short, institutionalized celibacy and priestly ordination are two very different vocations, and the Church needs more of the latter than there are authentic vocations to the former.

Clearly, then, to the second question posed above, I would answer that celibate monastic life should be continued. In fact, adamantly in the face of popular opinion, I am willing to predict that monasticism—within some decades—shall enter upon a period of significant worldwide growth. I am also willing to predict—in the face of mainstream scholarly opinion—that celibate monasticism will evolve so as to become a privileged site for new and unexpected (and *beneficial*) religious developments. Perhaps it suffices for me at this point to remind the reader that *historically*, and regarded from a global perspective, celibate monasticism transcends ideology and is cross-cultural. Besides the monks of Christendom, with their less than 2000 years of history, there is the 2500 year history of Southeast Asian celibate monastics who are 'atheistic', and the more than 2000 year history of Mahayanist monastics who reject the concept of 'omnipotent God' and whose ideal is 'compassion'.[28] Yes indeed, monasticism will remain with us. No doubt, there is much that Buddhist monks can learn from Christian ones, but there is also much that Christian monks can learn from their Oriental counterparts, especially in the matter of *orthopraxis* (how to breathe, diet, hold the body, etc.). In this regard, an intriguing twist is that some of the Oriental practices summon Christians back to traditions indigenous to their own history, but long abandoned. It turns out, in fact, that the principles of orthopraxis, of how to best structure monastic routine, say, or how to best dispose the psyche for meditation, operate in a surprisingly constant way. I am very convinced that Roman Catholic formation of celibates—in monastic life and seminary life—should work out a synthesis of Christian and Oriental disciplines. Novice-masters, confessors, spiritual directors, etc., should rediscover the rules of discernment elaborated by the medieval mystics, and the 15th-17th century mystics. And they should learn the time-tested

---

[28] It is a testimony both to celibacy and Chinese discipline that Chinese Buddhist monastics have conserved institutionalized celibacy to this day. Japanese Buddhist monastics, early on in their history, already put an end to it.

*psychologies* of Hinduism and Buddhism. The seething Unconscious in general and the erotic in particular surely number among the principle determinants of our human condition. One would think a Roman Catholic belief-system, with its doctrine that 'creation' is redeemed and good, would want to affirm these factors, discern their powers for good or bad, and teach how to deploy their good.

Biographeme:—One morning in 1958, during *conferentia*, Frater Robert asking, "Father Master [honorific for Novice-master, from *magister*, 'teacher'], in our meditative and imaginative life, how do you advise we treat sexual impulses?"... and Father Master answering, "Don't get involved in that. Exclude them. Pray for the grace to resist." In short, the Novice-master advised suppression (into the subconscious), and what he said served as well and at the same time to fortify repression (in the unconscious). Innocently vicious answer, this.

Biographeme:—One morning in 1961, during *studium*, a too frail and bony Frater Robert, muscles twitching and brains tensile, descending to the refectory to gorge some sugar. The symptoms of hypoglycemia, I know now. Too late.

Spiritual directors must learn to read the body, and treat the body as a working component of the religious life. Learn to practice the yogas. (How otherwise can these directors truly teach others?) Learn to practice the yogas. Learn to deploy the body in meditation. And especially, learn the holy sublimation of eros. Learn to sublimate up through the body-chakras. (Is not a prime value of celibacy that it facilitates spiritualization?) Learn, too, the deployment—through Oriental-style meditation—of the non- and off-rational mind.[29] More broadly and in general, learn to value, cultivate, discern the *intuitive*, and *artistic expression*, and *all* the behaviors linked to the 'right-sided hemisphere of the brain (= somatic left-side)'.[30] For a Catholic 'contemplative',

---

[29] The electroencephalograms of experienced meditators in deep meditation show a marked "increase of alpha-wave trains in the central and frontal regions of the brain," accompanied by "bursts of theta waves" and "synchronized beta spindles." The overall electroencephalographic pattern is unique to deep meditation, and indicates a calm alertness distinct from other forms of wakefulness. See the 'Brain Waves' section of the article on "Meditation as a Therapeutic Agent," in B. Wolman, ed., *Encyclopedia of Psychiatry, Psychology, Psychoanalysis and Neurology*, Vol. 7 (N.Y.: Van Nostrand Reinhold/Aesculapius, 1977), p. 69. I also recommend the more recent *Mindscience: An East-West Dialogue* (London: Wisdom Bks., 1991), the published proceedings of the Harvard Mind-Science Symposium, with the Dalai Lama, H. Benson, R. Thurman, et al.

[30] Scientific research into 'brain lateralization' has multiplied in the last few years, and is discovering much that is extraordinarily valuable. I began my

how scandalizing if the Christ-life is not one's *samādhi* ('meditative absorption').

O *Psychomachia* mine! ... ...

> *Wo ist das Geschlecht?* "'What about the sexual life of your *Dasein*?'
> they might have still asked."
> —Derrida, *"Geschlecht*: sexual difference, ontological difference"[31]

As for self-critique, undertaking it 'now' as it applies to the 'self' *then* is like entering a time-tunnel lined with Funhouse mirrors, or almost. Which is not to say that such a task should not be assayed,—it is fractured and distended but still functional—as any working psychiatrist would attest. In psychological terms, the only rationale I can find for the making and unhinging of my first 23 years is the following. First, the Making: (1) An only son of older very affectionate parents who were strict but over-protective (I had almost died of pneumonia at the age of 8); (2) Temperament—introspective, imaginative, intuitive; (3) Social maturation—other than at school and with relatives, socialization very limited; no girlfriends, under cover of 'having a priestly vocation'; and (4) Environment—religious, artistic (I painted, winning prizes at several exhibits), and literary (I read history, theology, literature *par trop*). Second, the Unhinging: Since I recall almost no occurrence of sexual arousal until my early twenties(!), I deduce that along the whole course of my adolescence, sublimation (or mere displacement?) came unconsciously, smoothly, with uncommon ease. After all, its wheels were uncommonly greased by the 'favorable' factors named above. And in psychological terms,

---

reading in this area with the article "Cerebral Lateralization of Function" in R. Atkinson, et al., eds., *Stevens' Handbook of Experimental Psychology*, Vol. 2 (N.Y.: John Wiley and Sons, 1988). Personally I am convinced that the decrees of Vatican Council II were miscarried *in their practical application* after the Council. This sad outcome could have been avoided if the following very concrete rule-of-thumb had materialized (it didn't):—Deepen what (psychologists now know) pertains to right-brain/left-hand activity (liturgy as mystery, prayer as non-discursive, etc.); and lighten-up on the enforcement of what pertains to left-brain/right-hand activity (proscriptions, rules). Of course, the applications which actually transpired did just the opposite.

[31] In *Research in Phenomenology*, XIII (1983), p. 71, translator uncredited. For the French 'original' of this essay, see *Les cahiers de l'herne*, ed. Michel Haar (Paris: Editions de l'Herne, 1983), pp. 419-30.

such would seem to account for the course of blissful 'consolations'—so overpowering, and sustained for a straight ten years.

I take sublimation to mean, by definition, the transmuting of unconscious libidinal energy: sublimation is thus therapeutic, healthful. If sublimation had been the name of my game for ten years, in the seminary it abruptly stopped. Otherwise, no slough of despair. I define displacement to mean the shunting of libidinal energy onto substitute-tracks which can't really bear the burden: displacement necessarily involves, then, quantum repression. Perhaps I had been both subli-mating and displacing for ten years—a mixed game—and then in the seminary displacement finally co-opted sublimation. Leaving for the semi-nary had meant leaving even parental intimacy: perhaps the latter had been the slim differential keeping my psychic machine on track, and able to take the curves.

> Du musst dein Leben ändern.
> —Rainer Maria Rilke[32]

Dressed down—as I now knew I was—by Rilke's non-negotiable imperative, soon after I returned to lay life I set about trying to change. Eating and sleeping enough for the first time in five years, I put together my wits and life sufficiently to resume my education. Realizing for the first time that a woman's intimacy was so important to/for me, I applied to co-educational colleges, but—with two years of credits already compiled from the seminary's baccalaureate program—I found no college would take me but a lay all-male college (at that time, Catholic colleges were still, almost all of them, gender-segregated). The cross marking my life seemed a 'chassé-croisé', indeed.

> chassé-croisé: n.m. (dancing) a dance step; (fig.) a series of moves or changes that end in nothing;...
> —*New Cassell's French Dictionary* (1962)

> (fig.)...mix-up where people miss each other in turn.
> —*HACHETTE Collins Gem Dictionnaire/Dictionary* (1979)

I read widely, not only in comparative literature but in philosophy/psychology/sociology—Kant, Voltaire, Rousseau, Marx, Kierkegaard, Freud, Russell, James, Sartre, Heidegger, Marcuse. In college and deferred from the draft, I anguished all the more over Vietnam,

---

[32] From his "Archaïscher Torso Apollos."

where—relative *naif* that I still was—I saw, transposed, my mother's Roman Catholicism (right-wing version) and my Father's red socialism[33] both fighting for the Good and against each other. At the seminary I had been too reclusive: at college I now practiced *giving* to people *directly*, by way of conversation, service, friendship.

> "        . . . . . . . of a rack
> Where, selfwrung, selfstrung, sheathe– and shelterless,
>         thoughts against thoughts in groans grind."[34]

At the time, my working Philosophy of Life? It had long been argued, of course, that Roman Catholicism is a highly efficient slave-machine, the cybernetics of which is so perfect that the Church's self-perpetuation is a Surefire Thing. (1) Impossible demands are made. (2) Nature thus sooner or later wins a victory, labeled a 'sin'. (3) As soon as it does, guilt arises [this works as the feed-back mechanism]. (4) The Church removes the guilt (confession, penitence). (5) The penitent, relieved, redoubles his/her religious obedience, thus ensuring sooner or later another sin. A perpetual and vicious circle. (Protestant Christians are in the circle too: an Evangelical's St. Paul does not obviate the machinery, only the Church as Middle Man.) A fiery and smoking Wheel. (Yet another Wheel in the pain-proliferating Circuit of *saṃsāra*, a Buddhist would say.) Nowadays Hélène Cixous talks about it, generalizing it into a secular pseudo-mystique of suffering, translating sin into Lack which is driven by a machinery of desire (for her, all of it an insidious male invention[35]).

At first, I decided that the slave-formula did not fit my case. I was not at all obsessed by the question of sin. Even sexual vigor (now that my Italian genes were activating their Erotic link) did not in the least embarrass me: for indeed true Christian Incarnationalists we

---

[33] The Italian church resisted the political revolutions of the 19th century, thus alienating in northern Italy several generations of the working class. In my father's youth, to be an 'Italian patriot' usually meant to belong to the Socialist Party. If, back then and before, the Church had backed a modified form of communism—which for Catholicism is theologically easy to do but (in most countries) socially difficult to do—the skin and flesh and bones and marrow of the world would be, just possibly, in much better condition today.

[34] From Gerard Manley Hopkins, "Spelt From Sibyl's Leaves."

[35] Cixous is partly right, but Lack seems to be part and parcel of the human condition no matter what—though of course we don't have a 'pure feminine experience' we can check (to see if it is a fertile not-lack-making desire). Women's lives are always affected somehow by men (and vice versa).

Wops (from dial.It. *guappi*) be. If anything, in my relation to God I felt not only innocent but, seemingly, victimized. The very fact I felt victimized, however, showed that the formulation did apply in the broadest sense. I was born into the Church, and the Church had messed me up, thwarting normal maturation. Vatican Council II was just then meeting. "We're changing—less triumphalism and rigidity, and more love, now!" priest-friends excitedly told me. Neither the Church nor its concept of God (nor any version of an omnipotent God) can get off so easily, though. I had concluded that already. Millions of human beings, in full belief and innocence, had maimed and been maimed *already*: an omnipotent God had *let it be* that people trying according to their own best lights *to be good* and *do good* had done frightful things to each other.

Example (numerically small)—An aunt of mine who in her twenties was abandoned by her husband and who, *relegated by Church law* to sixty years of loneliness, went near to crazy ("But the 'sufficiency of God's grace!'" do you protest?—Come now, do we dare blame her for going next-to-insane?). Example (big)—French Royalists rallied by the Church, fighting in defense of what was common *teaching* (Divine Right of Kings), and opposing democracy tooth and nail...(A scene repeated in Italy, with some differences, a century later). Example (bigger)—The medieval Church, on *biblical grounds*, institutionalizing the Jewish ghetto and its penalties; centuries later (but an old story), the Church, in the name of prudence, *allowing* German and Austrian Catholics to fight in World War II, when she could have barred it under pain of excommunication.[36] Example *ex muris* (big): God-fearing Moslems and God-fearing Jews, out of *love* for 'God' and 'His' People, killing each other: and an omnipotent God *letting it happen*. The standard theological answer is that 'there is evil in the world, and its workings are mysterious'. The answer seemed another vicious circle. If a human being, as best she/he possibly can, tries to do good, why should Evil result? The responsibility would belong to the omnipotent God, who thereby would be proven Evil. Or so a reasoning person would have to conclude. And even though the matter, in the formal sense, absolutely transcends human capacity to understand and judge, the fact is the omnipotent God has endowed us

---

[36] For some of the history, and a dismaying specific (the Bishop of Linz telling a young Austrian Catholic who refused induction into the Nazi army—'Military service is your duty'), see Gordon Zahn's *In Solitary Witness* ((N.Y.: Holt, Rinehart, and Winston, 1965).

with Reason and dignity (we are told): it would be a violation of how we are made *not* to judge according to our best lights. In short, having so made us, an omnipotent God—insofar as God is *good*—is bound in responsibility *to us*.

'Pop! The phoenix is out of the golden snare!' the Zen 'capping phrase'[37] goes; the meaning requires that one break out of the *epistēmē* within which a question is posed. Indeed, why be trapped inside the question, 'Is God good?' Break out!—Perhaps there is no God at all.[38]

> I shout my prayers at something
> Which,
> However hard I try
> To think exists, does not exist:
> Reason enough to cry.
> —Ishikawa Takuboku (1885–1912)[39]

It would seem an atheistic or agnostic model more easily suits human experience and the world that experience knows. Indeed, every sign or evidence of God (no matter whether the God[s] be good or evil or both), can be explained by science, or at least *explained away* by science (i.e., if science doesn't or cannot know the natural phenomenon in question, it is understandable that science doesn't or cannot know it: this is no proof whatever of supernatural involvement). The converse of all this is also true. There can be no sign or evidence of God(s), yet there can be God(s), even God(s) in control of the 'whole' universe. Clearly, in this case the God(s) would not at all match Christianity's concept of God, because a Christian God self-reveals, and a Christian God is self-obliged to goodness (with all that entails). As I was avidly reading comparative religion too, at this time, I charted a no doubt very cracked and incomplete Cracked Table of Possibles (which embarrasses me now) —

(1) -------------- God? Moral/amoral universe?
Unanswerable, therefore meaningless questions (avoid

---

[37] For a discussion of 'capping phrases', see I. Miura, R.F. Sasaki, *The Zen Koan* (New York: Harcourt, Brace and World, pbk. 1965), pp. 12-13, 28-9, 42, 55-6.
[38] I do not mean to press the likeness between sudden *'epistēmē-shift'*, an obviously western term, and the above Zen 'capping phrase', which is supposed to signal an experience with minimal (some would say *no*) conceptual component.
[39] The poem "Prayers," trans. Graeme Wilson, *Western Humanities Review*, 31, No. 1 (winter 1977).

anthropomorphizing the universe; only practical human
ethic is justifiable: how should I [we] act?)

(2) An amoral universe (chance, 'survival of the fittest',
etc.), with human means as a way of coping or escaping
(meditation, altruistic love, even selfishness, etc.). This
comes in various versions that combine variously:
With/without gods/spirits that help/don't-help.

(3) A moral universe (good deeds cause good, bad deeds
cause bad). With/without gods/spirits that help/don't-help.

(4) A split universe: Good Principle and Evil Principle,
in dialectical strife or cooperation.

(5) An omnipotent Good-and-Bad (-and-Indifferent,
maybe) God (the term 'God' implying Divine
purposiveness).

(6) An omnipotent Good God (or the alternative version,
omnipotent Bad God).

I thought over and prayed over my future course. At stake was
no less than my psychological survival. Here I was, to siphon from
Heidegger, *geworfen* in the truest sense—at sea in a life-world I had
not intended, and rung round with serried risks and needs. Most of
all, I now knew this Harlequin needed a Columbine, a woman

> . . . . . . . . lovely in her bones,
> When small birds sighed, she would sigh back at them,...

In my imagination, the image of a
comely maid[40] flitted to and fro now,—

> I kiss her moving mouth,
> Her swart hilarious skin;
> She breaks my breath in half;
> She frolicks like a beast;
> And I dance round and round,
> A fond and foolish man,
> And see and suffer myself
> In another being at last.[41]

Embodied, contingent, *lonesome,* I weighed
the Possibles not only abstractly but also (whether I wanted to or not)

---

[40] Unconscious projection of *anima* that Jung cautions against?
[41] Composite from Theodore Roethke's "I Knew a Woman" and "Words for the
Wind," both in *The Collected Poems* (Garden City, N.Y.: Anchor, 1975).

*existentially*. Life, after all, is not a tangram: pure cerebration never really calibrates a life-world.

   Out of my raw need for psychological support, I identified with the starving Christ spindled on the Cross, torso arched out and sagging, and I looked for solace to the dolorous Mother—

> Still falls the Rain -
> Still falls the Blood from the Starved Man's wounded Side:
> He bears in his Heart all wounds...
>
> The wounds of the baited bear, –
> The blind and weeping bear whom the keepers beat
> ...the tears of the hunted hare.[42]

Stabat Mater dolorosa
Juxta Crucem lacrimosa. . . . . .

The Church's (interpretation) of Christ was not *just* a trap, clearly, nor its theology of suffering sado-masochism.[43] Authentic love is unconditional: its purpose is to serve others, and this service must be committed *all the way*. Without this precise Christ-figure, archetype for me of sacrificial love—the 'milk and honey' drunk in with my very mother's milk, with my *italianità*—I could never muster the strength to *perdure*, to keep serving others. In my case, this was at least a *psychological* fact that had to be faced (for I still tried to keep service my motive everyday, no matter what the task: this was even the rheostat of my own *stability*). Moreover, Vatican Council II was pledging the Church to social service more than ever before—service to the persecuted and suffering, no matter what their ideology, in all the foul *oubliettes* of the world (or so it would seem: the Church would in the future renege all too often). Besides the more immediate social service (outreach programs in American cities, medical missions in the third world,...), the Church in general supplied a structure of meaningfulness, of cultural community, of emotional support. (Why, I thought, it might even send a nubile maid my way.) And there was this further consideration: even though for the space of a few dark years I had been 'at my limit', subjectively speaking, (indeed, I'd been even suicidal at times), on any objective scale my plight seemed

---

[42] From Edith Sitwell's "Still Falls the Rain," collected in her *Canticle of the Rose* [sic]: *Poems, 1917-1949* (London: Vanguard, 1949).
[43] Though the theology could be thus misappropriated in individual cases, or even group cases, and no doubt it sometimes has been.

trivial. Perhaps both my training and my ordeal had counted for something. To indulge in self-pity now would be shameless.

Perhaps, I decided, carved deep down into this swarming hodge-
podge of factors—at once idealistic and smarmy, pragmatic and (often)
subliminal— there was after all God's intaglio. Perhaps God's wee tiny
whisper—subtle and mysterious like in the Elijah-story—had been at
work even in the coils of (putative?) Freudian repression, and of
shocked stupor, "...Jack, joke, poor potsherd, patch matchwood"[44] that
I was. Perhaps the name of my game, even as a game of 'mere
displacement', had been at once infiltrated by the Holy Name
(filter/philtre, I would emphasize now[45]). Yes, at the end of much
prayer and soul-wringing, I tabled my Table of Possibles—my cracked
Table-Talk—and renewed my Act of Faith in the Church's Christ.

Nowadays I find it helpful to gloss, with a passage from Carl
Jung, my decision 'back then' to continue in the Church:

> ...we believe we can criticize religious facts intellectually; we think
> for instance like LaPlace that God is a hypothesis which can be
> subjected to intellectual treatment, to affirmation or denial. It is
> completely forgotten that the reason mankind believes in the
> daimon [deific force] has nothing whatsoever to do with outside
> factors, but is due to simple perception of the powerful inner effect
> of the autonomous fragmentary systems. This effect is not nullified
> by criticizing its name intellectually, nor by describing it as false.[46]
> The effect is always collectively present, the autonomous systems
> are always at work, because the fundamental structure of the
> unconscious is not touched by the fluctuations of a transitory
> consciousness.[47]

Whether the "powerful inner effect of the autonomous fragmentary
systems" adequates to a real daimon Jung leaves open, as inaccessible
to scientific psychology and outside its 'proper' purview.

In the years ahead, I was to prove more than motile enough in
the topsails: it was the underrigging—heart's cordage, as the poets
say—which was (fated?) again to do and undo me. (Given my green

---

[44] Gerard Manley Hopkins, from "That Nature was a Heraclitean Fire."
[45] Compare Derrida on *filtre*, in "Dénégations," 584; 53. And passim in his work.
[46] Though of course a Christian would say that to affirm this intellectual denial
would block a simultaneous 'act of faith'.
[47] Carl Jung, "Commentary," in *The Secret of the Golden Flower: A Chinese Book
of Life*, English trans. by Cary F. Baynes from Jung's German commentary and
R. Wilhelm's German trans. from the Chinese (San Diego, N.Y., London:
Harcourt, Brace, Jovanovich; Harvest ed. 1962), p. 112.

and callow history, I should have expected as much, but of course the callow never do.) Apropos of the topsails, I promptly processed the B.A. and processed through the sudatoria of the GREs. My GRE scores were uncommonly high, it turned out, high enough to win me a full fellowship in comparative literature at an Ivy League university. Ah Ivy League!--Your crenulated walls, your arch ogees and ogives, your Gothic abutments and Victorian undercrofts, your sweeps of quick-silver greensward. I remember thee. I am beholden to thee. I even much thank thee.

"Work hard and play hard," the rich and randy undergrads tried to teach us, but we—poor graduate grinds, scholarship kids all—spent all our time 'toting those library bales'. 'Tote those bales, shuck those blinders, flense those cauls', as our arch professors would have it. Night after night I lucubrated the bales. In seminar, I flensed the cauls of whatever insularity I had. The worldliness, the cold-eyed skepticism—they shucked whatever (academic) blinders I still wore.

I absorbed many good things—erudition, pluralism, some rela-tivism even. The university was not yet co-ed, though, and in my second semester—while visiting the town's Catholic church—I saw a Chinese girl descending from Mary's altar.

> "Oh langueo," gridai, e: "Causam languoris
> video nec caveo!" anche perché, un odore
> roseo spirava dalle sue labbra ed erano
> belli i suoi piedi nei sandali, e le gambe
> erano come colonne e come colonne le pieghe
> dei suoi fianchi, opera di mano d'artista.
> . . . . . . . . . . . . . . . . . . . . . . . . . . . . . .
> *stat rosa pristina nomine, nomina nuda*
> *tenemus.*
> —Umberto Eco, *Il nome della rosa* [48]

...adjective, noun (common or proper), immediately
nominalizable predicate (*rose, la rose, le rose, Rose* ["pink"
(adj.), "rose" (n.), "pink" (n.), "Rose"]...it retains,
out of context, the reserve of all those powers (Rose!) of a
name beyond names, the reserve that it still retains when it
becomes the last word...Here the translators might amass
references—to the Mystic Rose in *Miracle de la Rose* and in

---

[48] *Il nome della rosa* (Milan: Fabbri-Bompiani, 1980), pp. 249, 503; English edition, *The Name of the Rose*, trans. W. Weaver (London: Pan Picador pbk. / Secker and Warburg, 1984), pp. 246, 502.

*Glas*, to the same Mystic Rose in "The Secret Rose" by Yeats,...
—Derrida, "LIVING ON: *Border Lines*"[49]

...Verba homines facimus, nos quoque verba sumus.
—John Owen, *Epigrammata* (c. 1612)[50]

She had been kneeling at the altar and now she was coming down its steps. She was delicate-boned and fragile. A pale lotus parted by vermilion. Shimmering teeth. Alabaster skin fretted with maiden-hair. *Puella gracilis*. Transfixed, I stood in the back of the church a long time. Ensorceled. Six months later, in a grand Italian ceremony, we married. She had two personal names, her Chinese name and the Saint's name conferred by her parish priest back in Taiwan (upon the occasion of her Baptism, at the age of fifteen). But in this text we shall call her the Rose.

There (*là*), now—Rose. Rose, my Columbine.

One year into my Graduate School span (of five years), and seven months after first meeting with this Chinese maiden, I had married her. Without any real familiarity with women, and on the rebound from two seminary sequestrations, I had married much too early. If—as Umberto Eco reminds us—we all interpret others by acculturated names and codes, the *anima*-projection of an inexperienced man on an unknowing woman is worst (as Jung reminds us). Worst except, sometimes, for the *animus*-projection of that unknowing woman, who may carry—as this Columbine did—an even worse history of curtailments, of absences. (All told, God's own 'double-blind experiment'.)

---

[49] *Deconstruction and Criticism*, pp. 156, 158.
[50] In F. J. Nichols, ed. and trans., *An Anthology of Neo-Latin Poetry* (New Haven and London: Yale Univ. Press), p. 578.

La
rose

J'ai franchi
sur un pont de corail
quelque chose qui ne
permet pas le retou
r

—Claudel, *Cent Phrases*
*pour Eventails* [51]

From the start, Columbine tried to remake me: she wanted me to dance, host parties, be the envy of her Chinese friends. How much she had married me because I was an 'Ivy League man', and seemed in her eyes to guarantee a secure future, to this day I do not know. What I do know is that this Rose was definitely 'into puncture'. *Puncture*....Pink-eye and much more, I know this Rose gave me, ... pinking me, shearing me, searing me.

> Pin Lady is a woman with pins stuck in her couture, rows and rows of pins ...
> The embrace of Balloon Man and Pin Lady will be something to see...
> Balloon Man's arms will be wrapped around Pin Lady's pins and Pin Lady's embrangle will be wrapped about Balloon Man's balloons.
> They'll roll down the hill together...She's into puncture.
> —Donald Barthelme, "The Great Hug"[52]

But unlike Barthelme's Pin Lady, it seemed to me that mine both did and did not tell truth. At the end of our first year already, the Rose had disabused me of romantic illusion, of rosy scenario. This much of truth she had given me early indeed. Incessantly she vilified me for my Latinate tenderness, my displays of affection, and for what I took to be my esthetic tastes and intellectual bent.

---

[51] P. 708.
[52] Excerpted from Barthelme's "The Great Hug," in *Sixty Stories* (N.Y. Dutton, 1982), p. 315.

Pin Lady, how come you're so apricklededee? Was it something in your
childhood?
                                                    —Barthelme, ibid.

I'm convinced it *was* her childhood, and I do not mean at all to belittle.
On the contrary, as time passes I come to understand more, and this
feeds the hope I can someday come to forgive more. During the Sino-
Japanese war, the Rose was bombed for three years in succession by
the Japanese, and then—with her parents, brother, and sisters—was
tossed about in the fetor and hell-holes of the Communist vs.
Nationalist war (until 1949). Was Rose turning to Nightshade? Then
came the flight to Taiwan island, the separations and bereavements.
And then the pained adjustments to an island which must have
seemed so different in dialect and custom. Nightshade? The Rose's
parents had been from Northern China, of the landed aristocracy, and
her father was a full twenty years older than the mother. Before
marriage her mother had been quite a firebrand—she had gone south
on her own to Shanghai and even performed in Chinese opera, later
becoming an 'intellectual'. The Rose's father was a respected teacher,
a government official, and reformer. Given their disjoined personal
histories, and the general turmoil of the times, there must have been
much emotional distance between mother and father. Surely their
daughter my wife often hinted such had been the case. Nightshade.
The father died when Nightshade, who happened to be his youngest
daughter, was around fifteen years old: once, in a few precious
unguarded moments, she confided to me how his long pain-wracked
death from cancer had broken her heart. Nightshade, indeed. She was
to stay on in Taiwan for another ten years, finally leaving for the
United States in the mid-1960s, as her brother had done shortly
before her.

Our first daughter was born eleven months after our marriage.
She was the first of our Pasque-flowers. There would be two more—a
son born three years later, and a second daughter born a year after
him. (Indeed, the one successful collaboration between Columbine and
Harlequin would prove to be the children. No matter how outré the
harlequinade, these parents would, thank God, persevere in love and
service to their progeny.) Now grown, the two daughters and son are
happy, mature, capable of much affection. They are the three proud
and beautiful Easter-flowers of our own long long Lent.

My mother-in-law came to live with us in 1968, extricated from
Taiwan by the exorbitant monetary bond that her son and I together
posted with the U.S. Immigration Bureau. What became a horrid
ritual then began: Nightshade, in the face of every Confucianist
protocol, periodically evicted her mother from our house, usually after
several days of seething rage and bitter quarreling (screaming,
throwing things... this Chinese daughter could really throw the china).
When my parents visited (perforce seldom), she often threw them out
too, though they had from the start taken her to their hearts. It
seemed Nightshade could not be heart-*intimate* with anyone, least of
all with me (though she could be very gracious to other-than-kin and
to strangers: indeed, she would eventually become a nurse, a *good*
nurse). The incompatibility of our temperaments, much aggravated by
what was at the time the Roman Church's strictly enforced ban
against artificial contraception,[53] drove us to parallel but separate
lives under the same roof. Even when Columbine and Harlequin had
sex (and Harlequins always think they're adept at sex), Columbine
signaled she wanted only a mechanical operation, a gymnastic with no
accompanying love at all. And always from this darksome Rose's
distant past, from who knows what recesses of anger and thwarting,
there came her blind rage. Sometimes it came in slip-streams and
sometimes in a giant tsunami—but it always came. Nightshade.

My graduate studies progressed: classes for three years, then
the comprehensive examinations (called 'prelims' because they were
'preliminary' to the doctoral dissertation: failing them earned a Master's
degree, our university's 'kiss-of-death M.A.', a degree the Humanities
departments did not otherwise give[54]). When I look back now to those
days back then, what is conspicuous, strangely (not so strangely),
what *tweaks*, is not the intellectual osmosis, which happily happened,
which I am grateful for, and whose effects were like sweet water into a
sponge (to paraphrase Loyola[55]); what tweaks is the emotional trace,
the effects of deception, jealousy, ideological hatred, secret prejudice,—these whipped and stung like fast water off a sharp stone

---

[53] Artificial contraception was not only outlawed, but at least in our diocese
constituted the matter of a special promise: Catholics had to promise not to use
it, or they were not allowed a Catholic marriage.
[54] That is, one went straight through to the doctorate, which in comparative
literature at the time took usually six years (these six years were full-time,—we
did not do part-time undergraduate teaching).
[55] See "Rules for the Discernment of Spirits," in *The Spiritual Exercises*.

(Loyola again). Such vices are rife at all academic venues, of course, and reflect, sad to say, the human condition in general. But Apollinaire's famous observation had, back then, its particular relevance apropos of the Ivy League—

Le Paon ......

> By spreading his tail this bird so fair,
> Whose plumage drags the forest floor,
> Appears more lovely than before,
> but thus unveils his *derrière*.[56]

Such is the case because Ivy League professors used to do so much strutting—it was their national role. Thirty years ago, or thereabouts, this was perhaps especially true at my university in the various language and literature departments (less so, in the philosophy department), since rumor had it that the giant W.A.S.P. establishment was crumbling: the English department was under pressure to admit more Jewish faculty members, the German and French departments already had several Jewish professors, and the comparative literature faculty was, throughout my own Graduate School days, completely Jewish (in retaliation against the W.A.S.P.s, rumor had it). Into this clash of Titans (which on every count the Jews had of course the right to win), even we students—the five of us in comparative literature[57]—were thrown, and often... into the breach. As comparatists, we five took classes in several departments, inter-disciplinarians freecast into the fray, as it were. As an Italian-American from a Catholic undergraduate college, I found myself always odd-man-out,... roughcast, as it were.

I remember a hard-eyed W.A.S.P. brahmin, now deceased, who launched into anti-Catholic and specifically anti-Latin (anti-Spanish-and-Italian) tirades at every opportunity: how he loved to see me squirm. (There were eminently equitable professors too,—one of them, a Melvillean maverick, comes to mind at once.) Some of the Jewish professors were Europeans, refugees from devil-nazi fumaroles: they were wiry, endearing, and implacable. They were good to me. (My dissertation director seemed to have waterly-deep brown eyes and always an

---

[56] Trans. Roger Shattuck in W. Barnstone et al., *Modern European Poetry* (N.Y., Toronto, London: Bantam, 1966), p. 6.
[57] That is, there were five students in my entering class. I finished soonest, in five years—but probably because I felt, of the five classmates, the most stressed.

air of the bereft: he was both intelligent and kind.) Some of the American Jews were, from the first, crammed full of hate for me, infarcted with hate for me, impacted with it, blue-in-the-face with it. I came to feel their cold damp breaths more than once. Shades. Anamnesis: In seminar—Professor X, opining—"The Rosicrucians, a Catholic mendicant order, had a sinister influence on literature at the time." Mr. Magliola, remonstrating—"Rosicrucians were not a Catholic mendicant order." Professor X, rearing up in furious riposte—"Catholics are psychic cannibals, as is commonly known: witness their teaching on the Eucharist. Cannibals. Cannibals!"

Why have I bothered to remember all this? Why do I make it into so much of an issue? The reason is because I was unfairly tagged from the start; I was *stereotyped*, and it hurt. The stereotype, I am sure, was of a 'pious little Roman Catholic from a pious little school, who cannot think for himself, and who, like all his kind, is judgmental and rigid'. Further, I was made to pay, by way of abuse and contempt, for the crimes, no doubt the real crimes, of other Catholics, and of (all too often) the Roman Church itself. Especially, the heinous crime of anti-Semitism, the well-nigh 2000 years of it. This is why so many Jewish intellectuals were ready, apriori, to pillory me. Jewish brothers, sisters!—Some words to the Wise:—Backlash and reverse persecution just keep the vicious circle of hatred turning, that Wheel of *saṃsāra* spinning. Granted that my discomforts were unspeakably trivial next to the Crematoria, still I am human. I still flinch and wince. My tears still sting. I am not a saint (or I would—as Catholics say—simply embrace my suffering and 'offer it up', little as it is, in token reparation to God *for the sins of the Church*.) The likelihood is that you are protesting, dear reader, and thinking:—"*Tu quoque*, blithe equivocator!— The thrust of this your very 'apologia' is to show how much your Church *did* trap you, *did* distort and narrow you!" My answer, dear reader? I was born into an Italian blood-line and familial culture and into its Roman Church. These saturated my parents, my kin, my 'life-world'. Given a life-world is cumulative and sedimented, I can never outrun it. I can in retrospect gloss its early stages anew: I can negatively gloss it if I choose, and try as much as possible to start afresh. But given the nature of human psychology/biology, it would be impossible to excise its inevitable traces—even if I so intended. (Surely you know all this already!)

What is more (much more), the Italian tradition is so rich in 'humanitas' (sic), its treasures of intellect and art so vast, that I have—it should be needless to say—much to celebrate and *retain*. Even the 'end of man', the 'end of history'—*pace* Foucault et al.—cannot end them for me. And the Roman Church has played a positive role in this millennia-long narrative. This is not to deny that it has also played a negative role: Italians know this; we are no fools, and a characteristic Piedmontese anti-clericalism was amply represented among my many kin. We've had 'Petroleum politics' for a long time. Not (*non*) without (*sans*[58]) reason does the word 'petroleum' derive from Gk. *petros/petra* (stone, rock) and *oleum* (oil) from *ELAIA*, olive. Petroleum disseminates in many ways East and West. Why, even *brai* (F.) is a 'residue of oil and petroleum' (see Larousse).

Not entirely without reason does Derrida's Gérard Titus-Carmel (sic) deliver us the mischievous palindrome:

Léon, émir cornu d'un roc, rime Noël.[59]

I was trained from my youth in an Irish Christian-brother and then Jesuit tradition that is very humanist, and intellectually *informed*. (This tradition's defects—especially when/as it is transplanted/ cultivated in the United States—stem from *emotional* lacunae, experiential lacunae: THESE latter constitute the 'object' of this mixed critique, the bio-*catalogue raisonné*, which is both my 'apologia' and '*apo*-apologia'.) I recall to this day a dismaying incident in Graduate School: I dared to cite in seminar a Jesuit scholarly source, and my classmates—shifting uncomfortably in their chairs—began at once to titter and cluck. Fortunately, this time Professor XXX (rare polyhistor) was there to put them right—"Oh in Europe, you must understand, Dominicans and Jesuits participate in scholarly life; even in Germany and the Low Lands, they come to all the conferences. It is recognized, even by those who hate them, that they represent a long and viable academic tradition, and must be dealt with in those terms—as equals."

Please understand, dear Jewish readers, that many, many Catholics, and especially many Italians, are not and have not been anti-Semitic. Christ's suffering on the cross reminds us first of our own wickedness/weakness, and then of the wickedness/weakness which infects all humanity. My parents held Jews in high esteem, and in America lived near a community where Jewish and Italian

---

[58] See Derrida on 'non-*sens*' and 'non-*sans*' passim in his work.
[59] See *The Truth in Painting*, p. 251. *Roc*, R.O.C. too?

immigrants had worked side-by-side in the garment industry. Without diminishing the Church's crimes against Jews, we 'academics' should recall in particular the glowing periods in European history when there were happy exchanges of biblical scholarship between rabbinic and Catholic exegetes,—in tenth century Italy and Germany, for example; and the friendly collaborations between the Jewish and Catholic 'esoteric philosophers', as in 12th and 13th century Italy and France, for example. In the modern-day United States, if there have been a Father Coughlin (whom the Church silenced), a Joe McCarthy, and a Patrick Buchanan, there have also been Dorothy Day and the Kennedys and Mario Cuomo, and Fathers Merton, Berrigan, and Drinan.

Apropos of all the above, a scene in Charles Dickens' Bleak House has shadowed me since my graduate days, sometimes playfully, sometimes soberly. The scene constitutes the last part of Vol. III, chapter 7. From out of a ceiling-mural, the figure of a Roman—carefully painted there—points his finger down into the real room below:

> All eyes look up at the Roman, and all voices murmur, 'If he could only tell us what he saw!' ... He is pointing at an empty chair, and at a stain upon the ground before it that might be almost covered with a hand ...So it shall happen surely, through many years to come, that ghostly stories shall be told of the stain upon the floor, so easy to be covered, so hard to be got out; and that the Roman, pointing from the ceiling, shall point... with a deadly meaning.[60]
> —Vol III, ch. 7, "Closing In," *Bleak House*

For a Roman (Italian) and "Roman" (as Anglicans call Roman Catholics) like myself, the scene can be made to crazily allegorize in several directions (I'm on the ceiling, in the empty chair, and/or out of the room,...*ça dépend*). The Roman/"Roman" high up in the ceiling-mural becomes my *ascendance* (in more senses then one, here!), my Roman/"Roman" lineage, i.e., my ancestry,—for better or for worse. That is, I must celebrate Rome's good, repent for its bad. The indicting Index finger is also my (Freudian) super-ego: this is why the perpetrator of the crime is unknown (in the novel, only the mute Roman "sees" the actual crime, which is a murder). The Finger makes an effective Lacanian Other/other, too—unknowable, finite, and ever-changing as to its imputed 'meaning'. And the Roman/ "Roman" is also

---

[60] See also the accompanying illustration by "Phiz" (H.K. Browne), which is thus an illustration of a room having an illustrative painting on its own ceiling. I have used the Estes and Lauriat edition (Boston: 1895), interleaf pp. 120/121.

of course a deconstructionist (here perhaps I'm back on the ceiling). In the text of chapter 7 circumambient to our excerpt, however, Dickens chooses to emphasize the vain *projection*: the inanimate Roman is cast in a role *not* really his. Methinks (in my internal scenario) that whatever I suffered from scapegoatism is hereby depicted (and darker things too, that happened to me).

I passed the 'prelims' (comprehensives), wrote my doctoral dissertation (in phenomenology/hermeneutics) over the next two years, and graduated—earning that Ivy League Ph.D. at a time when the job market was drifting into its Dog Days. Because I was offered graduate-level teaching in comparative literature right away—beginning in the first year of my appointment, and specifically in that program's 'core', namely the 'methods' course and the doctoral seminar—I accepted an assistant professorship at "a leading Midwestern university," one of the Land Grant mega-universities. For once in a lifetime I was being a pragmatist.

Thus it was that Columbine and Harlequin and offspring, their belongings in tow, came to take up residence in the U.S. Midwest, far from their relatives and even further (than they thought) from the worlds they knew.

> Sleep has two gates they say: one is of Horn
> And spirits of truth find easy exit there,
> The other is perfectly wrought of glistening Ivory,
> And from it the shades send false dreams up to the world.
> —Virgil, *Aeneid*, VI, 893-6 [61]

In what the Hindu tradition calls 'Sleep-Dreams' I have often dreamt of late about the 'Awake-Dream',[62] part elysian, part sheol, and part grand-guignol, which was to constitute our *next fourteen years.*

> Noughts-and-crosses: chiefly Brit., [for] ticktacktoe*...a game
> in which two players alternately put crosses and ciphers in
> compartments of a figure formed by two vertical lines crossing

---

[61] Patric Dickinson, trans., *The Aeneid* (N.Y.: New American Library, 1961).

[62] I allude, only half-playfully, to two of the three states of ordinary human illusion, according to the *Aitareya*. See the Upanishad *Aitareya* and accompanying notes in *The Upanishads, Breath of the Eternal*, trans. Swami Prabhavanada and F. Manchester (N.Y.: New American Library).

> two horizontal lines and try to get a row of three crosses or
> three ciphers before the opponent does.[63]

>> *Ticktacktoe: (probably [from] ticktack). Also called
>> 'crisscross'. Ticktack: A steady ticking sound, as of a clock.[64]

Herewith a suite of Noughts and Crosses from those dreams of the
Dream: sometimes, after all, the crosshatches of dream carry a
mortal's 'truest' history ...

xxxxxxxxxxxxxxxxxxxxxxxxxxxxxxxxxxxxxxxxxxxxxxxxxxxxxxxxxxxx

A thin, loose-skinned man, Faulknerian-faced,
grinning, amicable: "Come in, come in...while I
am on sabbatical the house is yours..."

> A year later, another professor, fatter and ruddier
> and rheumier (upon entering our newly purchased
> home): [He points to the living-room wall, grim-faced]
> ... "You're in America now, Dr. Magliola.
> That crucifix must come down."

> A teacher who can arouse a feeling for one single good action, for
> one single good poem, accomplishes more than those who fill
> memories with rows and rows of natural objects, classed with
> name and form.
> —Goethe[65]

>> Teach a good poem.
>> Teach a good poem.
>> Teach a good poem.
>> Teach a good poem.

Gaudeo discere, ut doceam
('I rejoice to learn, so I may teach')
> —Seneca, *Ad Lucilium Epistulae Morales*, 6.4

---

[63] *Webster's Third New International Dictionary of the English Language*,
Unabridged (Springfield: Merriam-Webster, 1986). Henceforth, *Webster's
Unabridged.*
[64] See *American Heritage Dictionary*, New College edition (1969).
[65] *Elective Affinities*, trans. E. Mayer and L. Bogan (Chicago: Regnery, 1963), p. 25.

Cocktail parties (attendance *de rigueur*): They duck,
feint, and weave—the lusters after academic *appâts*.
The Look over the Shoulder, the Break and Dissolve
when a better Prize enters the door. A Flamen of
Flummery, perhaps? Look at how the Rank and File
parts (rank and vile) to let him pass! And then—ah!
—look at how they close in, the feckless flunkies—
the company-finks.

> Sunlit Sunday mornings: The children and
> Harlequin going to Mass. Most of the time
> Columbine comes too.

FFFF-Fantods of Fatigue From such a Fardel!—the burden of
    the bills,...

> Hear the tolling of the bills—
> Iron bills!...
> ...the rolling of the bills—
> Of the bills, bills, bills:—
> Hearken to
> the tolling of the bills—
> Of the bills, bills, bills, bills
> Bills, bills, bills—
> To the moaning and the groaning of the bills.[66]

Beetling and bristling,
  o'er brimming bills:—

> Of a heavy mortgage,

and Three sweet but ever-gaping mouths, and Columbine's tuition
(she is going back to college). Plus a supplementary fardel—
Housework (Harlequin, alas, does most of the Cleaning, half the
Laundry, and more than half of the Cooking)...
   ...All in all, (Domestic) Dengue Fever of the mind/body [Dengue
        Fever,–also called "Break-Bone Fever," and
        "The Bone-Crusher"]

...and Teaching and Writing and Committee-work in

> BRICK BUILDINGS ON BRICK DADOS
> BRICK BUILDINGS ON BRICK DADOS
> BRICKBUILDINGSONBRICKDADOSBR
> ICK BU IL DIN  GSO NB RI CKDADOS

---

[66] Cf. Derrida's (and others') Poe in Derrida, *Glas* (Paris: Galilée, 1979), p. 177.

Professorial ants, little pismires, run in and run out of many,
many doors all day long. The pismire is necessarily *(forcément)* a
committee ant. Some of them of the mired-in-the-quagmire
species of pismire.
*Formi-dable. Fo(u)rmi-dable. ...Forse.*

          [Upon doing Zen-sitting for the first time-[67]]
Beginning to 'ride backwards on the jade elephant'[68]:
There's 'a life-root to crack'.[69]
Zen-sit until 'the bottom falls out of the barrel of pitch'.[70]

      But an older one Professing in authority over Harlequin—
      and not kind and equitable like a woman—lies in wait, very
      ill-disposed: ...

                  ... sin [feminine] is crouching [masculine] at your door
                  and unto you its [masculine] desire (hunger),...
                              —Genesis 4:7 (Lit. trans. of the
                                Hebrew text, which marks gender
                                chiasmically here[71])


Summers, shafts of sunlight pierce the Plankton ...

France... *Bouquinerie,* academic *colloques,* and—at the top of
Montmartre's
        zigzagging steps—the *Basilique*
        *du Sacré Coeur...*

---

[67] I was guided by a trained (and 'advanced') Buddhist colleague. Unless one's instructor is an adept, it is potentially dangerous to attempt Zen-sitting.

[68] See K'uan Yü Lu (Charles Luk), *Ch'an and Zen Teaching,* Second Series (London: Rider and Co., 1961), pp. 137-8: The jade elephant symbolizes the Buddhist Path (of meditation). "'Reverse-ride' is the Ch'an idiom for 'going against the stream of birth and death'..." (by escaping its causality).

[69] "The Chinese idiom 'to sit on and to crack' is [more or less] equivalent to the Western term 'to break up'." In Zen-sitting one aims to 'crack' the 'life-root', i.e. the 'basis for life'. See *Ch'an and Zen Teaching,* First Series, p. 53. At this time, I learned the techniques of Ch'an/Zen meditation. Ch'an/Zen masters disagree as to whether the practice of Christianity necessarily renders a Christian's Zen-meditation a form of 'Heretics' Zen' (an old Buddhist pejorative).

[70] Master Sheng Yen, trans. Ch'an Meditation Center staff, Elmhurst, N.Y. (Elmhurst: Dharma Drum, 1982). p. 3.

[71] See the pertinent endnote, Jerusalem Bible (unabridged ed., 1966).

> Ah! la charmante chose
> Quitter un pays morose
> Pour Paris
> Paris joli ...
> —Apollinaire, "Voyage à Paris"

[And visits to Relatives: a great-uncle had migrated to Normandie, confecting: his progeny flourish there, layers upon layers of them: mille-feuilles.]

Italy ... Not so much for the 'bel pasticcio!' (which proliferates indeed), as for the contrary, the timeless decorum ...

> The bed, the books, the chair, the moving nuns,
> The candle as it evades the sight, these are
> The sources of happiness in the shape of Rome,...
> —Wallace Stevens[72]

(Rest, George Santayana, rest...)

| | |
|---|---|
| Quis te redonavit Quiritem | (Who gives you back, a Citizen |
| Dis patriis Italoque coelo;... | again to ancestral gods and Italian— |
| —Horace, Lib. II, carm. vii | sky?      —Horace, *Odes*, II, 7) |

Then, necessarily, Return to Plankton, and—

BRICK BUILDINGS ON BRICK PLINTHS
BRICK BUILDINGS ON BRICK PLINTHS

Professorial cathedrae:

"A chaque saint, sa gargouille!"........

"Saint(e)s"—J.A., C.S., B.B., D.K., M.M.R. (and more).
And among them, Professor W.K., akimbo in his office doorway.
THEN, of a sudden (for my benefit), 'high Camp' histrionics—
He throws up and out the graphemes of the word-sign
"BEWARE"... "There the word is," he points. "It is floating,... see?"
Then of a sudden, "The W has dropped out!" he screams (feigning
dismay). "BEARE" floats on. Then of a sudden, "The second E is
dropping out!" he screams (more dismay). "BEAR" survives, and
floats on. (Thunderously, then sternly, then wistfully, he repeats

---

[72] His "To an Old Philosopher in Rome," in *The Collected Poems of Wallace Stevens* (N.Y.: Knopf, 1965).

this word of Perdurance as it floats down the hallway and out of sight—): "BEAR!!"... "BEAR!"... "BEAR—" . . . . . .

> A resolute scholar and a humane person will
> never seek to live at the expense of injuring *jen*
> ['probity/comity', i.e., 'humanitas']
> —Confucius, *The Analects*, XV:8[73]

"Gargouilles"?—Alas, of too litigious an ilk for *parafes*.

### BRICK PLINTHS
### BRICK DADOS

*Front rows*
Bubble-of-maple, applebutter,
Coxcomb, Cobweb
Teal, Oatmeal
Vixen, Flaxen
Silversieve, Blackolive
Maraschinocherry, Gooseberry
Pompomyellow, Marshmallow ,...
> —A. L. Lazarus, "Girls' Heads Bent on Taking a Test"[74]

> Teach a good poem.
> Teach a good poem.

> Gaudeo discere, ut doceam.
> Gaudeo discere, ut doceam.

CROUCHING AT YOUR DOOR
CROUCHING AT YOUR DOOR
CROUCHING AT YOUR DOOR

---

[73] Sadly, the standard English translations of Chinese texts, and of Confucius in particular, usually *tra*nslate as male what is in Chinese non-gendered. Most of the translations from Chinese in my text are revised so as to represent the gender neutrality of the Chinese grammar (I have *cross-checked* with native Chinese scholars in each instance). For various *tra*nslations of *jen*, the beginner can consult the glossary-appendix at the end of Wing-Tsit Chan, trans. and compiler, *A Source Book in Chinese Philosophy* (Princeton: Princeton University Press, 1963). In my text, translations from Confucius's *Lun Yü* (rendered in English as *Analects* since James Legge's time) are derived from Lin Yutang, *Wisdom of China and India* (N.Y.: Random House, 1942). For those who prefer a more scholarly translation, my Chinese sources recommend D. C. Lau, trans., *Confucius: The Analects* (London: Penguin, 1979).
[74] In *Suit of Four*, p. 11.

"bk....confs....arts....prs@intl.convs....co-chr:doct.prog.
phil.&lit....esthet.(phil.dept.)...Latn.(for.lang.dept.)...
comp.lit.meth.&doct.sem.(comp.lit.)...comms....stud.eval.
tching v.gd....promo.assoc.prof."...rah!-rah!...rah-rah!
rah-rah...bray...bray...bray...bray...bray...*pouf! pouf!*

CROUCHING AT YOUR DOOR
CROUCHING AT YOUR DOOR

Hexagram 23: 'Disintegration'

("The season indicated is autumn,
when everything is beginning to rot
and disintegrate. The five *yin* lines
suggest weak, dark forces moving up
to overcome the strong. The shape of
the hexagram suggests a house with
only walls and roof remaining. The
structure is there, but is ready to
collapse.")

The Lines: Six at the bottom—The
frame of the couch
disintegrates. This way
brings destruc-
tion.
Ominous.
—I Ching [75]

---

[75] Riseman trans., pp. 37, 38.

No more Zen-sitting: I've become fat, and sudsy.


BRICK BUILDINGS ON BRICK DADOS ON BRICK PLINTHS
BRICK BUILDINGS ON BRICK DADOS ON BRICK PLINTHS
BRICK BUILDINGS ON BRICK DADOS ON BRICK PLINTHS

> Sunlit Sunday mornings: the children and Harlequin—
> laughing, holding hands—climbing up the Church-stairs
> to Mass. Columbine does not come.

Gaudeo discere, ut doceam.

Fuchsia in the face and bulbous, I gasp around the running-track...
I have joined Dr. I.'s experimental class of professor-joggers.
Dr. I., towering Egyptian and the university's specialist in the
'correlation of physical exercise and mental states'.
Boastful-yet-affable (a feat only Near Easterners seem able
to bring off), he loves to jog his joggers and they love
to be jogged...

> Dr. I., imperious, commanding his adulating flock (*y compris*
> many Jews): "Waist-bends! No, in the other direction! And STAY
> DOWN. Touch the floor with the tips of your fingers! [and then,
> impishly—] May I remind you, gentlemen, you are bowing to
> Mecca. To Mecca!"

BRICKS    BRICKS
    BRICKS
BRICKS    BRICKS
    BRICKS
BRICKS    BRICKS
    BRICKS
      France/Italy
BRICKS
BRICKS
      France/Italy

> Back to Zen-sitting. Thin again (130 lbs.).
> And much Hatha-Yoga (twice a day).

And Sunlit Sunday mornings: the three children and
Harlequin—giggling—bounding up the Church-stairs to Mass.
Nightshade doesn't come.

CROUCHING AT YOUR DOOR
CROUCHING AT YOUR DOOR

Hexagram 21: 'Biting
    Through'

("The characteristics of Li [Lightning, above] and Chen [thunder, below] are combined here. The hexagram shape suggests vigorous chewing [which bites through obstacles]...")

The Lines: Nine in the fourth place—he bites on stored, bony meat;
                receives
                coins and
                weapons.
                Benefit in recognizing difficulties, and in
                persevering.
                Auspicious.
                                —*I Ching* [76]


            Much rat-a-tat of typewriters: ratatouille of print.
            Rat-a-tat. Rat-a-tat.

Hexagram 58: 'Joyousness'

---

[76] Riseman trans., pp. 35, 36.

("The trigram Tui [Lake, youngest daughter, the joyous] doubled, forms this hexagram...Tui also represents success, and prosperity. It is thus favorable for business projects and new undertakings. But, for existing relationships and undertakings there may be misfortune and quarrels.")

The Image: The lake replenishing the lake symbolizes joyousness.
           Thus the superior person *studies and practices*
           *With his companions.*

The Lines: Nine in the fourth place—calculated joyousness is not a peace.
                    With cautious correctness, good fortune.

*—I Ching* [77]

[Upon finishing an academic year at the National Humanities Center, Research Triangle Park, N.C.–]... For ten months I have shuttled, woofing from 2nd floor office (dark and *yin*) down onto the Center's mezzanine (light and airy and *yang*) in order to learn, discuss, and agglutinate, and wefting back up to the 2nd floor office again, in order to think and write and concatenate. For the first time since childhood one has had the *time* to think meaningfully, to (so-called) create.

      Now their tiny tinny caravan, top-heavy with books and domestic debris, weaves its way back to the Midwest. Columbine in the Toyota and Harlequin in the Datsun and the children in both, on a high and windy bridge over the Ohio River they titubate for a moment, and then pass on.

                    Columbine comes to Mass sometimes, and
                    the children are going to Catholic schools.

Teach a good poem. Teach a good poem.

      [Upon profession as a Carmelite tertiary,[78] my period of formation having come to a close—]
      I look up at Mary of Carmel, olive-skinned and
      Jewish-Mediterranean in the old painting.
      Her White Mantle, once gleaming, is now turning ancient.

---

[77] Riseman trans., pp. 85, 86.
[78] A lay tertiary, so-called because s/he belongs to the secular 'Third Order' of a Community of Religious (in my case the Carmelites), and partakes—according to his/her state-of-life—in its duties, special charisms, and apostolate.

Not ashen, though, nor egg-white, but a sort of
old ivory—*blanc cassé*, the French say.
Her White Mantle is pinned with a yellow star.
Sometimes the star seems a Davidic yellow, and
sometimes saffron.
The Mantle is itself yellowing in patches, because of the
tempera paint, but only in patches.
Her Brown Robe is beginning to crackle too, criss-crossed with
jagged lines my soul can feel: the tempera paint
is turning very very old, but venerable Mary wafts an incense
all the lovelier.
Yes, thoroughly Ancient Mary.
And, indeed, thoroughly Postmodern Mary...
Of the twelve stars encircling her,
one is hidden behind her head and another is half-hidden.
The Carmelite motto floats below on its
Churrigueresque banderole, "Zelo zelatus sum pro Domino Deo
nostro," but the painter has occulted the letter U of
*sum* (Lt. 'I am–'), hiding it in a fold so only *s/m* shows.
The scapular around my neck has an image of Mary holding
a scapular, on which in turn Mary holds a scapular, on which
in turn Mary holds a scapular. . . . . . . . .
The image is sewn onto the brown Carmelite cloth in
noticeably large sutures.
The front and back flaps of the scapular are held together by
brown cord, and my head is in between, in the hole, this
interval.

Zen-sitting
Zen-sitting
Zen-sitting

A second book, and several more anthology-chapters, come to
completion. Harlequin is promoted to the full professorship. Rah-
rah. *Pouf!*

"He walks on the tiger's tail: the tiger bites him. Misfortune."[79]
                                        Misfortune
                                        Misfortune
                                        Misfortune

In Taiwan, next, all five of us settle down for a sabbatical year abroad.

---

[79] See *I Ching*, hexagram 10 ('Treading')—six in the 3rd place (Riseman trans., p. 22).

The children and I, breathless with delight.
But Nightshade is loth: viscous memories shingle her eyes,
their dampness creeping cold along her skin.

Tamkang University, in the mountains but over-looking
   the aquamarine China straits.
Nicknamed 'the Garden university'.[80]
      Imperial Palace-style architecture:
         Carmine-red pillars,
           Vaulting tile roofs,
              Cloud-railing bridges.
      Sunken-gardens laced with worn stepping-stone.
      Orange camellias—banks and banks of them.
      Dark lotus-ponds.
      Surrealist mountains—
        diaphanous in the dawn-mist,
        steamy and lush in the tropic-day.
      Rows and rows of rice terrace,—and, their backs flecked
with busy white birds, the lumbering water-buffalo.

[Upon returning to the Midwest and the university,
after the sabbatical year—]:

Hexagram 47: 'Oppression'

---

[80] Chiang Kai-shek's evacuation to Taiwan (1949) brought with it hundreds of
thousands of young, unmarried Mainland recruits. In time, these soldiers—many
of whom, far from home and kin, remained unmarried—were mustered out in
work-battalions of sorts (with their own syndicates, privileges, camaraderie). At
Tamkang University they supplied a goodly portion of the cooks, mechanics,
maintenance men, gardeners. Especially,—gardeners. Teams of them fanned out
over the campus everyday, transforming it into a fabulous and vast Oriental
garden. I moved to National Taiwan University, Taipei, in 1988,—but my later
sojourns back to Tamkang alarmed me. The ugly *bétonnage* of urban life was
beginning to encroach even the 'garden university', creeping up the mountains,
wiping out the rice terraces. And the gardeners were in their late middle-age.

(This is one of the major 'danger signs' of the *I Ching*, signifying extreme difficulty... Exhaustion is symbolized by *K'an* [water] lying under *Tui* [lake]. The lake is empty and its water drained away. The lines— one weak holding down two strong and two weak enclosing one strong—suggest restriction, obstacles and oppression.[81])

The Lines: Nine in the fifth place—oppressed by the figure with scarlet trappings,

> His nose and feet are cut off.
> Accepting this, joy comes slowly.
> Benefit in sacrifice.
>
> —*I Ching* [82]

## CROUCHING AT YOUR DOOR
## CROUCHING AT YOUR DOOR

"the whisperer who hides away"
—From Sûrah xciv, *The Holy Koran* [83]

the whisperer who hides away
the whisperer who hides away
the whisperer who hides away

> Some people, because of their irresistible desire for fame, wealth, and power, have become cultured by education, art, religion, etc., and may exhibit on the surface a dignified character and noble deeds. Yet, hidden in their hearts lie secret burning ambitions, mean ideas, and dirty tricks... Therefore there are in this world well-educated hypocrites and robed devils.
>
> —Ch'an Master Sheng Yen[84]

## SCARLET TRAPPINGS
## SCARLET TRAPPINGS
## SCARLET TRAPPINGS

---

[81] The commentary continues—"All six lines are unfavorable, but the most extreme misfortune bears the seeds of great regeneration, if one can understand and absorb the hard spirit of the time" (p. 70).

[82] Riseman trans., pp. 69-71.

[83] See T. Cleary's endnote to Sûrah xciv, in T. Cleary, trans., *The Essential Koran* (N.Y.: Harper, 1993).

[84] Master Sheng-Yen, *Ch'an*, bi-lingual text (Taipei: I-Yu, 1979), p. 23.

> And her teeth in me,
>      ...... Rose *dentata*,
>                    for over eighteen years.
>              Shimmering teeth in me.

> Slow trepanning of the brain,
>    skewering of the skull. Spit-work.

> Slow despiteous spite-work
> via the spit-work.
> Spite-work on the spit-work.

> NO MORE.
> NO MORE.
> NO MORE!

Malfeasance: 'wrongdoing'.
Defeasance: 'rendering void, nullification'.

## THE MALFEASANCE/DEFEASANCE OF GOD?

> Increase. Benefit in setting forth.
> Benefit in crossing[85] the great water.

> *—I Ching* [86]

> Resigning from my university position in the
> United States, I accept an appointment as
> distinguished chair professor in the graduate
> school of Tamkang University, Taiwan.

From behind the Mega-university's purdah-curtain,—

come remonstrations of friends: "Robert, you're in good standing and
have a bright future, NEH grants, national posts someday, and
possibly a Guggenheim...You are a tenured full professor, with the
attendant perquisites...Why throw everything away?"
.........

---

[85] Not that the problematic of crossing is ever so simple. Indeed, this 'my' text is
through-and-through a treatment of crossings. Compare *La dissémination*, p.
392: "Le miroir se traverse *de lui-même*, autrement dit ne se traverse jamais."
Nagarjuna, the Indian Buddhist philosopher, makes much the same point.
[86] The 'Judgement' from Hexagram 42, Riseman trans., p. 63. For the pertinent
'Line', see Six in the Second Place (p. 64).

come snickerings from the ill-disposed: Maleficent Mangonels,[87] they
fling balls of burning pitch,

>          of Obloquy—
>              "Ah, male menopause, Dr. Magliola?"
>              "Middle-age crisis, Dr. Magliola?"
>              "Too hot in the kitchen here?"...
>              "Aren't American women docile
>               enough for you?"
>          of Derision—
>              "Sold out to/for the Chinese? The
>               geekie Chinese, with their rinky-dink
>               buildings and rube goldberg economy?
>               The caterwauling Chinese and all their
>               gew-gaw? Our Yellow Adversaries?"

>     A big BUDDHA-LAUGH to them.
>     A big BUDDHA-LAUGH!
>     At last I have learned how to give
>     a big BUDDHA-LAUGH.

>     "Six in the fourth place: Entering the belly of the dark
>                     through the left side.
>                     He wins the heart of the dark:
>                     he slips out the gate."
>                                 —*I Ching* [88]

xxxxxxxxxxxxxxxxxxxxxxxxxxxxxxxxxxxxxxxxxxxxxxxxxxxxxxxxxxxx

[On the other side of the world I stand, two months later; in front
of me, eighteen Chinese graduate students: I open the seminar in
phenomenology and deconstruction]—

>     In the *Inferno*, Dante descends to 'il punto al qual si
>     traggon d'ogni parte i pesi' ['the point towards which—from

---

[87] "Mangonel: (ME *mangnel*, fr. MF *mangunel*, prob. fr. ML *manganellus*, dim. of
LL *manganum* ballista, mangonel, fr. GK *manganon* philter, ballista; akin to GK
*manganeuein* to deceive, MIr *meng* deception, ruse, Toch A *mank* guilt, error; Skt
*mañju* beautiful; basic meaning: to beautify):—a military engine formerly used
for throwing missiles (as stones or javelins)"—excerpted (there's even more) from
*Webster's Unabridged.*
[88] Hexagram 36, 'Darkening of the Light', but here the dark becomes a means of
escape. Very Oriental, perhaps.

all sides—weights are pulled'[89]], makes a half-circle turn,
and then—edging along a slender passageway—positions
himself so he can climb upward through this other half and
come out on the diametrically opposite side of the round
earth from where he had begun his initial descent. When
he comes out, he finds an island-mountain right there, and
on the top of the mountain is the Paradise, the Walled-in
Garden [Eden].

I too have emerged here, at the mountain with the
beautiful Garden-University on top. Thank you for
receiving me.

[I do not tell these same students until later that in Dante the long
way up the mountain is Purgatory: beginning students—and
human beings in general—do not accept talk of deconstruction
readily. (And what could Purgatory be but deconstruction, even in
what is called "the most technical sense"?[90])]

Indeed, Taiwan—and the teeming/glorious *Umwelt* of Chinese culture—
were about to become for me an Eden and a 'purgatorio' and then—thank
God—some Braille-work on a mountain-top.*

> * Braille: (after L. Braille, French teacher of the
>             blind) A system of writing for the blind that
>             uses characters made up of raised dots in a
>             6-dot cell *arranged in two vertical columns...*
>
> Braille tablet: see Braille slate.[91]

---

[89] That is, by gravity. See *Inferno*, xxxiv, 111.

[90] That is, it can be said—if and when one aims to operate within the parameters
of Catholic theology—that purgatory purges both sinful and neurotic constructs,
and prepares us to celebrate the salubrious logocentrisms-as-deconstructed
which constitute our psyche. Buddhism, for its part, has of course its own very
different ways of dissolving logocentric constructs, including the psyche. Compare
Derrida on "psyche" in the title essay of his *Psyché: inventions de l'autre*.

[91] Both entries are from *Webster's Unabridged*.

PART ONE


CURRICULA VITAE




Section Two




Curriculum Vitae Novae:
Psycho-bio-graphemes in Saltire
with Convoluted Borders


—For the BBC's "What's My Word?"

To slip out the gate, to turn upside-down, edge along the ambage, and head in the new direction required that I die a kind of death. Goodbye, brick plinths and dados. Death's *glas* takes its toll...

> Abba, dark death is the breaking of a glass.
> The dazzled flakes and splinters disappear.
> The seal is as relaxed as dirt, 'perdu'.
> —Wallace Stevens[1]

Is it bemusing that the 'official' Chinese name for the mega-university I had just left is, in English,—(the Buddha's) "Universal Ferrying-Across"? (A 'phonic translation', linguists call it.)

> 'Universal Ferrying-Across' (Sanskrit *viśva pāramitā*), the Buddhist's 'Crossing Over' to liberation from *saṃsāra* (the wheel of lives and deaths).[2]

(The 'official' Chinese translation for my Ivy League university starts with the very same word: old Shakyamuni's *viśva*... has been tracing me, tracing me.)

Why did Harlequin choose to leave American university life, and indeed, the United States itself? He was gagging from the forcemeat of pain which was his marriage, his paste-up of a marriage. To a wife who behind his back derided him to her friends: that he was so tedious, so

---

[1] From "A Golden Woman in a Silver Mirror."
[2] In Taiwan the Chinese term for *viśva pāramitā* also refers to the grand folk-ceremony whereby disembodied spirits are helped across from a worse spirit-state to a better one.

unromantic. He was fleeing his mock-up of a marriage to a wife who—
during stints of cold sulk lasting a month or more—would not even bid
him a 'good morning'. "Tant va le pot a l'eaue qu'il brise" ("So much
the pot takes water, it breaks").[3] Harlequin was detecting in himself
more and more signs of mental malaise: his behavior was becoming
quirky, the price of not repression but prolonged suppression.
Harlequin had not in all those years given his body to another: yet
Columbine chose ninety percent of the time not even to sleep in the
same bed with him. She never once told him *why*, nor ever opened her
heart to him in anything, despite his pleading.

> Some say the world will end in fire,
> Some say in ice.
> From what I've tasted of desire
> I hold with those who favor fire.
> But if it had to perish twice,
> I think I know enough of hate
> To say that for destruction ice
> Is also great
> And would suffice.
> —Robert Frost[4]

Not that she wasn't suffering too, inside: Harlequin's logic told him
she must have been—He was sorry for that. When they finally separated, they were already well into middle-age.

What could have been the dear sweet Rose's gloriole years, and
my years of strapping *virilità...*, were irrevocably past. Her springtide
and mine, unspent, lay cold-dead in the water. "Reason enough to cry."
O *Sancta Mater Ecclesia*, you should have given us more options,
somehow. Somehow.

The first reason, then, that Harlequin left America was to escape
from Columbine in a way that was surgically clean, a way which
would avoid the bloody domestic mess that comes from merely moving
'to the other side of town'. His children, although already grown-up,
had to be protected from the *sub rosa* gossip and febrile fits which can
arise when estranged parents live in hostile proximity to each other.
His older daughter was beginning college; Harlequin arranged that

---

[3] From François Villon's serio-comical 'ballade',— "Tant grate chievre..."
(fifteenth century). By all means read this pre-modern 'ballade' for its wise
postmodernity.
[4] "Fire and Ice," in the *Complete Poems* (N.Y.: Holt, Rinehart and Winston, 1949),
p. 268.

the other two children come to pass time in Taiwan, and alternately go to school there. Indeed, over the intervening years they have—considerably more, perhaps, than their mother does—come to appreciate and cherish Chinese society: they are now, thank God, internationalists in the best sense. (Harlequin arranged to supply the family very well financially over the many years ahead, and he signed over to Nightshade his entire academic pension[5].)

> A person's relations with his fellow man must not be based on the desire to triumph over him. This ruins the whole relationship and is the undoing of truth. For when a person has in mind only triumph over his fellow, he strives to establish his own point of view or his own wish, regardless of whether it is true or false...
> —Rabbi Menahem ben Solomom Ha-Meri, from *Bet Ha*
> *–Behirah* on *Pirkē Abot* (Judah Goldin trans.)

Another reason for Harlequin's leaving the United States was a long-*standing*/deep-*seated* dissatisfaction with American academic life, and he had had experience in three sectors of it—the 'public State' system, the 'private denominational', and the 'private Ivy League'. Too much of an American professor's life is necessarily consumed in the minute discriminations and parcelings-up of Power: even a full professor cannot escape these, since to refuse to 'play the game' of this *grimoire* inevitably provokes retaliation, sinister retaliation. Some university super-committee or some Dean will *hatchet* one's most altruistic aims as an intellectual—perhaps to teach a graduate elective course, or to win a stipend enabling research. (I remember seeing a graphic documentary showing several lions and a pack of hyenas shredding and pulping each other: dollops of bleeding meat went splashing in all directions. Nature Red in Tooth and Claw. American academic life is worse—*invisible*, its Darwinian combat *suppurates*.)

> Before he gets his post, he is anxious to get it, and after he has got it, he is anxious about losing it, and if he begins to be anxious about losing it, then there is nothing that he will not do.
> —Confucius, on those whose passion is to rule over others, *Analects* [6]

---

[5] Which was already being dispensed: the nation-wide pension plan in question begins monthly payments when one leaves the American university system.
[6] Trans. Lin Yutang, *Wisdom of China and India.*

The hypocritical "You see to my publication-grant [though it is not deserved], and I'll deliver my committee's vote for your pet project [though it is not deserving], and all under the cover—of course—of 'legal justifications' (because we can trump-up so very very well)." Weasels, it is said, can suck the egg yolk from a little *puncture* while leaving the eggshell looking perfectly intact.

On the national level, not to say the international, academic life is ofttimes just as immoral. Notice, please, how pervasive (and exclusive) the 'Old Boys' Network' is (though nowadays it is not limited quite as exclusively to the male gender).

> "The Master was an old Turtle—we used to call him Tortoise–"
> "Why did you call him Tortoise if he wasn't one?" Alice asked. "We called him Tortoise because he taught us," said the Mock Turtle angrily ... "Reeling and Writhing, of course, to begin with,... and then the different branches of Arithmetic—Ambition, Distraction, Uglification and Derision."
> —Lewis Carroll, *Alice's Adventures in Wonderland* [7]

Surely you are familiar with the scenario. Let us say Old Tortoise #1 (Old Boy Number One), teaching at a prestigious university, writes his fifth book: it is hastily written and slight (during its writing his attention has been on university politics instead—wheeling/dealing for a deanship, maybe). Another professor, at a minor campus of a state university, and thus a 'peripheral professor', writes a book on the same subject—a very good book (his job is not at a prestigious university for reasons which should be irrelevant: he is a loner, maybe; or writes slowly, so his publication is not quantitative enough). The manuscripts of both men reach the editor at the same university press. It being a prestigious press, the editor knows Old Tortoise #1, and is also friends with Old Tortoise #2, on the press's editorial board. Indeed, Old Tortoise #2 has done him many a favor. In the case at hand, Old Tortoise #2 has applied for a prestigious national grant, and Old Tortoise #1 sits on the grants-committee. What are the chances that our peripheral professor's manuscript will be sent on to the official Readers at all? Or, if sent on, what are the chances it will survive other types of illicit ambush along the way? The chances are hardly better than "hitting a needle's point with a tiny mustard seed"

---

[7] *Alice's Adventure's in Wonderland*, ed. D. Rackin (Wadsworth, 1969), p. 187.

(as the Chinese say), or maybe even finding "hair on a *tortoise's* back (as the Chinese also say)."[8]

There is more to the scenario, of course. Grappling hooks inevitably find each other. In a recent appearance on a public broadcasting station, Dan Rather, the television journalist, lamented the triumph in America of *to do well* over *to do good*. University presses must—in a so-called free market—*do well* according to market norms. Since the academic establishments secure the readership of academic books, and groom the authors fed to the readership, university presses must needs conform. Thus the circles of self-interest (Buddhism's *tṛṣṇā*, 'thirst/craving') interlock and lock closed.

At the American mega-university, Harlequin taught at the main campus, and his publications, though not prolific, were always deemed adequate. He was a loner, though, and what complicated matters was that he was very idealistic. From the beginning, Hermeneutics was for him a means/end whereby he pondered on the human experience, and especially on what are somewhat deceptively called its 'ultimate concerns'—love, spirituality, suffering, beauty, sex, frustration, evil,... and so on. These construings constituted the how/what of his academic work, materializing as the philosophical and literary problematic he was publishing on/about at the time. (This is what a humanist/posthumanist *should* do, it seems to me.) And no matter how or where a promising 'path' through the problem-at-hand 'opened up', he would weigh the intrinsic feasibility of following. If a coherent rationale developed, and time, ability, and resources were *ad hoc*, he followed through. Not that he dehisced 'in omnibus partibus', mind you. When a path turned, heading in a new direction or towards a new intersection, he would surely take measure before acting. But *political* considerations, i.e., the effects such a turn would have on his public career—his career's 'visibility', advancement, and so on—entered into his calculations hardly at all.

Thus, when Harlequin opted to leave the American university system, his complaint was not with his own philosophical itinerations, which in fact (it seemed to him) were making a kind of 'unstately

---

[8] Respectively, see and compare K'uan Yü Lu (Charles Luk), *Ch'an and Zen Teaching*, First Series (Berkeley: Shambala, 1970), p. 58; and Miura/Sasaki, p. 113. But remember too what C.A.S. Williams, in *Outlines of Chinese Symbolism and Art Motifs* (Tuttle, 1974), reports on p. 405: "Chinese authors describe ten sorts of tortoise; one of them is said to become hairy in its old age, after much domestication."

progress', but with academe itself. That the style of his intellectual life was so interdisciplinary already made any adjustment to the institution difficult, and this was doubly so because he targeted his conference-papers according to what he happened to be writing at the time. When in his early years he was writing on literary theory, he delivered papers at the MLA (Modern Language Association) and at comparative literature symposia. Later, when he was writing on Husserl, Heidegger, and Derrida, he switched more to SPEP (Society for Phenomenology and Existential Philosophy), and the IAPL (International Association for Philosophy and Literature). He switched to religious studies when he was writing specifically on Buddhism and Derrida (after an interval of a few years, he gathered-in Christian theology again, too). In each of these disciplines, he earned acceptance, and then recognition, by the pertinent specialists. In comparative literary theory—by Beardsley, Bloomfield, Falk, Hassan, Krieger, Martinez-Bonati, Scholes, Wellek, and others; in philosophy—by Holthusen, Inada, Schrag, Nota, Ricoeur, Wu Kuan-min, and others; in religious studies—by Altizer, Panikkar, Streng, Wyschogrod, and others;... all of whom warmly recommended his work in their respective fields.

In terms of personal itineration, these phases seemed to unfold 'naturally', (?), perhaps inevitably. They were, all of them, ranged under (and in due time over/inbetween) the sign of Hermes—that is, of hermeneutics, the intent study of how texts/life-texts are read. The Geneva School in literary criticism/theory was 'concrete, spiritual, and personalist' in the broad sense. In phenomenology, Husserl was introspective, and—according to Husserl's own lights—radically 'experiential'. Heideggerian phenomenology, because of its new epistemology,[9] the 'mutual implication of inside/outside', enabled Harlequin to better explain how to deal with texts (both secular and religious); it also helped him to better understand how he interacted with 'his' circumambience—its events, people, things. Heidegger also brought Harlequin home to ontology, and facilitated an opening towards Oriental philosophers.

In the meantime, my study of Carmelite prayer and my Zen practice/study helped me towards that dissolution of concept (and of reliance on the ultimate integrity of concepts) which—in conjunction

---

[9] Though Heidegger, of course, would not agree to call it such, for well-known reasons which it is not the role of this account to rehearse.

with Derrida—was to transform into the 'differentialism' of my own future work. Derrida, whom I turned to in the late 1970s, taught me to distinguish between destruction and deconstruction, a distinction which—while at the National Humanities Center—I found as well in Nagarjuna, the great Madhyamikan Buddhist philosopher. The intersection of Nagarjuna and Derrida proved to be the most fecund discovery of my study-life. Concomitantly I had been reading Karl Rahner's Trinitarian theology, so when I went on to derive the maneuver of 'pure negative reference' ('under erasure', of course) from both Nagarjuna and Derrida, I saw—to my astonishment—that this maneuver satisfied Rahner's requisite marks for the Trinitarian function[10] ('under erasure', of course). All along, of course, I was fortified in the task of life by some saintly people, and by my favorite literary figures,—many from the medieval and Baroque periods, and many from the more recent past,...Dickinson, Mallarmé, Faulkner, Stevens, Robbe-Grillet, Endo, Ashbery, and so on. Nonetheless, in American academe, to let scholarship rather than opportunism habitually *take the lead* in one's career-decisions becomes— eventually—self-defeating.[11] This I had to face up to, and also I had to face the fact that my involvement in 'orthodox' religious theory and practice was not at all politically correct among my peers. Indeed, it alienated my peers from me. (The American Catholic establishment was in its own way just as bad: its liberal theologians tended to be elitist groupies, and its traditional theologians rejected 'deconstruction' on apriori grounds.)

And there was more reason still to be disheartened. Harlequin had to face the fact that his work was much more interdisciplinary than is usual: and that even though his credentials in comparative literature, in philosophy, in Buddhology, and in Christian theology—in the *four* (consult Derrida on *four*)—were being repeatedly confirmed by papers and refereed publications[12] in *each* of these four disciplines, still his very *interdisciplinarity* was self-defeating. Why self-defeating?

---

[10] Which is not to deny that Jung and Derrida, in their very differing ways, square the Triangle.

[11] Unless one is truly extraordinary, or nearly so (which I surely am not); and unless one is at the 'right' place at the 'right' time.

[12] Which, besides his books, went on to include book-chapters with Macmillan/U. of Mass. P. (on hermeneutics), FuJen U.P. (in comp. lit.), Penn. State U.P. (phil.), Reidel (phil.), Mayaguez U.P. (phil.), Routledge (theol.), Rodopi B.V./National U. of Singapore (theo./herm.), Cornell U.P. (Buddhism/Christianity), Scholar's P. [AAR] (Buddhism/Christianity), National Taiwan U.P. (herm./Buddhism/ Christianity).

Simply put, because the way to acquire institutional influence on a national/international level is to frequent the large conferences of a single discipline (or at most, two disciplines): one should go back year after year to the same several conferences affiliated with that discipline, each year presenting papers and 'networking' (in the discipline of literary studies, for example, one should 'present', annually, at the national MLA convention, a regional convention, and one or two more specialized conferences, the ACLA national meeting,[13] for example, or the Twentieth-Century Literature conference [each of these are conduits to MLA national convention structures as well, making them solid pragmatic choices]).

Eventually, the ambitious scholar can stand for election to a regional committee, and then a national committee, of the parent organization (the AAR, say, or the APA). Not that I am suggesting the ambitious scholar is not publishing *too*: indeed, much publication is indispensable, and with good university presses. I am not suggesting that ambitious pragmatic scholars aren't smart, or not very good at their discipline. What I am suggesting (and more than suggesting) is that *if* one does not gain *institutional* influence, in the long run, even one's publication suffers. For one's manuscript to gain a truly equal chance with others in the same qualitative bracket, one must give priority to *marketing* oneself; afortiori, the kind of reception one's publication enjoys is normally in proportion to one's national visibility. What I am protesting is that some scholars, myself included, do not like this marketing-principle (and its accompanying mind-set), and we are convinced that we should not have to like it and practice it in order to enjoy an equal chance at scholarly communication with our colleagues. Nor should we have to stomach the disdaining last kiss-off, "You're jealous [i.e., 'envious'] because you're not up to snuff."

In Harlequin's special case, the several shifts in conference venue according to his evolving research have made it more difficult for him—even up to the present day—to experience that collegial and

---

[13] The American Comparative Literature Association (ACLA) is according to its own lights 'interdisciplinary', of course. But my point is that the ACLA, for example, is housed within the *power-structure* of literature. One doesn't find many literary comparatists, MLA comparatists, who specialize in 'philosophy and literature' *and* in fact 'present' at American Philosophy Association meetings as well as their own MLA meetings (for one thing, the two annual conventions, that of the APA and that of the MLA, were convening almost simultaneously, at geographical venues distant from each other).

cordial acceptance which the involved organizations normally extend to their members (and this even though he has faithfully retained ties, down through the years, with all these organizations). Ironically, the impediments were greater for him at the time I have been discussing, before his departure from America; now that he commutes in from the Orient to American conferences, as he sometimes does, the acceptance is warmer. It remains the case, unfortunately, that if, let us say, an esthetician from the APA expects equal opportunity from MLA seminar-organizers in "The Esthetics of Literature," s/he can expect to be disappointed, even if s/he belongs to the MLA and has demonstrated expertise in the 'esthetics of literature'.. Likewise, when the APA recognizes a Buddhologist-member as a specialist in Buddhist poetry, s/he may very well be cold-shouldered if s/he joins the AAR and seeks equal access to an AAR panel on Buddhist poetry.[14] (Typically, these alienations prevail even in the case of allegedly 'cross-over' topics such as 'literature and sociology' say.) The inequities occur—for all but the most exceptional figures—because it is so very difficult (and—except for the exceptional—maybe by definition impossible) to breach several exclusivist in-groups. The 'Internet' system, beginning to boom as I write this, seems to be making matters still worse: academic coteries are and will continue to recodify themselves within the net by way of 'protected access' and the like.

The prolonged famine which had been my marriage—for I had merely exchanged the deprivation in the seminary for the deprivation in loveless matrimony—had just about broken me. And the prolonged frustrations of my work-life had just about broken me. (Some elder American colleagues had accosted me—"We made you a full professor so young, how can you be so ungrateful!": they missed the point; freedom to dialogue nationally/internationally with my peers was important to me, not any security or honor per se.) But most of all, the Church had broken me. Indeed, even the failure of my marriage-life and work-life could be laid at the Church's door. Of my marriage-life because my Catholic formation had not encouraged the socialization I

---

[14] The territoriality defended by one's official doctoral subject is very much involved, of course. In the hypothetical cases I have just cited, the MLA would be defending its Ph.D.s in literature against Ph.D.s in philosophy; likewise, the AAR would be protecting its doctorates in religious studies against encroachment by doctorates in philosophy. And the APA, for its part, is just as defensive, of course.

needed to make an informed and mature choice of a partner[15]; and the Church's condemnation of sexual intimacy before marriage had pressured me to marry *too soon*; and the Church's ban against contraception had gotten my marriage off to a bad start; *and* the Church's intolerance of divorce and remarriage had shut off all possibility of intimacy with another woman. And the disappointments of my academic work-life could be laid at the Church's door, or at least so it seemed to me at the time. For *if* I had not resisted assimilation into the Ideology of the American academic mainstream, I would quite naturally have *thought like* the mainstream all along, and my crises of conscience over world-view would not even have arisen. That is, *apriori* I would have excluded the grounds for feeling alienated and confrontational.[16]

Even my life-style, though it was no doubt abetted by genetic predisposition, bespoke a far-off time and place: that I rose from bed early every morning, and retired early, and that the pace of my daily writing—its rhythm, if you will—alternated prayer/meditation and actual composition (even when dealing with the most 'secular' subjects) bespoke a monk-scholar much more than a modern academic. Does a monk-scholar find it easy to 'network', in the evening making the rounds of cocktail parties? How much had my early identification with European Catholic history—my reading in Benedictine hagiography,

---

[15] The case was so bad for me because I had even been torn out of the traditional Italian settings—where young people used to 'eye' each other (sic) at dances attended by all the neighborhood families (youngsters attracted by each other could then initiate further contacts, under the watchful eyes of relatives). And all the families used to promenade through the piazza after Sunday Mass, affording time for mutual inspection. Failing these, matchmaking used to be invoked, often by concerned friends and relatives. 'Thrown' into America, I could hardly avail myself of these.

[16] How much to compromise and how much not? A tremendously difficult and delicate problem, of course. Jewish friends have told me some offspring of strict Orthodox Jews afortiori undergo this ordeal of conscience. It can seem the Orthodox Jewish community is caught in a vicious circle, as if the rules which make the community rigidly exclusive (so a member normally does not even take meals with a non-Jew) foster divisiveness between it and the circumambient culture; and in the long haul indirectly invite persecution. Perhaps then, in our society, strict Orthodox Jews in particular can empathize with my plight. Though in my case, perhaps unlike theirs, staying strictly *inside* the community did not seem to work either: prima facie its rules were, at the time, driving me literally to madness.

for example—planted a contemplative's[17] life-style in my unconscious as its so-called 'ego-ideal'? Apropos of these last, even while I was diagnosing them—the vicious circles of the stubborn/lonely alien, they might be called—I still realized at the same time that they were not wholly vicious: that my very differences had potential to do good for my surroundings (and could/would have done so, in a more tolerant world: more tolerant than the United States, I mean[18]... Asia, I was about to discover, would take me to its heart). Furthermore, when the *why* of a situation is so entangled, and so much of it is irreparable and irreducible, its good and bad are—at least within human purview— irreducible too.[19] You see, I was already back then, before my many Taiwan-years, beginning to come to terms with a most pervasive Catch-22. The cosmic game of Blindman's Buff. –Bluff?

> Anamnesis: While paging through a casual magazine published in Taipei,[20] I come across a diagram of CHIROMANCY'S Left Hand. Though not a practitioner of divination,[21] I am interested in the psychology of the system and I give a look. The diagram shows the center of the palm, called the QUADRANGLE, to be framed by four lines, those of the Heart, Hand, Fate, and the Sun. (Interesting that Christian iconography puts a crucifying nail precisely through Christ's 'quadrangle'.[22]) I look spontaneously at the quadrangle in my own palm: a deep skin-crease runs from its upper left corner to its lower right corner, and, intersecting this diagonal at mid-point, another skin-crease runs

---

[17] In traditional Catholic terminology, a 'contemplative' is one who cultivates an attentive 'inner gaze' on the Divine Indwelling, that is, God's 'presence' in the soul: if/when the Indwelling is tangibly experienced, it is usually reported to 'localize' psychophysically in the solar plexus.

[18] French and Italian scholars had been very supportive of my work when I had given papers in Europe. But if the French and Italians were ideologically open to me, their bureaucracy wasn't. To teach in their university-systems I would have had to process all over again through to their own systems' government-approved doctorate. Already with a wife, and three children to feed, I found this move economically infeasible.

[19] Which is not at all to say there is neither good nor bad.

[20] *Taipei City Magazine*, #49 (Feb. 1990), p.28.

[21] I still am not.

[22] The traditional iconography belongs, of course, to the zone of 'authentic' meaning sometimes called myth: to this extent, it does not pertain that the historical Christ was probably nailed through the wrists.

diagonally from upper right corner to lower left—that is, the quadrangle is filled with a giant X.

In his account of spiritual/psychological maturation, Carl Jung speaks of the transition from late-phase *melanosis* to *leukosis*, and the several moments of this delicate transition.[23] My death to 'my' old self/s marked a moment of radical disillusionment,... palm-in-saltire. For the reasons already recounted, I had broken with my wife, distanced myself from American academic life, and now I was gradually drifting from Roman Catholic practice (the Mass, sacraments, etc.). After all, all my life I had prayed every day, tried (or so I thought) to love and serve people, and attended weekly and often daily Mass; I had prayed with my children every-day, given them catechetical instruction, and—when I could afford it—sent them to Catholic schools; I had taught Sacred Scripture on weekends, and become a faithful Carmelite tertiary. 'Evangelical Protestant' Christians would insist, of course, that the aforesaid list of good efforts only shows my refusal to 'take Christ as my personal Savior' whose grace is a gratuitous gift. The name of my false game, they would say, is Arrogance—I assume good works can merit grace.

The Evangelical's argument, in my very sincere opinion, misconstrues what an orthodox Catholic Christian believes. A Catholic Christian confesses that through the Holy Spirit's initiating grace, the Catholic Christian takes Christ as his personal Savior and then cooperates with the Holy Spirit, out of loving gratitude and service, in the doing of good works. (Indeed, I was never taught otherwise, though our explanatory catch-phrases may have differed from those of Protestant Christians.[24]) Through the doctrine of 'sufficient grace', a teaching affirmed by Catholic Christians and many Protestants, God is supposed to give us sufficient grace to resist backsliding. But during my period of radical disillusionment, the rub

---

[23] See C. G. Jung, *Psychology and Alchemy*, trans. R. F. C. Hull, Vol. XII of the *Collected Works* (Princeton: Princeton University Press, 2nd ed., 1968), pp. 228-232, and passim (see appendix). 'Leukosis', Gk. 'whitening', whence also the word 'leukemia'. Umberto Eco in his *Foucault's Pendulum* implies that Derridean deconstruction (which is figured into Eco's Dantesque allegory) is leukemic, that is, cancerous, and that it thus can lead the human race only to destruction. Eco does not seem to recognize that the 'leveling' of value can be a phase on the way to salvation/liberation.

[24] My point is that Evangelicals misunderstand Catholicism on the matter. This is not to deny there are significant differences between the Evangelical and Catholic theologies of faith/good-works.

was precisely that I did not—and had not—experienced in any way, shape, or form the sufficiency of God's grace. It is hard (farfetched?) to believe that the good God sees to it a disciple goes crazy (or even that the good God 'let's it happen'). Yet now my whole life had backfired— spitting smoke and fouling the air, and finally blowing up in my face. In *Moby Dick*, Herman Melville parodies a Shakespearian deep sea-change with one of his own, and tolls the tocsin which in my dark moment sounded mine as well:

> The sea had jeeringly kept his finite body up, but drowned the infinite of his soul. Not drowned entirely, though. Rather carried down alive to wondrous depths, where strange ships of the unwarped primal world glided to and fro before his passive eyes; and the miser-merman, Wisdom, revealed his hoarded heaps; and among the joyous, heartless, ever-juvenile eternities, Pip saw the multitudinous, God-omnipresent, coral insects, that out of the firmament of waters heaved the colossal orbs. He saw God's foot upon the treadle of the loom, and spoke it; and therefore his shipmates called him mad. So man's insanity is heaven's sense; and wandering from all mortal reason, man comes at last to that celestial thought which, to reason, is absurd and frantic; and weal or woe, feels then uncompromised, indifferent as his God.[25]

I felt that I too—having plumbed the depths of loneliness—had 'come up knowing then'. Knowing not so much that God was 'indifferent' but that there was no personal God at all. No doubt Buddhism, because of its philosophical humility, its commonsense, its refusal to invoke a creator-God or alleged supernatural Revelation, fortified and comforted me throughout this time, as it continues to do, in differing ways, up to the present. Being a well-read person, and also open to experience (I would eventually pass a half-year living in a yogic ashram, for example), I was familiar with the myriad of religious alternatives, but found them variously unavailable for/to me. The other grand Near-Eastern religions, Judaism and Islam, seemed to share the same ultimate notorieties as Christianity. They are intolerant of 'pagan' religions, the beliefs of which they grossly misrepresent; and they interpret history in terms of global confrontation between themselves and various 'non-believing' peoples. Their scriptural texts—precisely because they are textual but afortiori because, even among texts, they are extraordinarily ambiguous—contain moments which lend them-selves to the most dangerous appropriation (witness how horrendously

---

[25] *Moby Dick* (N.Y.: Random House, 1950), ch. XCIII, p. 413.

they have oft been used).[26] Dom Aelred Graham, scholarly British Benedictine, puts it this way, and I concur:

> *"The Bible*...It is made up, for the most part, of historical or supposedly historical documents, extravagant denunciations, and exclusivist devotions, requiring long and deep research before they can be properly understood. Parts of the Old Testament, the Gospels, and the Pauline Epistles abound in memorable, heart-touching sayings; but most of them call for careful elucidation before they can be correctly grasped and appropriately applied."[27]

The efforts of liberal Christianity, especially liberal Protestantism, to escape biblical faith nonetheless retained, I found, the anti-Asian (and anti-African and anti-native Indian) prejudices of their mother denominations. Moreover, it seemed to me ironic that what was positive about religious liberalism, namely its humanistic universality, was in inverse proportion to its recognizable Christianity. It made more sense, it seemed to me, for Christianity to reinforce those beliefs and practices necessary for right-hemisphere of the brain activity,—repetitive chant, for example, and *contemplatio* (non-discursive deep meditation), and adoration, and the like. But Gregorian chant and the rosary, and non-logical/non-emotional contemplation, and adoration of the Blessed Sacrament, say, were utterly unacceptable—indeed, reprehensible— to liberal Protestants; and they were eschewed since the 1960s by liberal Catholics. A sad situation, it seemed to me, because in the Catholic tradition, anyway, these right-brain/left-side activities were considered clearly and uniquely Christian, not blandly 'universal'. Yet their respective deep structures—formulaic prayer, alpha brain wave deep meditation, and devotion-in-sacred-space, were analogous to those in the non-Semitic religions, and thus facilitated an equable/equitable opening-up towards (and dialogue with) these other religions.

---

[26]  Derrida's version of the so-called 'law of recurrence' is perhaps most succinctly broached in "The Question of Style," in D. Allison, ed., *The New Nietzsche* (Albany: S.U.N.Y. Press, 1977), pp. 185-88; see also "Dénégations," pp. 551-2, 581-3; 19, 50-1.

[27]  *The End of Religion* (N.Y.: Harcourt Brace Jovanovich, 1971), p. 235. Recognizing the vast likelihood for wrong-headed, indeed malicious, interpretation of Scripture, the Jewish and non-Evangelical Christian traditions, in their diverse ways, have established mechanisms for the 'safe-guarding' of Scriptural 'truths', but even these seem—on too many occasions—to have botched-up in the concrete.

Process theology, which after a dormant period was processing quite rapidly at the time, I read attentively. It suffered, I found, from the frailty I just ascribed above to liberal Christian religiosities—its best ideas failed to be Christian at the same time. Not that this was bad for philosophy or even formal theology, but it was bad—I was coming to realize more and more—for religious practice. Bad for religious practice simply because practice can only come to terms with the human unconscious if/when it is enmeshed in a collective religious tradition.[28] The archetypes inscribe themselves into a Christian as concrete Christian ectypes—the Christ-child, the virgin birth, the baptismal initiation, the sacrifice of the Cross, the Eucharist, etc. A Christian must either fix on these[29] or—if her/his conscience so leads—switch to another religion, Judaism or Hinduism or Buddhism or shamanism, say.[30] I had already concluded that if I were to continue interest in Christian theology, it would have to be a theology which serves religious practice.[31] The process theology I was reading offended me because its tone seemed so damned 'American' in the worst sense—so naively optimistic, a Pollyanna theology blithely blind to its own fulsome selfishness. The televised 'Nature' documentaries came to mind again—the cold-eyed stalking, the biting and tearing, the scarlet dollops. 'I've experienced life to be like *that*', I thought. 'And what I've found in all history and see all around me is *that*'. Ofttimes it is masked by seeming professionalism or piety or—Lord knows—patriotism, but it is still *that*. Schopenhauer's bloodthirsty and ravenous Will, which—as he tells us (did he take it on faith?)—can be transcended by deep meditation.[32] To whitewash aggression as necessary

---

[28] Despite the fact he was much out of favor among theorists, the Carl Jung whom I had read long before was having a growing influence on me—largely because I was finding again and again that his theories were confirmed by what I witnessed in the world, and experienced in myself.

[29] Deconstructing them *as mere concepts*, and restoring them at the same time: this is how I do deconstructive theology (of which I write elsewhere).

[30] Even the Roman Church grants this,—saying, however, that the Christian is responsible before God for acting in accordance with what s/he should know through Revelation and Church-teaching.

[31] Ironically, process theology would concur here. It is just that the process theology I read described the process but consistently excluded the traditional concrete content.

[32] Schopenhauer deployed Buddhism in order 'to cope'. There are many Buddhisms, with differing emphases. I have never been helped by the kind which would simply affirm the good and evil in the world as the 'inevitable play of *saṃsāra*'.

evolutionary process is blindly complacent, and ultimately inhuman in a very repugnant way. (At its most secular level, I appropriate 'transcending' to mean a periodic 'distancing' or 'abstracting' via meditation *so that* one can cope without going mad in the face of pervasive cruelty[33]: I do *not* mean escapism, because I believe and have always believed in direct action to make the world better.) Liberation theology, which despite papal cautions had continued to spread throughout the 1970s, expressed my Leftist concerns very well: if religious practice is a work of the deep-psyche (as it should be), it must simultaneously engage in the world to stop oppression/ aggression. By the time I was setting out for Taiwan, I had already been a committed socialist for many years[34] (which, perhaps needless to say, had alienated me even more from my old Midwestern colleagues).

Death-of-God theology would seem on the face of it to have suited my disillusionment, but I was thrashing about for a philosophy of life that I could not only affirm intellectually but which I could deploy concretely in order to ensure mental health and a modicum of happiness. Apropos, nothing in the Buddhist *Tripiṭaka* has ever spoken to me with more tender immediacy than Shakyamuni Buddha's simile of the man dying from a poisoned arrow.[35] With a flick of his hand, Shakyamuni dismisses as idle speculation all questions as to the whys and wherefores of the arrow, and instead, sets about removing the arrow. The Death-of-God theology I was reading, fabricated as it was out of nordic Protestant substance, did not supply the right-brain/left-hand orthopraxis (meditation, chant, prostrations, icon-concentration, etc.) I required for psychic survival.[36] For—as will become clear later—I

---

[33] I do not mean to say this is the aim of orthodox Zen meditation. Zen teaches that the world must be accepted *as it is*, 'good' and 'evil' (though one continues doing all the good one can). Most Zen masters reject the notion of any 'hidden' or 'deep' meaning behind 'things'. In the Theravadin Buddhist tradition, some teachers—*for beginners*—deploy meditation in the way I am suggesting.

[34] Went to Taiwan, so capitalist a country? More on this matter in a moment. Apropos of Marxism, it failed (in Eastern Europe) in large measure because its professed high ideals can only be kept alive within the context of a religious society: only a loving religion, constantly renewed, would be able to motivate the broad masses of humanity to overcome selfishness. Only a spiritual people can keep alive the holy maxim, 'From each according to her/his ability; to each according to her/his need'.

[35] In *Sutta* 63 of the *Majjhima-Nikāya*.

[36] Not that Death-of-God theology did not passim invoke Buddhism: it sometimes did, but the appropriation was only intellectual.

was groping more and more towards a mode of deep consciousness modulated through traditional religious forms. Protestant Christianity, having from its beginnings purged such forms as idolatrous, was on this account utterly impotent to help me. *My version of Death-of-God theology, if I had chosen to absorb the term, would have adapted/ adopted the Buddhism of Nagarjuna's 'two truths' ('*saṃvṛti* is *paramārtha*'), more familiar to Westerners in their Prajnaparamitan version, in the *Heart Sutra*'s "Form is emptiness; emptiness also is form." If I had indulged Death-of-God theology, I would have applied the 'two truths' to at once affirm God (*saṃvṛti*, logocentrism) and void God (*paramārtha*, deconstruction of logos). In any case, the ideas I worked out privately in terms of Death-of-God were to variously reappear, years later, in my treatments of postmodernism.[37]

Demythologizing, in its several generations of scholarship, I followed carefully. Its scientific quest for the 'historical Christ' was no doubt necessary—the time for such a mission had come. The attempts of some to 'phenomenologically reduce' Christianity to the early faith-community seemed to me naively scientific, and in need of deconstruction in turn. Ultimately, according to my lights, the goals of demythologizing were misplaced: I had already converted to the idea[38] that religion does not function in terms of 'historical validity'. As for the so-called 'secular' philosophies that really drove American life, sovereign but for the most part unacknowledged, they—needless to say—swarmed all around me. They seemed to be no more than modern-day versions of hedonism at the worst and epicureanism at the best: neither could expose the pretenses of the American dream. Was I being too harsh on them?—An interrogative already moot in the broaching, I'm afraid, for I had long found life so painful that hedonism was for me impossible and epicureanism out of the question: a much more radical approach to life was needed, if I were going to survive. That much more radical means was Derridean deconstruction, which for me had never been a fashionable trend, but an 'authentic' (tsk, tsk) way of doing philosophy; and it was becoming, increasingly, the means of my survival.

From the start, I had taken Derridean deconstruction in its most technical sense, as—(1) the tracking of the thought-processes of a putative logical sequence; (2) the exposing of flaws in that sequence,

---

[37] Most of these in Far Eastern journals, in the Chinese language only.
[38] Not a novel idea, certainly, but I along with many others had long resisted it.

and of the cosmetic repairs deployed to conceal them; (3) the pursuit, no matter what, of the more logical conclusion which the cosmetic 'fix' had blocked; and—if the larger logical frame of reference requires—(4) the placement of this 'more logical conclusion' under erasure[39] (postmodernism—as I practice it—is largely a description of these 'alternative conclusions under erasure'). I concurred with Derrida that when trained on the two founding principles of classical (and later, humanistic) philosophy, viz., the principle of identity and the principle of personal identity, deconstructive maneuvers show these principles themselves to be radically defective. I also concurred that any deconstruction is at once a constituting of yet another holism which awaits deconstruction in turn. But unlike Derrida (perhaps), I found all of this a confirmation of Buddhism, which deconstructs personal identity and indeed any holistic formula—including the principle of identity itself and the logic it founds; and especially I found deconstruction is a confirming of early Madhyamikan Buddhism, which—unlike Yogacara and some other Buddhisms—steadfastly refuses to recuperate identity into a new mystic holism of any kind. Surprisingly, deconstruction West-and-East had become for me a sort of existential hermeneutic (tsk, tsk). My experience of life— throughout—had been precisely the falling-apart (often, the concealed falling-apart) of putative holisms, no matter how microscopic or macroscopic nor what the kind—cultural, political, religious. After Vatican Council II the Church in particular was falling apart, splintered by stubborn right-wing churchmen making embarrassing decisions and mindless liberals selling away our cultural birthright of Sacrament and Mary and other archetypal signs. Seemingly drawn off from lower and lower in the gene pool, what few new clergymen we had, appeared—too many of them (not all)—to be cultural Philistines bloated by self-importance and pampered by worldliness. Heaven send us more saints. Saints like St. Francis who heeded Christ's dinning cry from the Cross—"Francis, Francis, go rebuild my Church!"[40]

---

[39] All of this is explained in detail elsewhere in my publications.

[40] This work does *not at all* contradict deconstruction as I practice it. Deconstruction should, in my opinion, (1) thrash out the *false*, and (2) expose the inadequacy of even the true (that is, even concepts which are true 'so far as they go' still *come apart* against the measure of a more Divine reality). Thus deconstruction can help *rebuild* the Church.

"...for a time, two times, and half a time" (Daniel 7:25);
and Rev. 11:2,3,9,11;
12:14;
13,5;
see also Rev. 11:4 for its
two Olive trees (*elaiai*)
and two Lampstands (*luchniai*)

And note, dear Reader, how the following names double, with
(perhaps) yet a half to come:—

a time:    John XXIII    (1958-63)
            Paul VI      (1963-78)

two times:  John Paul I   (1978)
            John Paul II  (1978-?)

half a time:  ?           (?–  ...

> "But in Gethsemane the lean and dried-up branches of the olives straggled in the moonlight—in the convent they had some branches of olive trees that had been brought from the castle where their father, Saint Franciscus [It. 'Francesco': 'French one'], was born... Among these bitter, withered bushes He [the Christ] had lain upon His face, sweating blood, as He saw at the bottom of the chalice all the evil that the race of Adam and Eve had committed and shall commit from the dawn of the ages until the Day of Judgment."

—Sigrid Undset, *The Son-Avenger*[41]

"DE GLORIA OLIVAE" [L "From the Glory of the Olive/ Olive-tree"]
— *Prophecies of St. Malachy* (Mss., 16th cent.[42])

---

[41] Trans. from Norwegian by Arthur Chater (N.Y.: Knopf, 1930; pbk. ed. 1964), p. 125.

[42] Consult Suzzane Jacquemin, *Les Prophéties des Derniers Temps* (Paris: La Colombe, 1958); and Georges Vouloir, *Les Prophéties pour les Temps Actuels* (Paris: Editions Médicis, 1948). The manuscript was "discovered" in the 16th

"De Gloria Olivae,"—the Prophecy's
cryptic phrase for the Next-to-last
Pope in history; according to the
Prophecy's list, after John-Paul II,
there are to be only two more Popes.

April 21, 1996: Romano Prodi's *Ulivo* [the 'Olive-tree'], a
          Left-Center coalition, wins the Italian
          general elections.

"Then shall the Great Vicar of the COPE be put back."
—Nostradamus [Michel de Nostredame], 16th cent.
          "Michael of Our Lady," a
          Franciscan Tertiary of Jewish
          descent, is said by some to be
          here predicting a future Pope of
          ancient *Cap*etian lineage; but this
          prophecy is sometimes confused
          with others predicting a temporal
          leader of *Cap*etian descent, and
          very holy, who shall protect the
          Olive (the Jewish People) and the
          Church and the human race, as
          the End draws very near. He
          shall lay down his scepter on the
          Mount of Olives. Some
          commentators, however, take the
          "Cope" to signal a Pope from an
          Order that wears a cowl, like
          Franciscan *Cap*uchins.[43]

When a cardinal springs from an olive-branch,
have mercy on us, O Lord, and heed the prayers
of Blessed Mary and the saints.


          Influenced by Buddhist deconstruction, my own work exposed
not only how logic deconstructs itself, but how supposedly rational

---

century, and is attributed to St. Malachy (12th cent.). Some call by the name
"uncanny" its perceived accuracy over the last four-hundred years.
[43] Consult M. P. Edouard et Jean Mézerette, *Michel Nostradamus* (Paris: Belles
Editions, 1947); and *Les Prophéties de Maistre Michel Nostradamus* (Sarlat:
Michelet, 1946).

wholes are often deconstructed by what is called the "uncanny," and also by the gratuitously non-logical—by emotion, passion, and the like (which—as deconstructive agents—also then go on in-turn/out-of-turn to dissolve). I described what I called the off-rational meditation of the Madhyamika, and the Madhyamikan claim that through this meditation, Nagarjuna's 'two truths' can be realized.[44] This is to say, it can be realized that matters-which-go-on as broken in infinite 'regressio', as *devoid*, can at once be frequented as phenomeno-logically intact. Like Derrida, I remained committed to the worth of logic despite, or more correctly *because of*, logic's necessary ongoing self-deconstruction. I remained committed to ethics, and to working out the project of goodness-at-all-costs. During my own meditation—which was Zennist, disciplined, and in strict *padmāsana*—«I» (entre guillemets) sometimes experienced the constitution and negation of the going-on. My experience was calming, affirming, and even 'benevolent' in that it seemed to empty itself out and frequent what was 'close' and what was 'far'. This very description attests, for those who are informed about such matters, to the limited nature of my meditative practice. I was still far from the wisdom and compassion (and egolessness) ascribed to true liberation. From day to day, my meditations made the rounds of several phases. On my darkest days, meditation would—I knew—at least bring quietus, a sort of benign yet active quietus, in the face of the Ravenous Mad World. And after the meditation period, I knew the ensuing state of mind/heart would continue on for several hours, motivating me towards active compassion in the midst of the day's rat-race.

Involvement in Derridean deconstruction meant productive exchanges with Freudian and Lacanian psychology, with Italian *pensiero debole*, and with Cixous, Irigaray, Kofman, and Kristeva. Freudian thought and its extensions and its spin-offs helped me, as it has helped many others, to unveil the sick and tangled tics of human behavior. Freud knew enough to warn that 'human nature' is a recipe for unhappiness—unhappiness that even sex for one reason or another cannot *obliterate* (in fact, sex often *literates* it, i.e., displaces-and-repeats it). Shakyamuni Buddha marshaled our humanity to cope with this inevitable residue/sur-plus of grief; Freud at most was able to resign (re-*sign*?) himself to it. At the time, in the throes of

---

[44] See my *Derrida on the Mend* (W. Lafayette: Purdue Univ. Press, 1984;86), pp. 119-24, and passim; and Part Two of this book.

disillusionment, even polymorphic Hinduism was too theistic for me, too logocentric—I needed the astringency of Zen.[45] However, Hinduism *did* reconfirm for me what my Italian forbearers instinctively knew— that the body is good, its so-called *animalism* is good. Only Mosaic or Protestant puritanism could/should be embarrassed by the coded reappearance in religion of the psycho-biological. Then why, I wondered, were liberal Americans, *soi-disant* liberated Americans, so embarrassed, snickering at traditional Latin Catholicism for its symbols of womb-comfort and breast nourishment, of linga-and-yoni and death-drive? What the early Christian Church had concluded to, after much struggle, was as relevant as ever—

> Iconoclasm new or old has the same results for all its fervor:
> Priceless treasures forever lost, for white-washed walls pale
> inspiration and a neutered divinity makes impotent love.
>                                                        —Macrina[46]

Religion is not *only* up to this game of symbolism, but it is up to it, and why shouldn't a religion expect its Divinity to animate the game? But for a latent puritanism, why would liberal Americans snicker at such (relatively) transparent symbolism? Yes, a sophisticated Hindu would proclaim, in religious ritual I do introject and I do purge, sometimes.[47] Glory to the God for it! And Christian clerics should be sophisticated enough to heed the same proclamation in their own tradition. (If enough of them had, the modern Catholic Church, for one, would have been saved the outrageous sexual scandals of the present-day, the sad result of manifold *repression*.) Along with Derrida, my work in the future was to turn more to religion: in my case, some of it to the role of archetypal signs—their moment of phenomenological form and their

---

[45] Specifically, what I call 'differential Zen,' i.e., Zen the theory of which does not reduce to absolute logocentrism (such as the 'one Buddha-nature', etc.). Fortunately, in Zen it is the meditative practice which is important, not the teaching manuals. Thus I have found that *how* the verbalized instruction of a given *sangha* glosses the meditative experience is not nearly as determining as it would be in dogmatic (intensely ideological) religions.

[46] Trans. in *The Catholic World Report*, San Francisco, Cal. (Feb., 1992).

[47] These behaviors are understood to function in many registers at the same time, from the most primitive to the most sublime. A Catholic introjects the sacred host in Holy Communion, s/he purges in confession—even these should function in many registers, all good. In postmodernism, we would say the primitive and the sublime and the in-between registers displace-and-repeat each other in a glorious ongoing tangle. All good.

moment of dispersion/devoidness. Jungian signs and their archetypal roots belong, I argued, to *saṃvṛti*. To rationally deconstruct these roots, rendering them irreducibly rhizoid/rhyzogenous if you will, is to work conceptually towards *paramārtha*, a devoid moment that can only be frequented off-mystically (and not logically). That is, analytic deconstruction can be at most a *prajñapti*, but—as such—*prajñapti* can be very useful indeed.[48]

> Heaven and Earth are ruthless;
> For them the Ten Thousand Things [= all things] are but as straw dogs.[49]
> —Lao Tzu, *Tao Te Ching*, 5[50]

What Lao Tzu, the founder of philosophical Taoism, meant by the above famous lines is open to dispute. On my saddest days I appropriated them to represent my own sense of desolation. As for the concept of Fate, either as arbitrary or as a consequence of acts preceding my birth—I could not for various reasons accept the notion.[51] I appropriated in particular the following poem not for its apparent fatalism, but because of its exquisite hopelessness:

---

[48] Especially when deployed by *upāya*, 'skillful means'. For Madhyamika Buddhists, *prajñapti* in its first sense means any 'language/thought construct' which would 'name' anything (the 'anything' is empty, the Madhyamikans say, and nothing in it corresponds to the putative 'name'). *Prajñapti* in its second, more specialized sense, means only those 'language/thought constructs' which can lead, via Buddhist discipline, to the truth. By concealing-revealing emptiness in a unique way, these special forms of *prajñapti* can function as 'clues' (to *śūnyatā*). See Mervyn Sprung in his anthology *The Question of Being* (University Park: Pennsylvania State Univ. Press, 1978), p. 110. For a more detailed definition, see Douglas Daye, "Major Schools of the Mahayana: Madhyamika," in C. Prebish, ed., *Buddhism: A Modern Perspective* (University Park: Pennsylvania State Univ. Press, 1975), pp. 81-95. I am arguing that analytic deconstruction can work as a *prajñapti* in the second sense.

[49] Straw dogs were used in ancient sacrificial ceremonies in China. "When the ceremony ended, the straw dog was discarded, indicating an attitude of indifference" (Chang Chung-yuan, *Tao: A New Way of Thinking* (New York: Harper and Row, Perennial Library ed., 1975), p. 15.

[50] Arthur Waley, *The Way and Its Power: A Study of the 'Tao Te Ching'* (N.Y.: Grove, 1958), p. 147. For those requiring a more recent scholarly translation, see Ellen M. Chen, *The Tao Te Ching: A New Translation and Commentary* (N.Y.: Paragon House, 1989).

[51] For example, I could find no factual confirmation of individuated *karma*, no proof whatsoever. The most I could possibly affirm is that good deeds in general lead to later good deeds in the broad sense (and conversely, hate breeds hate). This even humanistic psychology confirms, and with much evidence.

> Drain off water on level ground—
> It will flow separately towards the east, the west,
> the south, the north.
> Human lives too are fated,
> How can I sigh walking and grieve while resting?
> —Pao Chao (period of Six Dynasties)[52]

Through most of this transition period, though, I consciously adopted as far and away the most logical the philosophy of tychism—the claim that absolute chance operates the universe (tychism does not exclude repetition, of course: see the various 'probability theories', and compare current 'chaos-theory'):

> We that have done and thought,
> That have thought and done,
> Must ramble, and thin out
> Like milk spilt on a stone.
> —William Butler Yeats[53]

The title of Yeats's four line poem is "Spilt Milk": we invariably head towards our final dissolution, but—perhaps—we shouldn't cry over it. Buddhism accepts this dissolution, 'knowing' that what we call 'identity' as such is just a moment-by-moment convergence of factors. Christians in their own more moderate way affirm the value of ego-lessness ("For you have died, and your life is hid with Christ in God"[54]), but still their drive towards 'personal fulfillment' more often feeds their egoism, justifying it, plumping it up. From Buddhism in Taiwan I was to learn—among many other things—that I could survive by letting the spectacle of the world go on without me (i.e., without *me*): I would try my utmost to do good, and for the rest—affirm (and observe with keen interest[55]) the rising and cessation of all 'things'.[56] As for the oncoming dissolution of this moment-by-moment

---

[52] Trans. by Hsiang-fei Liu in *Bulletin of the School of Liberal Arts*, National Taiwan University, 37 (Dec. 1989), p. 83.

[53] The *Collected Poems* (N.Y.: Macmillan, 1956), p. 235.

[54] Col. 3: 3.

[55] Not that I take literally the 'mirror' metaphor so dear to Buddhist rhetoric. The 'convergence of factors' which is momentary 'Robert' necessarily influences the mundane 'outside', the 'others', the samsaric non-Robert. In this world, even 'mere mirrors' are convex/concave. Heidegger/Gadamer are right—'To know something is to change it'.

[56] In the Christian tradition, the maxim of St. Teresa of Avila is not the same but surely analogous: "Lord, give me the grace to change what I should change and to accept what I cannot, and the wisdom to know the difference."

composite called 'Robert', it was not in the least to be feared. Everything rambles and thins out like spilt milk on stone, and ever new 'things' arise (compare Buddhism's *pratītya samutpāda*). I recognized this discontinuous flux so easily because Jacques Derrida had already trailed the traces for me.[57] Yes, I knew the discontinuous flux by many postmodern names already—the 'spastic slide of displacement-and-repetition', the 'chance-ridden ever drifting dance'. But in Taiwan I was to better learn how to live it ('frequent it'), not just talk about it. (In proportion to how successfully one frequents the flux as *paramārtha*, there is of course no 'one' and no 'it'.[58])

## NEITHER TANGRAM NOR T-TOTUM

To shake (O.E. scean): – vt....
(3a:) To cause to quake, quiver, or vibrate...
. . . . . .
(5a:) To free oneself from: cast off [had *shaken* his bad habits][59]


Strange, though. Here I was, having earlier thought a God-filled cosmos a Tangram artfully designed, and now thinking a Godless cosmos a T-Totum arbitrarily tossed, and yet here I was, behaving according to neither. Even during the times when I was trying to shake (sense 5a) belief in God, I found myself praying to God to help me shake (5a) belief in God. And when I was most dispassionate, letting the world go on around me and in me without *me*, I prayed to God to help me achieve this letting-go/letting-be. Sometimes the thought crossed my mind that God was *letting me* shake (5a) belief in God so as to shake (sense 3a) the *notion* of God I had. Of course, an orthodox Buddhist—if agreeing to comment—would probably say that such invocation proves I had not let go completely yet: I was still *fabricating*. However, throughout this 'apo-apologia', I aim to limit myself, for better or for worse, to an account of my own experience—on the off-chance that some readers may find what I say interesting or helpful. I do not lay

(

---

[57] Jacques's deconstruction of the other Jacques (Lacan) helped too. My other James the Greater and my other James the Less. (Grammatically, I here leave the respective antecedents in doubt.)
[58] Though as *saṃvṛti* there is still 'one' and 'it'. Do you get the notion of the 'two truths'? And there is more, the further off-mysticism of '*saṃvṛti is paramārtha*'. More of the latter later in this book.
[59] *Webster's Unabridged.*

claim to absolute or universalized truth.[60] And it just so happens that my experience, what the case was (and, in a different way now, is) *for me,* is that I carried on prayer to God continually (not continuously but at least continually).[61]

Ch'an/Zen is classified as a 'self-help' school of Buddhism (as opposed to the Pure Land sects, say). In Ch'an/Zen the practitioner normally marshals her/his 'own' resources—variously said to be the 'Buddha-nature', the 'true' (non-empirical) self, etc.—rather than depending on a Bodhisattva for merit-transfer. Yet I note that in Taiwan even the famous Sheng-Yen, a Ch'an master known to be more negative than most Ch'an masters towards theism, can say— when speaking of his early monastery days—"... I prostrated to Kuan Yin [a Bodhisattva] five hundred times at night, and again in the morning before the other monks woke up... To this day I believe Kuan Yin gave me assistance."[62] (Aside—A Bodhisattva is not a God but is ritually addressed as *Other* and does *assist.*) For me, openness to Other-Power is constitutionally necessary, an existential imperative. Even Derrida, in "Dénégations" (which belongs to his 'later phase'), points out that deconstruction of constative discourse does not apply to 'prayer', which is another kind of speech-act altogether.[63] I suggest that for most people the invocation of some kind of Other-Power may be constitutionally/psychologically necessary—perhaps it is animated by a Jungian archetype.[64] Later I was to come to a clearer notion of the

---

[60] Except for one conviction, which I insist is binding on all: the obligation to loving-kindness.

[61] I acknowledged at the time that this 'interior conversation' might well have been my equivalent of a more secular person's 'constantly talking to him/herself'. That I called by the name 'God' the 'alter ego' addressed in 'my' interior monologue would then have been the result of childhood conditioning. The secularist who verbalizes to her/his alter ego would be confirming at least an innate need for communication. Would s/he even feel sometimes the 'alter ego' was helping? A fictitious helping by enabling a fictitious circle of communication? All of it a grand simulation? This problematic was not to be 'relatively' resolved for me until much later, when it became clear that 'neither I nor not-I' were doing the conversing. I say *relatively* resolved because I do not treat such a 'resolution' like a Grand Tunck supplying all the answers (while really supplying none, as the Grand Tuncks of satirical infamy are wont to do).

[62] See his 'Autobiography' in *Getting the Buddha Mind* (Elmhurst, N.Y.: Dharma Drum, 1982), p. 1. See also p. 9: "I attribute this not to any native intelligence, but to the discipline of practice, and to the compassion of Kuan Yin Bodhisattva."

[63] Pp. 571-4; 41-2.

[64] Which would mean that it is not universally necessary—not all archetypes need be or can be enacted by every individual.

epistemology of (what is called) Other-Power, as I shall indicate in due course.

> China, with the seductive allure of superior culture, conquered all her conquerors simply by being passive, getting underneath, and absorbing their barbaric hardness with her civilized softness.
> . . . . . . . . . . . . . . . . . . . .
> Chinese gods are not jealous.
> —Daniel Reid, *Reflections of Taiwan* [65] (sic)

Chinese gods are not jealous, but American gods most definitely *are* jealous[66], and most of the time.[67] It seems to me that the preponderance of Americans—in paroxysms of noisome self-stroking—primp and preen themselves over their own national generosity. Their myth trumpets how unselfishly they rescue the huddled immigrants from those 'disinherited' countries which compose the rest of the world! But woe if you are an American citizen and opt to go in the other

---

[65] *Reflections of Taiwan*, R. Ian Lloyd and Daniel Reid (Singapore: R. Ian Lloyd Prod., ltd., 1987), pp. 16, 131.

[66] Seemingly, the Judaeo-Christian God is too—at least as anthropomorphized in the Old Testament. In the Hebraic tradition, to anthropomorphize the Divine is supposed to be idolatrous. Isn't the Old Testament idolatrous by delivering a God who is jealous? For a popular but insightful contrast between American cultural assumptions and eastern Buddhist ones, see Tatsuo Motokawa, "Sushi Science and Hamburger Science," in *Perspectives in Biology and Medicine*, 32, 4 (summer 1989), pp. 489-504. Be cautioned, though, that Motokawa sometimes gives Buddhism a particularly Japanese slant.

[67] To the point, I find in my personal records the following note, dated October 1993 (when I was visiting with my Mother) and born out of what was my very *ad hoc* rage:—Somalis loyal to General Aidid have released an American helicopter pilot, after holding him hostage but giving him adequate care (antibiotics, etc.). Little or no mention on American television news that a Nigerian soldier attached to the U.N. force was also held hostage and later released. (He doesn't count,- he's not an American). Only over short-wave, from RFI (Radio France Internationale), do I learn that the Nigerian—unlike the American—was stripped and beaten during his captivity. One would think the American press owes this United Nations ally some attention too, even some credit and gratitude. But no,... he doesn't count,- his body and blood don't count at all, 'worm and no man' that he is. The trope of countability in its several senses often is a cruel sociological marker. For how enumeration, and finity/infinity, relate to the act of sorting, see Edith Wyschogrod, *Spirit in Ashes: Hegel, Heidegger, and Man-Made Mass Death* (New Haven and London: Yale, 1985), pp. 36-41. Her interpretation of Zeno's Paradox likewise suits, in my opinion, the way the American government reported/represented the recent Gulf War: American casualties were enumerated, counted, but Iraqi casualties were not (in fact, the U.S. government named them 'uncountable'). Though human and finite, the Iraqi soldiers were treated as infinite 'reserve', as 'evil infinite'.

direction—indeed, to emigrate! Then the American hubris—the overweening American hubris, I dare say—turns well-nigh psychopathic: most Americans simply cannot accept that some people might want, might just possibly want, to leave United Statesian culture.[68] These generous Americans don't have the decency to grant that sometimes, for some good people and for some good reasons—temperament or whatever—another country might be freer, more intellectual, even more civilized. Ye be fell, O Liberty Bell, and ye canst not ring 'cause ye be most foully crackyd. Mega-dittoes. (See 'dittology' too.)

"By leaving America, you slap us in the face and make a fool of yourself," my right-wing American colleagues had told me. From the likes of them, an indictment to be expected, I suppose. I was dismayed to find, however, that my 'liberal' colleagues shared their disdain: they behaved as if I were consigning myself to scholarly oblivion, and to cultural troglodytism. In other words, even so-called 'enlightened' liberals, self-declared 'cosmopolitans', either did not know or refused to believe (1) that Far Eastern culture is just as civilized and educated and ultimately 'wise' as Western culture; and (2) that East Asia's institutions of higher-education—those of Japan and the 'four little tigers'[69] (Taiwan, Hong Kong, S. Korea, and Singapore)—are just as rich in scholarship and opportunity as their Western counterparts. True internationalists—those who have inculturated in several cultures on several continents over respective spans of several years—testify, in fact, that America's vaunted 'quality-of-life' is already surpassed by that of western Europe, and, increasingly, by that of Japan and the little tigers as well. Of course, for those who prefer the values of Asian culture—so different from American values—the supremacy of Asia has always been the case, regardless of material norms. Here, however, I am addressing (and including) even those values the American myth takes to be supremely its own—material prosperity, and—much to the point—the wide-spread and democratic educational system which such prosperity can and should afford.

"The Chinese [Taoist] gods are not jealous." What I found in Taiwan is that Chinese are comfortable enough with their own civili-

---

[68] Try this little test of American goodwill: next time you hear an American telling a 'Polish joke', a joke s/he will no doubt claim is 'harmless', tell in turn an 'American joke', and watch the reaction.

[69] The Chinese more often say "the four little dragons," but the feisty goodwill associated with Oriental 'dragons' refuses to *transfer* in *transl*ation.

zation that they can celebrate their historical culture and welcome an incredible diversity of others as well. These others they give parity and respect: these others they often learn or at least learn from. In short, the Chinese don't only give lip-service to a 'policy of inclusion'; they really practice it. Here are some telltale examples (which I purposely keep small and a little bigger, leaving the reader to extrapolate on her/his own):—

(1) Take the phenomenon of the olive. A typical American likes only two kinds, a pimento-stuffed green olive pickled in strong brine, and a larger black olive bathed in light brine. The Chinese have long had scores of 'prepared olives' of their own—in many shapes and colors. And salted or sweetened or dried or soured or sweet-and-soured or dried-and-sweet-and-soured or salted-dried-sweet-and-soured. Now they also import the Italian and Spanish and Greek olive (Gk. *ELAIA*), olives in their hundreds of shapes and colors and varieties. The same goes for mushrooms. And for honey. And for peanuts. And snails. And ice cream.

(2) Take the phenomenon of fast-food. A typical American eats fast-food at McDonald's and its clones, and Kentucky Fried Chicken and its clones, and Taco Bell and its clones. The typical Chinese in Taiwan chooses from hundreds upon hundreds (no exaggeration) of traditional snacks, plus from the menu of McDonald's and Kentucky Fried Chicken and Taco Bell (all in Taiwan now), plus from the offerings of Japanese fast-food chains (where sometimes the food circulates on the flatcars of miniature trains—around and around the serving counters they go...).

(3) Take the case of cinema. A typical American only watches American films (and yuppies attending 'foreign film festivals' insist on English subtitles). The typical Taiwanese regularly sees Chinese movies, American movies, Japanese movies, French movies, Spanish and Italian and East European movies, and can comprehend original English-language and Mandarin and Taiwanese (and sometimes Japanese) sound-tracks.

(4) Take the case of high-school students. A typical American student doesn't know American history, not to speak of 'world history'. The

typical Taiwanese student knows Chinese history and American history and 'world history'. S/he shall have read Chinese classics plus Chinese contemporary literature plus European and American classics and contemporary literature. S/he will be able to tell you the name and chief works of the current year's Noble Prize in Literature. *Au contraire*, American students fare so badly on tests of academic competence given in sample countries around the world that the American establishment—though it necessarily publishes these comparative results—refuses to *publicize* them.

(5) Take the phenomenon of language. A typical American, at least a generation after his parents' immigration, writes and speaks only English. A typical Taiwanese can speak Mandarin and Taiwanese, read and write Chinese script, and get by well in a third tongue, usually English (plus, increasingly, Japanese or a Continental European language).

Taiwan has over 25,000 students studying in the United States, the largest foreign contingent in American universities.[70] Many of these attend American universities because they have failed (or know they would fail) the entrance examinations to Taiwan's university system. Taiwanese graduate students obtain student visas not out of any generosity on the part of the U.S., but because these students can do for America what most American graduate students cannot do—be this the teaching of Oriental languages to undergraduates, or, as in the preponderance of cases, the computing (and testing) necessary for the function of academic science. By doing a disproportionately large amount of the day-to-day 'lab work', computer programming, etc., Chinese research assistants—along with Asian Indians and other Orientals—carry the hopes of American technology on their backs.

(6) Take the case of university professors. American professors in the humanities know their discipline, surely, be it empirical psychology or comparative literature or whatever, but—in my opinion—typically fall short in breadth, i.e., in general humanistic knowledge. Their counterparts in Taiwan have by comparison much more extension: whatever the liberal discipline they have individually chosen as their specialty,

---

[70] Statistic as of 1987. Since then, the proportion of Chinese from the People' Republic has become much more noticeable.

the chances are that they will know both the Oriental and Western intellectual traditions in general—not only Confucius and Lao Tzu but Plato and Aristotle and Kant, and—due to Taiwan's 'Arabic diplomacy'—perhaps some Arab philosophy too. And you can count on them to know the conventions of Chinese art *and* European art, Chinese music *and* Western music (including the heavily Africanized American styles). If we resort to western terminology, we would call them 'renaissance wo/men', or 'wo/men of all seasons'. They are fun to talk to.

> If a person loves kindness, but does not love study,
>  the shortcoming will be ignorance.
> If a person loves wisdom, but does not love study,
>  the shortcoming will be having fanciful or unsound
>  ideas.
> If a person loves honesty, and does not love study,
>  the shortcoming will be a tendency to spoil or upset
>  things.
> If a person loves simplicity but does not love study,
>  the shortcoming will be sheer following of routine.
> If a person loves courage and does not love study,
>  the shortcoming will be unruliness or violence.
> If a person loves decision of character and does not love study,
>  the shortcoming will be self-will or headstrong
> belief in oneself.
>                 —Called the 'six shortcomings', Confucius, *Analects*

What I came upon in Taiwan is a culture where scholarship retains the same high place Confucius recommended for it some 2500 years ago. And as a consequence, academic life commands more prestige than any other sector of society. Indeed, shortly after my arrival, I remember that the published results of a recent poll of the general populace named 'university professor' the most respected of *all* occupations. Businessmen/women may control the private wealth of Taiwan but in my experience they invariably yield honor of place to scholars: the millionaire's proudest boast, in fact, is that his or her grown children 'teach in the university'. The current president of the country holds an American doctorate, and ten out of his thirteen Cabinet members hold doctorates (always in hock to businessmen and politicians, the U.S. Cabinet at one time during Reagan's presidency could hardly muster even one doctorate among its members). To be in Taiwan (what in the United States is called) an 'egghead' does not Gorganize voters, it magnetizes them (and sometimes, distressing to say, mesmerizes them—an abuse, of course, but one showing, at least, that the people's sympathy is in the right place). There are now 25 national universities and institutes in Taiwan, and many private universities and colleges. Admission to higher education is determined by one's rank on rigorous national examinations. National Taiwan University, at which I took an appointment beginning in 1988, is the premier university in the country. Though Chinese native scholarship is of course well-represented on the faculty, the majority of my colleagues hold foreign doctorates, from America and Europe: the government in Taiwan has encouraged *cross*-fertilization and internationalism.

To what I have said above, at first blush two objections (at least) can be raised. First, one may object that a doctorate, while admittedly important for the school system, is irrelevant to good management, and government officials are managers, after all, of/for the *res publica*. My philosophical disagreement with resort to the business-model as the proper governmental model is so profound that for me to properly explain it would de-train us here (and entrain us on a political track for this book's remainder). But 'my' *curricula* [plural] *vitae* is what I proposed willy-nilly to graph, not sociology. Thus I must here content myself with no more than affirmations. To wit—It is good in general for the whole country when scholars rather than business or military leaders or entertainers (from TV, movies, music) command pride of place; and it is good for government when political leaders can establish their academic credentials (no one is denying that these leaders also need much governmental experience). Second, one may object that my earlier indictment of academia is hereby contradicted:—if academia is so entrepreneurial, why do I so privilege the academy in this present discussion? My answer is that Taiwan's educational establishment differs—in my opinion, differs favorably—from that of the United States: my plea, just made, for a prioritizing of scholarship in 'national life' presumes a corresponding change in the style of a nation's scholars. That is, American academia should no longer mimic the entrepreneurial model. I whistle in the wind, of course. My 'beau geste'.

  —Pollution of the air and water and soil.
  —Unsafe work conditions in many factories.
  —Widespread flouting of the hygienic code.
  —'Sweetheart' contracts that endanger the public safety...

Taiwan can be said to have had these magots, its own magots, unique in their carving and grotesquerie (magot: 'Oriental figurine, often rendered in a crouching position'[71]). Nowadays the situation is improving rapidly, but even during my early years on the island, Taiwan still had rows of these magots (rows of nightshade too, and other pharmaceuticals which—be assured—I never indulged!). So believe me, I do not simply idealize or romanticize the Far East. Lord knows, I am not so naive as to fall for the pipedream of exoticism at my age. And I have been in Taiwan long enough—nine years as of this writing[72]—to know both its high art and its kitsch, its grace and its offal, its 'honnetes hommes' but also its peculators and pikers. Everywhere on the earth's face, humanity is frail/ flimsy. No doubt, idyllic passages bestrew this book, when I talk about the Far East. This text purports to be—I remind the reader again—a report of 'my' experience, and much of Chinese culture has touched me irrevocably, charmed me, made me over, and I do try to represent these moments. In my *Lebenswelt* these moments tag and mark the 'Orient-to-me': they *psychologically* define it for 'me'.

As for Taiwan's own 'academia', it plays the game of factionalism and infighting too, sometimes vicious infighting, but the rules are different from America's. What from the beginning singled out for me Taiwan's university-life is the Confucianist concept of the 'true scholar'—who is precisely one who does *not* market him/herself.[73] Not that most university professors in Taiwan practice this ideal. Far from the case. Most professors, I dare say, engage in the rough-and-tumble of university politics, and have pokers in many other fires as well. HOWEVER, in proportion to how much they do these things, they forego real respect from their peers and society-at-large. And gross self-promotion causes an irrecoverable loss of face. Would-be academic Trumps would lose face if they trumped (afortiori if they trumpeted it). Most important for my case—A scholar who studies/researches and teaches and writes does not have to 'network' in any western

[71] Throughout the Far East, art vendors hawk the 'magot', "A Chinese or Japanese figurine, usually grotesque and rendered in a crouching position"— *American Heritage Dictionary* (1976).

[72] That is, of the writing of this portion: the book has been pieced together over several years.

[73] There are now many women professors in Taiwan. The status of women's rights in the society-at-large is difficult to gauge. In some ways modern Chinese women are more liberated, and in some ways less liberated, than their western counterparts.

sense.[74] S/he is not at all judged inhuman and aloof on this account
(the Chinese are not Japanese, remember). Another appeal of the
Chinese concept, very dear to me, is that 'true scholarship' is
*necessarily* multi-disciplined: whatever the specialization, a scholar is
also a Poet, and is on familiar terms with Art and Music (even an
empirical scientist in Taiwan will know these subjects). To top off the
advantages, a 'true scholar', given his/her work has the merit, has
more access to publication rather than less. I am sure this Chinese
rationale has its flaws and cosmetics too: any deconstructionist knows
such is the case. Given time, I would be willing to argue, though, that
it holds up very well. Like the lava-stone Obsidian come up from the
depths, it is by and large much *better*, more *valuable*, because of its
special sort of cracks.

I arrived in Taiwan at a good time, the early 1980s. An historical
quirk had transformed a so-called 'backwater' island (not that it was
ever really such) into a scintillating marvel—a microcosm of all China.
After the civil war, the millions of refugees from the mainland, from
the score and more of provinces and regions, had transferred their
respective cultures onto this island of about 14,000 square miles, the
approximate size of Holland.[75] What the mainland Chinese had
traditionally called the five Grand Cuisines were here juxtaposed with
the native Taiwanese Cuisine, and the plethora of regional menus
from all over China. And the glorious heterogeneity of Chinese arts,
customs, festivals. And a gala of scholarships too. Literati of all China,
for good reasons and/or bad, had gathered here, concentrated
themselves here... on this little island. The technical advance of Taiwan
was so rapid that by the 1980s its 20 million people boasted the
world's fastest growing economy, and held the second largest foreign
cash reserve in the world.

The government spent much of its money wisely—on education.
Students were and are treated well. The fees at state universities,
which are completely subsidized, are of nominal cost. Professors were
and are treated well. A new National Library was constructed at great

---

[74] One does *socialize* with one's peers in Taiwan, but the model is familial,
*Gemeinschaft* not *Gesellschaft*—there are banquets and dinners where one stays
put in his/her seat and gets to know one's companions well. If one wishes to
circulate, in between two of the courses s/he stands and goes toasting from table
to table, making sure to get back to one's own table in time. I never saw a
'cocktail party' in Taiwan.
[75] Or Connecticut and Massachusetts combined.

expense. Prestigious national scholars hold places in the Academia Sinica, which functions somewhat like a cross between France's C.N.R.S. and its Académie Française. State-university faculty receive professional discounts from many state-owned enterprises, and even some private ones (more than one hotel clerk—upon seeing my university I.D.—has knocked 20% off the price for me, *without* my asking). The National Scholarship Council even pays full business-class round-trip airfare and a generous per diem to university professors giving papers at foreign conferences—in Europe, North and South America, Africa, the rest of Asia. It fully subsidizes sabbatical years abroad, at a university or research center of the professor's choosing (and besides this, the professor's annual salary is directly deposited into a home bank account at the same time, so one is in effect provided two concurrent sources of income when on sabbatical). Our libraries are excellent, and each year a book-order list is circulated on which we can add whatever titles we want purchased.

Taiwan was good for me. I threw away my checkbooks and credit cards, and car keys,[76] and lived in free housing on campus, with free electricity and air conditioning. Free medical service—doctors and medicines and hospitalization if need be. Other material needs were tended down the first street off-campus: vegetables, fruit, canned goods, pastries oriental and western, and the sundries,... each touted from their own family-run shop—in a carnival of Chinese color and strobe light, an 'impasto furioso' of them. The Chinese lay their glitter on thick. And temples and tea-shops and coffee-bars. Every street was an extravaganza. Goodbye to the distant shopping malls and gray parking lots of United Statesian suburbia. I could stroll right out of my home, and browse and shop, now.

O Postmodern China—Gaudy Taoist shrines, laden with 2000+ years of ritual, and next door, a technicolor disco. Side-by-side. And ragtail assemblies of scabrous stray dogs,—they're frightened of their own shadows ("We can't 'put them to sleep'," an earnest official told me, "It would be counterproductive for them, it would foil their karma: the best thing is to leave them alone—they must work off their bad karma, there's no escaping karma"[77]). From a corner a curmudgeon of a vendor hawks the latest craze, chestnuts roasted Italian-style in a black iron brazier ("Genuine Italian brazier, imported"). Germans and

---

[76] Whereas the typical middle-class Chinese was learning to acquire all three.

[77] Most Chinese are folk-Buddhist/Taoist, a highly syncretistic affair.

Frenchmen and Dutch and Arabs pass by, sauntering in clusters...
Artists, intellectuals, business people, they speak their own languages
aloud (Why do foreigners in America feel constrained to speak English
in public, even to each other?). Every few blocks, Buddhist nuns with
their begging bowls; ... in the midst of the throng they stand poised
and perfectly still: the crowd gives them their holy space, a circle of
silence about ten feet across. There's prompt taxi service too: taxis are
so cheap and there are so many that *they* chase *you*. "We're better
Buddhists than the Buddha," a Taipei cabbie told me. "The Buddha
only comes when you call him; we come whether you call us or not."
Pell-mell the omnipresent taxis whisk me Neapolitan-style (against
traffic or on sidewalks) to the opulent new National Theatre and the
new Concert Hall, and to art galleries and foreign-film festivals. One
time, a Taiwanese cabbie—in order to regale me as we were thus
speeding against the grain—delivered himself of this intentional
(quasi-)non-sequitur: "I'd sit in the back with you while I'm driving,
where it's safe, but if I sit up here in front, right in back of the wheel,
not only can I reach the wheel better...I'll also die first, and my body
will shield you!"

"For shame. You are defecting to a Fascist corporate-state!"—my
friends of the western Left lambasted me. They're wrong about
Taiwan, as anyone who has lived on the island a long time will testify
(unless perhaps they're holed up in an expatriate enclave, and flop
about in panic—like live fish on a plate—whenever they venture forth:
for my part, I live among Chinese). The so-called '*capitalism*' in Taiwan
allows for a communitarian presence which is quite pervasive, and
*native* to the Chinese tradition. It is so pervasive that I dare say a
western capitalist would label it downright 'socialist'. Among state-
university faculty, for example, even the square-footage of free living
space is strictly allocated 'per capita', and without regard for rank.
Proprietors of companies incur, *mutatis mutandis*, an equivalent
obligation to allocate perquisites according to traditional Chinese
justice, which is remarkably equitable *pace* the negative western
stereotypes. Between owners and workers there prevails a delicate
balance of power: the balance functions according to an unwritten code
centuries old, and I have known several instances of it. If someone in
authority is perceived to abuse those below him, the 'grannie-network'
will 'stick it to him', and really fast. The old grannies and aunties who
initiate and regulate all Community Opinion in Taiwan will within a

week turn the owner's name to Mud(d). And the tradespeople will start on him/her too—mysteriously, the owner's telephones will go dead and the electric lights black-out (the policemen will 'look the other way': *their* relatives are workers too).

As is well-known, for years one party controlled the government. What westerners didn't seem to realize is that Chinese one-party rule involves so many factions *internal* to the party that a kind of democracy prevails in any case. However, some important points of view *were* excluded by brute force from the political process, as is also well-known. Reform *was* desperately needed. I do not mean at all to deny this. Now there is a multi-party system which is edging closer to the Occident's democratic model. Do not, dear western reader, underestimate the resourcefulness and sophistication of the Chinese. Do not jam a western template on them, in some mad messianic rush. In the Orient more than anywhere, matters are not limited to how they seem/seam. This is the case, believe me, with Mainland-R.O.C. relations too. The more so rather than the less so since the most recent confrontations. Don't just fall for surface-texts. There are sub-texts. And sub-texts.

Discoid Discombobulations of computer-noise,
      of 'floppies' and hard disks—
  White Noise. And side by side with white noise, the
 Black Silence of fast Chinese written script (called 'grass-style'),
      and the mystic
 Black/White Silence of calligraphy—elegantly brush-painted script.
      My Taiwanese students—
      postmodern *diskoboloi*—groove on all of them.
And what of
Cataphrenetic Cachinnations of
   Black Noise, of modernist typewriter and teletype?
    Taiwan had largely bypassed black noise, at least in Chinese, for
    Chinese typewriters perforce horripilated with so many rods and
    prods, and perforce were serviced by so many
    key-faces,[78] that the Mechanical Age was best bypassed. Best to
    leap to the Technological Age. Leap to it, but keep the
    Traditional side by side.

---

[78] Because the language is not alphabetical. Chinese typewriters can still be found, but their use was never widespread. On the occasions I have seen the performance of Chinese secretary-typists, their dexterity, or rather, ambidexterity, has left me Speechless.

So Taiwan bypassed Modernism[79] (which rejected the Traditional) and
    settled into the
        Postmodern (which juxtaposes Black/White Silence
        and White Noise, and alas sometimes—
        at the discotheques—just plain Noise).

    Arriving in Taiwan, I found hermeneutics all the rage in both
literature and philosophy. My students, after my first year all of them
graduate students, throve on literary theory: in fact I can say that
several of them read each issue of *Critical Inquiry, Semiotext(e)*, and
the *PMLA* as soon as the airmailed copies reached Taiwan. At National
Taiwan University and Tsing-Hua University, Gayatri Spivak, Michel
Butor, Murray Krieger, Tzvetan Todorov, J. Hillis Miller, and Fredric
Jameson visited and lectured. Amazingly, I beheld myself assuming
the cautionary mode of my American and British peers, at least those
in better schools: That is, like them I felt obliged to caution my
students to learn the 'basics' first (especially, before undertaking to
deconstruct the 'basics'!). Our students in Taiwan work very hard—I
can honestly say that most of them did master/mistress the philosoph-
ical/literary 'canon(s)'. In the long run, their authentic postmodern
mind-set would accept no less. Hired as I was to teach western
hermeneutics, I taught only Master's and Doctoral degree students (in
two or three seminar-series a semester—each time choosing syllabi of
my own choosing). I had no committee work, only the directing each
semester of several Master's theses and a doctoral dissertation or two.
My research efforts in Buddhism could redouble, and at last I was
liberated from those features of the academic profession which were
for me—'type B' personality[80] that I am—both onerous and hobbling.
    Psychologically, Chinese culture was for me analogous to what
Carl Jung calls a 'crucible' (*crux* is the word's etymon, Jung also
notes). I found out so many matters the West takes for granted as

---

[79] In literature courses we of course study and celebrate modernist authors—
Yeats, Valéry, Rilke, Cummings, and so on, but insofar as we juxtapose them
with other authors/periods we are implementing—according to my specialized
definition—a postmodern agenda.
[80] For comparative profiles of Type A and Type B personalities, see Aron Siegman
and T. Dembrowki, eds., *In Search of Coronary-Prone Behavior—Beyond Type A*
(Hillsdale, N.J.: L. Erlbaum Assoc., 1989). For the sake of their victimized Type
B friends, if not for themselves, Type A personalities should also look at M. P.
Janisse, ed., *Individual Difference, Stress and Health Psychology* (N.Y.: Springer-
Verlag, 1988).

*natural* are in fact *artificial*: the Orient does them an opposite way it thinks is 'natural'. (Which is why, if I may supply here an allegorical reading, the story says St. Peter was crucified upside-down: so he could 'experience', all told, from *opposite* directions.) During the first years in Taiwan, my scholarly work continued and indeed increased, and concurrently my conscious mind and its ego-constitutions yielded much terrain to my unconscious (a dangerous phase in the growth process, Jung notes). Sometimes my ebullitions came smack up against Chinese protocol—

Hexagram 50: The Cauldron

The Lines: Nine in the fourth place—the legs of a *ting* [cauldron] break,
the noble's food is spilled upon the noble.
Misfortune: blame.

—*I Ching*[81]

I² faced my Shadow(s),—to again invoke Jungian terminology— acknowledged these shadows as my 'own', and then began at last to let them melt away. Hopeful too in the beginning that I² could still find a sweet woman's love, a love like that between my mother and father, I came to the conclusion that it was for me to walk 'alone but not lonely'—

Nine in the third place—showing force in one's face is ominous. The
superior person is determined and walks alone
through the rain.
Is caught in the flood; is hated. No blame, in the end.

—*I Ching*[82]

---

[81] Riseman trans., p. 75.
[82] Riseman trans., p. 65. Hexagram 43, 'Determination'.

I[2] was learning how to live peacefully—given my temperament—in the ever shifting negative-overlap between consciousness and the unconscious.—

The Judgement—    Returning, Success.
There is no mistake in going out and entering again.
Friends enter without harm.
The course of the Tao is to and fro.
On the seventh day, returning.
There is benefit in one's undertaking.

*—I Ching*[83]

The Chinese taught me to treasure true Community—

Nine in the second place—tolerating the unevolved, fording the river,
neglecting neither friends nor what is far away.
Thus one is able to take the middle way.

*—I Ching*[84]

The Chinese taught me how to keep social surface fluent yet cope with sub-structures that crack and slip; and to do this *without* injurious repression/deplacement (that is, without destruction). Between the surface and the lurching depth is this 'way of the between', a way ever differing, sliding, negatively overlapping. Perhaps without their knowing it, the Chinese taught me much about how to forsake the destructive and live (not just *think*) the deconstructive.

The influence of scholarly Buddhism is represented by what I say in the later sections of this book, as is also—I hope—the influence of Buddhist meditation. The general influence of popular Chinese culture on me, in the positive and the non-positive—and folk Buddhism/Taoism in particular plays a role in this culture[85]—is too amorphous

---

[83] Riseman trans., p. 39. Hexagram 24, 'Returning'.
[84] Riseman trans., p. 23. Hexagram 11, 'Peace'.
[85] Though the role of syncretistic Taoism is considerably greater. Taoism is too this-worldly for me: after experiences such as mine, the side of Buddhism which avers the illusory craving and madness of *saṃsāra* has its obvious appeal.

*Curricula Vitae*                                                95

for adequate treatment here. Chinese culture in Taiwan[86] sometimes
involves clear *juxtaposition*,—the structures are intercalated but
strictly distinct. 'There are many Taiwans in Taiwan'. In ideology
alone one can already name and differentiate: official Confucianism,
Pure Land Buddhism, Ch'an Buddhism, esoteric Buddhism, disparate
Christian churches, and Islam (and, side-by-side with all these, large
chunks of westernized secularism). Chinese culture in Taiwan is
sometimes a matter of bewildering *syncretism*: mainstream Taoism
with its Confucianist-and-Buddhist elements, smaller Taoist sects,
Ming-dynasty 'harmonized' Buddhism, and many independent cults
(and mixtures of some or all the foregoing with westernized and/or
Japanese-style secularism). The most I can do here is represent the
dizzying heterogeneity/homogeneity of Taiwan by way of the several
'decoupages' which follow.

\*\*\*\*\*\*\*\*\*\*\*\*\*\*\*\*\*\*\*\*\*\*\*\*\*\*\*\*\*\*\*\*\*\*\*\*\*\*\*\*\*\*\*\*\*\*\*\*\*\*\*\*\*\*\*\*\*\*

—Ju Lai Buddhist vegetarian restaurant: on most days I eat here for
lunch. Each patron assembles his/her own dinner from carts carrying
forty or fifty different selections, each artfully designed, and then
queues up and pays not according to the content of one's plate but
according to its *weight*. In the background, a soft Buddhist chant from
the establishment's cassette-player. Suddenly, today it switches to a
Christian but very non-Roman "Amazing Grace." Exuding *odium
theologicum*, I rush to the restaurant-owner. "Don't you realize the
Fundamentalist Christians around the corner slipped you that tape in
order to infiltrate, convert you? And they don't even let their converts
as much as put a foot on your temple's ground!" The reply:—"I know!
But we like the melody. And the Christ was a great religious leader
too. All that matters is compassion-and-wisdom, compassion-and-
wisdom! Every great Master has unworthy disciples! Why get all hot
and bothered?"

—The beleaguered old lady confides in me: "I've had a sad life, and
what makes it even sadder is that I'm a woman. We have a harder life
than men, what with menstrual periods and all. I'm reconciled to my

---

[86] There are non-Chinese aborigines too, most of them in the mountains. Their
plight is much like that of the American Indian—exploitation, underemployment,
alcoholism.

fate, though. My suffering is not my own doing—it's from the bad karma of a previous life. And after all, that wasn't me who did the bad things! The Buddha denied transmigration of souls." [Yes, he *did* emphatically deny it.] Night's shade was falling, but she could "sense what was going on without a light," she said. Huddled under her Lamp-stand without a light, she smiled, gestured in the air with her crackled old hands, and concluded, "Why should I feel guilty for what I didn't do!" (Very complex philosophy/psychology at work here: don't be fooled; not that I mean to affirm all of it—there is much in traditional Chinese culture which can fall in an anti-woman way.)

—The student is plump for a Chinese, and her classmates tease her about it. She stands next to me and gestures towards the grand mountain on the other side of the river. "If we look at the mountain skyline from this angle," she declares in a matter-of-fact voice, "it profiles the Kuan-Yin Bodhisattva we have today—a slender Kuan-Yin. But if we go up the river a few kilometers and look again, the angle changes and she's a Tang-dynasty Kuan-Yin, a plump Kuan-Yin." [Kuan-Yin Mountain is said to silhouette the feminine manifestation of Avalokitesvara, the all-merciful Kuan-Yin—her head-dress and coiffure, her face and bosom, and her flowing dress.]

—I sit down across the little table from a colleague, a woman professor. She gets up at once, sits at a diagonal from me, and continues our conversation (leaving the chair across from me vacant). I am early on in Taiwan—it takes me awhile to learn she means no offense. She shouldn't sit *across* from me. I am neither her husband, nor—she being unmarried—her boyfriend. Symbolical *deployment in/of Space* is very important for the Chinese.

—I give a painting, as a house-gift, of five cranes flying in formation across the sky. My host and hostess become uneasy. I am early on in Taiwan—only later do I 'put two and two together'... Realizing I hadn't put two and four together, much less, even associated the painting symbolically with the household for which it was meant. The host and hostess had four children, thus constituting a household of six, not five.[87] *Symbolic numbering* is very important for the Chinese. (Even the postage stamp one chooses for an envelope counts—What scene

---

[87] There's even more to it, but this gives you the drift.

does it depict?  What *situationally* can the depiction mean?[88]) [Aside: FOUR is a very inauspicious number in Chinese folk culture, because its Chinese phone is like that for DEATH.]

—The gigantesque sea-turtle (310 kg.) straddles the cart, eyes crusted closed, dry head sagging in the noonday sun. The burning noonday sun. The turtle's captor, a fisherman, is auctioning it off to the richest benefactor (who, as a 'good Buddhist', expects to earn merit by liberating the animal from captivity). With luck this particular turtle will be returned to the sea, but it had been there in the first place, before the enterprising fisherman trapped it so it could be liberated again—at a price. The Practice of Liberating Animals is not supposed to work this way, but Buddhism has its abuses too.[89]

—The 'architectural drawing', neatly sketched and color-tinted, hangs in a place of honor in the lobby. "But that doesn't look like this neighborhood at all!" I exclaim. "Trees and sweeps of green lawn are painted in where there's nothing but concrete and rows of shop-stalls!" "Of course! Of course!" my host, a philosophy professor, readily agrees. "Everyone knows that! But we Chinese like to idealize everything. And then we deconstruct it down to reality again. That's why

---

[88] Derrida says it, of course:—postal signifiers do dislocate. Dislocation belongs to their condition as *postal*, ultimately as *human.*

[89] Popular Buddhism has its share of abuses: they remind me 'mutatis mutandis' of their counterparts in Italian popular culture of an earlier day. Monastic Buddhism, which usually models the structure of Buddhism in the West, has its own more sophisticated pitfalls. See the pertinent discussion in Yoel Hoffmann's *The Sound of The One Hand* (N.Y.: Basic Books, 1975), pp. 23-25 and passim. And the whole of Tim Ward's *What the Buddha Never Taught* (Berkeley: Celestial Arts, 1993). My own experience has been that especially in the West the Buddhist *sangha* often attracts dependent personalities whose fixation on a manipulative master actually serves to arrest their spiritual growth. Even meditation, which at least collaterally should serve to resolve neuroses, can instead continue repression by way of a psychic compartmentalizing and pseudo-disidentification. Fortunately, the western *sangha* is now facing and learning to deal with these potentials for misuse built into the nature of its monastic structure. See, for example, Jeff Rubin's informed psychoanalytic critique in *Drang Den* (Dec. 1989), pp. 13-4, and the other reports in this issue from the third annual Buddhism and Psychotherapy conference. *Inquiring Mind*, the newspaper-journal of the Insight Meditation movement (Vipassana), discusses these same issues with an equal candor and scientificity. Perhaps needless to say, though here I say it—meditation for those who are ready for it and with proper guidance accomplishes marvelous liberations. I practice and encourage it.

postmodern artists and photographers are so popular here. One of their favorite techniques is to deconstruct classical Chinese art-motifs—by showing how the idealized subjects *really* look. Lotuses with some brown edge and an occasional blemish, bamboo stands with some breakage and dry-rot!" *Chen-ju / Zhen ru*[90] (*Skt. tathatā*). Buddhist 'suchness'. Celebrating things the way they 'really' [sic] go on.

\*\*\*\*\*\*\*\*\*\*\*\*\*\*\*\*\*\*\*\*\*\*\*\*\*\*\*\*\*\*\*\*\*\*\*\*\*\*\*\*\*\*\*\*\*\*\*\*\*\*\*\*\*\*\*\*\*\*\*\*\*\*\*

> The Buddhist Saints are the incomparable saints
> Mooing continue of lovemilk, mewling
> And purling with lovely voices for love,
> For perfect compassionate pity
> Without making one false move
> of action,
>
> Perfectly accommodating commiserations
> For all sentient belaboring things.
> Passive sweetsaints
> Waiting for yr Holyhood,
> Hoping your eventual join
> In their bright confraternity.
>
> Perfect Divines. I can name some.
> What's in a name. They were saints
> Of the Religion of the Awakening
> From the Dream of Existence
> And Non-existence...[91]

For my part, I love the Buddhist incomparable saints *and* the Catholic incomparable saints. During my ninth year in Taiwan, I think God began to shake me down. Perhaps atheistic Buddhism, with its compassion-and-wisdom, helped God shake me down. All I know is that I began—slowly—to awaken from my Wake-Dream. Not that I am claiming much. Mine is not a classical Awakening. A large part of my awakening—my exiguous awakening—is precisely to affirm God's darkness. (The late Father Bede Griffiths, O.S.B., who lived for decades in a Christian ashram in India, wrote with a special relevance of the

---

[90] One of the several Chinese terms used to render *tathatā*.
[91] Jack Kerouac, 236th chorus, *Mexico City Blues* (N.Y.: Grove-Atlantic; orig. 1987), p. 238. Chinese Buddhists whom I know would be dismayed at Kerouac and American 'Beat Buddhism' but they would love this poem. So do I.

"cave of the heart" and the "divine darkness"[92] in the *tropics*, the Sun can be a less than benign metaphor.[93]) And I am admittedly dubious about many (not all) who either look straight into the Sun, or claim to.

The Awake-Dream I woke from was the expectation that within my life experience, my *Lebenswelt*, the world could be perceived, could be *detected*, as a *just* world.[94] I mean 'world' in the broadest sense— Nature, the universe, the human and non-human, all that goes-on insofar as it is available to my awareness. By 'justice' I mean a reliable correlation between moral actions and consequences. I woke from the dream that the *world-as-I-know-it* could be counted on, relied on—to be just. (This does not deny that there could be at least some apparent justice sometimes.) Of course Christianity is based on the 'justice', 'righteousness' (Gk. *dikaiosunē*) Christ supplies so we are 'put right' with God though we and everything are blighted by/in the consequences of the Fall, but what I woke from here was the expectation that this *dikaiosunē* would perceptibly make the events in my Life-World fairer, more equitable, or even *God's apparent dealings with me* fairer, more equitable.

---

[92] Bede Griffiths, *Return to the Center* (Springfield, Illinois: Templegate, 1977; orig. ed. London: Collins, 1976), pp. 65, 28, respectively. At least two S.V.D. priests also direct Hindu-style ashrams in India: Fathers Philip Lukose and George Proksch (see *Divine Word Missionaries*, 24.4 (winter 1982), 3, 19.

[93] Of course in Hebrew scripture God is identified with the Sun-metaphor, but Moses cannot look into the Divinity's blinding Light. In the New Testament, Christ the Logos is said to make the Light 'manifest' (such a Translucency is for the Jews theologically impossible, and becomes one of the grounds for their rejection of Christianity). Christ does say, however, "Unless I go, the Spirit cannot come to you." Any Christian theologian worth her/his salt (and saltire) knows that in traditional theology God by definition must transcend all metaphor, and conversely, that God creates and creates-as-good *both* darkness and light. And traditional theologians would say that in Jewish and Christian scripture God 'adapts' to the metaphors meaningful to Semitic culture.

[94] This question is old stuff, I know, and the reader surely knows its permutations, at least its most memorable permutations, from Old Testament times through to Tolstoy and Dostoevsky, Kafka (*especially* Kafka), and Foucault and Irigaray. I am not here pretending any contribution to the theoretics of justice and expectation. (Whatever contributions I hope to make come in other sectors—the epistemology of meditation, for example.) On the subject of theodicy I am almost old-fashioned. Please read Deleuze/Guattari, Baudrillard, and so on, for innovative re-thinkings of expectation. What I am here reporting, rather, is what (I think) was—existentially—my psychological state-of-affairs, unoriginal as it happened to be.

Tu muerte más bien divertida [Thomas] Merton
(o absurda como un koan?)
—Ernesto Cardenal, S.J[95]

I did not only wake *from.* I woke *to.* I woke *to* the realization that Binds and Double-Binds constitute the only *phenomenological* descriptions that makes sense-for-me out of my life. And they go a long way towards making sense-for-me out of the unspeakable injustices one can perceive in the world of human history (injustices in my individual life pale in comparison, of course[96]): the total or near-total extinction of whole peoples—the total extinction of the Hurons after their well-intentioned conversion to Christianity, the near-total extinction of the Cambodian people by Pol Pot, of Black African ethnic groups by other Black groups and by Whites, and now of many Indian tribes by right-wing Latin American governments, and so on and on.

Bind, looser sense: for me, = the logic of dilemma. Either option is
conclusive against the agent.
"What a bind!–Damned if one does; damned if one doesn't."
—Represented ahead by two lines cutting across each other,
as, *for example*, in a Greek X (chi)
or Roman x
or Christian +.
Bind, stricter sense: for me, either (1) = the logic of the Catch-22,[97]
or (2) = the logic of the Mobius-strip (the causality of
which is more perverse). The Catch-22 situation:–e.g.,
"What a bind! To sleep, one must be free of high anxiety
[the cut], but to be free of high anxiety, one must sleep!
[crosscut]."[98] The Mobius-strip situation:–e.g.,
"What a bind! One's wanting to sleep generates the high
anxiety that thwarts sleep." Analogically, the 'wanting' is
here like the twist in the Mobius-strip which ensures that
though one planes along *all* the surface [cut], one still can't

---

[95] See "Coplas a la muerte de Merton," in Cardenal's *Antología* (Buenos Aires: Carlos Lohlé, 1971), p. 196.
[96] Alas, the relative triviality of one's own plight does not diminish its *existential* import: the parents of three children who lose one to murder are not significantly consoled by the realization that some parents have lost all their children to murder.
[97] Which can also be called the vicious circle.
[98] See the many examples of Catch-22 in Joseph Heller's own *Catch-22* (N.Y.: Dell, new ed. 1970): the classic defining example is found on pp. 46-7. See also the several definitions of Catch 22 in the Addenda section, *Webster's Unabridged.*

see 'the other side [crosscut]'.
   —Likewise represented ahead by two lines cutting across
     each other,
     as in X
        x
        +.

Double-Bind: for me, = two intersecting Binds of any kind. (Bind$^2$,
    Bind-squared: it is with 'good reason' that *quadrature*
    pervades deconstruction.) Double-Bind situation:—e.g.,
    "What a double-bind! One's wanting to sleep generates
    the high anxiety that thwarts sleep! [cut]. And if one
    *doesn't* want to sleep, that undermines health and in any
    case one *still* doesn't sleep!
    [crosscut]."[99]
      —Likewise represented ahead by two lines cutting across
       each other, quartering their purview,
       as in X
          x
          +.

I found that situationally these binds and double-binds do not work in
a paradoxical way: for example—to use again the case I invoke
above[100]—high anxiety does not in the long haul *nullify* or *cancel-out*
sleep; rather, high anxiety *thwarts* sleep—that is, some sleep will
come, but in fits and swatches. To deploy my more technical
language—as I necessarily do in this book's next Part—the going-on
meanders by way of negative overlap (here, specifically in the
occasional overlap of sleep and anxiety, a negative *differential* which
constitutes 'fitful sleep', a thwarted but not 'absolutely canceled'
sleep).[101] What is more/less—my life-experiences, phenomenologically

---

[99] There are many Ch'anist *kung-an* which deal with this same problematic of the
double-bind: their influence on me shall become apparent. So too will the
influence of St. Paul's famous double-bind, and how he deals with it: "For I do
not do the good I want, but the evil I do not want is what I do" (Romans 7: 19). In
Paul's double-bind, 'to will the good' induces a contrary correlate, a most
unwanted correlate, yet 'to not will the good' is not at all a viable alternative for
him.
[100] The binds/double-binds I have cited earlier and later in this text are my
personal ones: this example, involving sleep and anxiety, happens not to be from
my general experience. Harlequin usually sleeps well.
[101] Not that negative-overlap is necessarily 'bad' or 'good'. I use the term to mean
a 'mixed' (undistributed) neither-nor. (On distributed/undistributed forms of the
third and fourth lemmas, see ahead passim, and *Derrida on the Mend*, endnote

On Deconstructing Life-Worlds

described, are a meandering or 'errant' going-on of binds and double-binds. This is not to say that relative closure, that sometimes *plenum* and other times paradoxical congruence of good-and-bad, do not appear: sometimes they *do* appear. But somehow, some way, there always lurk the binds or double-binds. They reassert themselves—so much so that the mark of Bind and Double-Bind appears irreducible. History seems an 'infinite retreat' of these marks, always replicating-with-a-Difference. Marks that stagger-about, ...seemingly punctured by chance, seemingly shunted this-way-and-that by chance. Thwarted but not caving-in, not collapsing. Meandering ever. The mark of X (chi), x, and +, (—all the same-with-a-Difference), erected over skulls, branded into foreheads—

legible only to the Blind,...
read only by the fingers of the Blind.[102]
Braille.

...So muss dein Hertze vor zu einem *Ölberg* werden.
—Angelus Silesius (1624-77), as cited by Derrida in
"Post-Scriptum"[103]

A BINDIARY of BINDS ('personal' Sampler)...

Harlequin's so-called 'personal' life had been—throughout his marriage—bound by dilemma. He could submit to emotional battering from Columbine but at least nurture his three children; or he could escape her emotional abuse but concomitantly distance himself from the children. Loving the three children so dearly, he of course chose the former, but emotional abuse is a substance with an incredibly long 'chemical half-life'. That is, the psyche takes years to reduce its residue of pain even by half. The other half is lodged in him still. Two in one flesh. Later, in Taiwan, another dilemma: Harlequin could forego any chance to find a new wife, but forward his salary to his three children in college; or he could establish a new household (in Taiwan an educated woman's family insists she marry 'well', i.e., into a very sizable income), but abandon his children to their own financial

83.) The 'goodness' or 'badness' of the negative overlap depends on 'what is missing' and what one's attitude is towards the 'absence'.
[102] Some can be even off-funny, of course. Brand X?
[103] Derrida, "Post-Scriptum," in H. Coward and T. Foshay, eds., *Derrida and Negative Theology* (Albany: S.U.N.Y. Press, 1992), p. 312.

resources. Of course he chose the former, but he paid the price in loneliness. And later, when the children graduated from college, and Harlequin was seemingly 'available'—by *that time* he was too old, at least too old for a college-educated woman in Taiwan (and older women are simply not available: it is a conservative country). Throughout, though marital prospects were better for Harlequin in America, he disliked the American life-style so much that this aversion over-whelmed all other considerations. As for Europe, beloved Europe, it was foreclosed to him because so late in life and without a degree from a European university, he would not be able to teach *en permanence* in a good state university (Europe's rules are very strict in this regard).

Apropos of Harlequin's (so-called) *professional life*, his publishing career was doubly-bound: *what* he necessarily chose to set forth in his writing, and *how* he set it forth, necessarily thwarted the likelihood it could be set forth, especially to Western readers (this is still the case).[104] Earlier, Harlequin had found that his second book had been taken by many readers in either naive or malicious ways which grossly misconstrued *even its available lexic senses*.[105] Yet for him *not* to set forth, and not to set forth *as* he did and *how* he did, was an impossible alternative. For he did not write *in order to* publish; rather, he always sought to publish in order to *tr*ansmit the writing. This situation led severally to a Double-Bind.

Even Harlequin's body generated its bind. Vigorous physical exercise was necessary for his bodily and mental happiness, but it invariably made him too tired to write very efficiently. If he *didn't* exercise vigorously, he became fat and sluggish. Nor was a 'golden mean' workable[106]—his adrenaline would not 'kick in' without exercise that was strenuous, and without adrenalin the physical/mental benefits did not activate for him. (Attached to this bind was a more trivial,

---

[104] Any claim, Freudian or Sartrean in provenance, that he unconsciously *wanted* the bind, *wanted* his work to be thwarted, is—in my opinion—very wrong. Having carefully attended to these theories and their possible application in his case, I dismiss them. The bindiary is not a mere bindery. Likewise, I dismiss the Buddhist 'karmic' explanation: there are no pointers to it in my experience (nor Harlequin's), and I, for one/two, cannot take it 'on faith alone'.

[105] To be distinguished from readings which are contrary to the author's 'willed intention' but lexically possible. Any deconstructionist worth her/his salt and saltire realizes such readings, these latter kind, are sooner or later inevitable.

[106] Another example of what I call in *Derrida on the Mend* and elsewhere the 'centric between' and its failure. 'Centric between' differs, of course, from 'differential between'.

even comical one: if he exercised vigorously his face became much too
gaunt for his body, and if he *didn't* exercise vigorously his body
became too fat for his head. Clearly, Harlequin's very genes [his
genetic *script*] did not bother to synchronize head and body—they
wrote his head and body to be ever disproportionate.)

> And St. Francis said to Brother Masseo: "...I command you to twirl
> around in this crossroad, right where you are standing, just as
> children do, until I tell you to stop."
> —*I Fioretti di S. Francesco*, I.xi[107]

Harlequin's *academic study* was at Cross-purposes with the
above binds but for an unexpected reason:—it *didn't* trip them up. It
confirmed them. Derrida's deconstructive work exposed for me one of
the most sinister of historical binds: the philosophical Tradition's *hot
desire* to know how 'matters really go on' (sic) had again and again
generated the argumentative sleights-of-hand which had thwarted
chances for a closer approximation of how matters 'go on'. Derrida also
showed me how the 'intention to mean' necessarily commits itself to
'repetitive' structures (grammar, lexic, etc.) which thwart, displace,
intention. A necessary human Bind! Of Humans-in-language! The
bariolage (from Fr., *barioler*, 'to variegate', prob. blend of *barrer*, 'to
cross-out', and *rioler*, 'to cross-out'![108]) of my own deconstructive work
barrelled towards religious concerns of more interest to me. Towards
Buddhism's inquiry into bind/double-bind and the nature of Desire,
and the Madhyamika's use of Bind-theory to deconstruct holism. And
towards Christianity's study of the Blessed Trinity, where I found that
Trinitarian theology promotes-without-knowing-it what are very
*differential* parameters (not perimeters) of Trinity: the God of
Conciliar theology seems to work as a Bind (see Part Two, ahead). It is
precisely *thinking* which helped me find this trinitarian Anomaly, the
ongoing intellectual perusal of which gives me (rare) cause for
celebration. *Deconstruction edifies* in more ways than one. I am not
called to the exclusive No-Thinking of much centric Zen Buddhism:
the Buddhist sages whom I most admire *off-think*.[109]

When I began to awake from my Wake-Dream, I felt a (holy-)
watermark. Children growing up during and after World War II were
routinely overtreated with penicillin: my doctors had used it on me for

---

[107] See the trans. by Raphael Brown, *The Little Flowers of St. Francis* (Garden
City, N.Y.: Doubleday, Image pbk., 1958), p. 64.
[108] See full entry in *Webster's Unabridged.*
[109] On this, for this, Dogen is a good case in point.

every illness, including many for which—we know today—it is completely ineffective. Ever since, my natural immunity to disease can throw up only the frailest of defense-lines. Whenever a wave of nasty microbes sweeps through, I am decked for at least a week. For at least two days I become violently ill—fever, raw throat, an engulfing stomach-and-back pain. I reflected that whenever I was thus in the maelstrom, or for that matter, whenever I was in the sluices of depression, I *clung*, and *clung tenaciously*, to the Catholic signs-and-practices which had imprinted the majority of my life. Images of Christ, of Mary, of the saints—big Teresa, Francis, Ignatius,—our Catholic 'mandalas'.[110] *Spontaneously* (sic), with all my heart, I repeated the traditional recitations, our sacred 'mantras',—"Heart of Christ, once in agony, have mercy on the dying," "Flos carmeli... Stella maris, ora pro nobis!" And many others. And I fingered a rosary,[111] repeating and repeating the *ave*. 'A far cry from *non-clinging*!' a Ch'an/Zen monk (but *not* a Pure Land monk) might very well declare! (Or again, under some circumstances he might very well not.)

    *Crucially,* etched into each mantra, each prayer, I felt a crux,[112] a riddle, a *chi*, a bind—a bar and transverse-bar cutting across each other. The cruxes, with the mantras their sacred writing, replicated themselves with-a-difference: they staggered-about,... punctured, and shunted this-way-and-that: they meandered, and kept streaming off the page. I had eluded the experiential fact long enough—that my psychic skin was reading this cross-hatched writing; ... that my psychic depths were fingering a Divine braille in the darkness. A Divine braille[113] read by mystic *touch*, not sight. I returned to the full practice

---

[110] I invoke 'mandala' and 'mantra' here in only a broad analogous sense.

[111] Rosary indeed. From M.L. *rosarium*, representing Mary's 'crown of roses'. One decade of the rosary: A rose is a rose is a rose is a rose is a rose is a rose is a rose is a rose is a rose is a rose. A decade of the rosary X fifteen constitutes the 'complete' rosary.

[112] Crux (fr. L. cross, torture, see 'ridge'): a puzzling, confusing, or difficult problem; an unsolved question. Consult *Webster's Unabridged.*

[113] In Scripture there is Divine braille—crosses, seals, and Name inscribed into foreheads (e.g., see Ezk. 9:4, Rev. 3:12, 7:3, 22:4), and Evil's braille—its name and number written on hands or foreheads (e.g. Rev. 13:16). In the Ash Wednesday service, Christ's cross is inscribed with ash on the foreheads of the penitent. This Divine braille should mark us to become 'other Christs' (*alteri Christi*), consecrating our marks of suffering through/with/in His marks:—"I have been crucified with Christ [*sunestaurōmai:* 'co-crucified']; it is no longer I who live, but Christ who lives in me" (Gal. 2:20). (Ash Wednesday: 'Mercredi des

of Catholic Christian faith—the Mass, confession, communion, and through them, utter entrustment to Christ. Shortly after, the Lord— no doubt to impart further courage to my paltry will—reinforced this 'second conversion' with a Seal, a very perceptible Seal:—to my astonishment, the *consolatio* of my youth returned, after an absence of more than thirty years.[114] Yes, *for me*, a *chi* necessarily hatches as a *Chi-Rho*,[115] and an x-bind is always also a + -bind, the 'Sign of Contradiction' (Luke 2:34). No longer would I cling to the Cross only when in desperate 'straits': I could suffer this kind of Bad Faith no longer. (My personal and ineluctable need for *This* other-power—a need which I would think runs parallel to some 'other' in my unconscious[116]— explains why Ch'an/Zen Buddhism is not alone enough for me.)

That my rational mind pulled in one direction, limiting reality to a universe of (cruel) phenomenal randomness [the cut], *and* my Christ-faith pulled in another, expanding reality to more-than-phenomenal meaning [the cross-cut], was *already* a Crux (riddle, Cross). It was a Bind that put my personhood on a Cross and pulled it in two directions. In this sense, one could say the Cross is Perverse, severally and variously perverse—but that's the very point(s) of it. Satanic evil has its hand in this perversion, but Christian theology maintains that the cross—by pulling in two (or more) directions, by *excruciating*—is the means whereby evil is conquered. The cross may be perverse, may excruciate *because* of sin, but the victimhood which can be thereby achieved is *good,* and conquers sin. The resurrected Christ invites Thomas to read-by-touching His five sacred marks (*stigmata:* 'marks'). As Gerard Manley Hopkins says, Christ's "work was done by being broken-off undone,"[117] that is, by being Thwarted. As for those doctrines of Christianity which make no sense in terms of

---

*cendres'* in French, thus another permutation in Derrida's cendre/sender reinscriptions; see Neh. 3:15; cf. John 9:7—"*Silōam,* which means 'Sent'").

[114] So much for the thesis that the *consolatio* of my youth was 'only body-chemicals'? If 'only body-chemicals', the chemicals were back after mid-age. I suppose God can work through chemicals too, of course. God is the God of bodies too, and of chemicals. The 'body-mind dichotomy' isn't only un-Oriental. It is also un-Jewish and un-Christian.

[115] The superimposed Greek letters *chi* (X) and *rho* (P), the first two letters of *khristos* ('Christ' in Greek), and used as a monogram.

[116] An archetype, perhaps? My ongoing investigation of psychology adapts Jung and Lacan, albeit a most star-crossed of combinations.

[117] In *Correspondence of Gerard Manley Hopkins and R. W. Dixon,* ed. Claude C. Abbott (Oxford: Oxford U. P., 1935; 2nd ed., 1955), pp. 137-8.

available phenomenal evidence—the Fall, grace, Providential care, eternal life, the existence of the soul, etc., I opted to accept them because they are contingent upon (part-and-parcel with-) the Christ-experience I was (and still am) tangibly frequenting.

Even the institutional Church, with all of its human corruption and scandal and cruel streak, from the cowardly apostles down through the latest appalling episodes, I would accept. The Church which had so often left me to hang, and to twist slowly slowly in the wind, I would accept *for Christ's sake*—even though its bar had so often trussed me up and its sharp cross-bar thrusted sideways into my heart and shafted straight across. For all I knew, I was in my own way this much of a faitour too: the Saints tell us 'mutatis mutandis' we *all* are. (So, noting the etymology, I decided on 'No more Harlequin!': no doubt I *did* store up too much rancor, much too much rancor, the Devil's own very 'bad blood'... His/her/its bad blood-juice; Yes, I had to learn to *forgive* instead, to forgive even gargoyles.) Next, apropos of the rational intellect, I· did (and do) find it helpful to combine and adapt Jung and Levinas into the following protocol (like and *unlike* Kierkegaard's). For me, acceptance of the Christian belief-system is not mere adherence 'pure and simple' to the literal definition of 'grace', say, or 'original sin', say. Rather, it is acceptance that each of these doctrines is a specialized register within our human race's compass—limited as this compass is—of what is really so Other that its real workings are beyond our human comprehension. That is, the reality of each particularized doctrine is in this sense an 'X-function', an 'unknown'.[118] Not only the Biblical stories, but Doctrines—the Teachings themselves—seem to work almost like (T.S.-) Eliotesque "objective correlatives" of/for the divine Other[119] (which does *not* mean we should be less attentive to doctrinal intricacies). Thus scientific 'demythologizing' as such is irrelevant, unless it serves this same function (which it *can*).

---

[118] This does *not* mean Revealed doctrines are 'untrue'. They are true insofar as they go, but any formulation in a human register must necessarily 'fall short'.

[119] Or better, as we shall affirm ahead, 'of/for the Neither I nor Not-I' (conversely, 'of the Neither Other nor Not-Other'). The doctrines and biblical stories are the enfoldment, or better, the *gaine* (F.), of the 'Neither Other nor Not-Other' in us human beings. See Derrida on *gaine* passim in his work, and do not let Derrida's Jean Genet scare you off: Derrida is, perhaps,· quite religious (L. *religiosus*, from re + *ligare*, 'to bind back').

The Black Robe of Braille

[ _____ Debré

Debray

Dobrée]

débraie

*l'Ebree* (It.)

*ça*, 'March of the Hebrew Women'


Shortly after my second conversion, I resumed my old practice of doing meditation before the Blessed Sacrament. Sometimes, deep in meditation, I would feel a cross begin to tilt over, until it became an x, a 'crux decussata' (and thus a cross still: 'a supposed variety of the cross of crucifixion consisting of two intersecting beams set up in the form of an x'[120]); and sometimes a cross would cross-breed and cross-hatch and graft on/in, until it was at once a Buddhist *sauvastika* (—in China, now, the more usual age-old sign marking a site as Buddhist: the crampons turn to the *left*, as opposed to the 'swastika', the crampons of which turn to the right[121]). And crosses would go through many other mutations, splices, superimpositions... some involving graphic modification, some involving similar or dissimilar meanings—but they *all* reiterated somehow a line and crossing it a transverse-line.

What happened next did not come in sudden vision: rather, it came like writing comes—slowly, cryptically. It was *not* grand. And it came with many intertexts, Derridean[122] and otherwise. Moreover, there was a Surplus (sur +) in the writing.

Va doblando la punta el San Juan de la +

. . . .

o *gana*[123] decía San Juan de la Cruz

infinita gana—

—Ernesto Cardenal, S.J.[124]

---

[120] See 'crux decussata' in *Webster's Unabridged*. Also called 'St. Andrew's cross'.

[121] See W. E. Soothill and L. Hodous, rev. Rev. Shih Sheng-kang et al., *A Dictionary of Chinese Buddhist Terms* (Kaohsiung: Fo Kuang Pub. reprt., n.d.), p. 203.

[122] Baited but (almost) free-floating from the "+ R" section of *Vérité en peinture* (or see "+ R [Into the Bargain]," *The Truth in Painting*); and *Glas*, p. 216 and passim; and *Carte postale*, pp. 420, 543, and passim.

[123] If you want (not if you don't want), see an etymological dictionary and compare Derrida's French *gaine* again.

[124] *Antología*, p. 205.

For me, henceforth, the line and transverse-line—no matter how many its permutations—would also reinscribe Christ's Cross and His Bind/Double-Bind written in Blood. (Even a Crucified man's Body is in a Bind:—Don't take a breath and you asphyxiate; take a breath, straining and heaving your torso up and out, and you double your fatigue and further wrench your hands and feet.)

But—no doubt about it—there was a surplus in the writing. Maybe from Christ's surplus but surely it was a surplus. It was given over, handed over, and is among other reasons the main reason for this book. It is meant for *all* people who, like me, sense their life is a bind/double-bind. (For those many who *don't* sense these binds, yours is Another way: this writing probably cannot help you.) No matter whether you are Buddhist or Christian or a dual-practitioner,[125] or whether you are an absurdist or materialist or determinist or atheist or agnostic or deconstructionist or animist or monotheist or polytheist or whatever—if you have an inkling of binds/double-binds and suffer from them—I will give you a way to cope. I shall *not* ask you to change your *ideology*: the writing is a grid of permutations, a stream of siglia, of braille-marks. Join it where you want.

To cope: [ME *copen, coupen*, fr. MF *couper*, to strike, cut off, ...]
2a. to maintain a contest or combat usu. on even terms
or with success, used with *with* ... b. to face or encounter
and to find necessary expedients to overcome problems and difficulties ...[126]

...this interval that constitutes it [the 'present' element]
in the present must also, with the same stroke ['du même *coup*'],
divide the present in itself, thus dividing, along with the present,

---

[125] 'Dual practice' has become the accepted if ambiguous term for those who practice both Buddhist and Christian meditative forms. I mean to include in this number those who—like myself—think that whatever beneficent 'sameness' comes from Buddhism and Christianity is constituted precisely by their mutual *difference* as religions. Most 'dual practitioners', especially Catholic ones, take another tack. Zen says its 'truth' cannot be verbalized, and some Zen traditions even distinguish the 'Zen-experience' from Buddhism (which they associate with Buddhism-as-institution, its dogma, rituals, etc.). Thus it is fairly easy for a Christian to justify dual practice in traditional Christian terms, if s/he wants to. Several Catholic clergy, in 'good standing' with their Church superiors, have been officially installed by Japanese Zen masters as *sensei* (Zen teacher). So have Christians of other denominations. And Jews. Contact in Japan the Japanese Society for Buddhist-Christian Studies, and in the U.S.A. the Society for Buddhist-Christian Studies.
[126] Abridged, truncated, from *Webster's Unabridged*.

> everything that can be conceived on its basis, that is, every being,
> —in particular, for our metaphysical language, the substance or
> subject.
> —Jacques Derrida[127]

How much the Buddha is crosshatched in(to) the writing, the
Crosshatch, which follows below—I leave for you to figure (if you
want). How much or little the Buddha—from off the page—writes me
and writes this crosshatch which follows below—I leave for you to
figure (if you want).


+ + + + + +·+ + + + + + + + + + + + + + + + + + + + + + + + + + + + + + + + + + +


## CROSSHATCH


xxxxxxxxxxxxxxxxxxxxxxxxxxxxxxxxxxxxxxxxxxxxxxxxxxxxxxxxxxxx

—Even that *différance originaire* which—*while* binding into them—makes
'No' and 'Not-No', human 'negation' and 'affirmation', *possible,*-
thus making our *humanity* possible...,
Even *différance originaire* is a double-bind:—

> To what mode does this discourse belong, then, both that of
> Dionysius [pseudo-Dionysius the Areopagite] and that which I hold
> about him? Must it not necessarily keep to the place, which cannot
> be an indivisible point [*pace* Heidegger], where the two modes [the
> secret, mystical; the philosophical, demonstrative] cross—such that,
> properly speaking, the crossing itself, or the *symplokē*, belongs to
> neither of the two modes and doubtless even precedes their
> distribution? At the intersection (*croisement*) of the secret and of the
> nonsecret, what is the secret?
> —Derrida, "Dénégations" (557; 24, 25)[128]

> There is a secret of denegation and a denegation of the secret. The
> secret as such, *as secret*, already separates and establishes a
> negativity, it is negation which de-nies itself. It de-negates itself.

---

[127] As quoted in *Derrida on the Mend*, p. 33. I revised D. Allison's trans. slightly,
towards increased literalism.
[128] The first three citations below are likewise to Derrida's "Dénégations." I have
altered Frieden's translation in several places, in favor of greater literality.

This denegation does not come upon it by accident, it is essential and originary (*originaire*). (557;25)

But if the risk [that intention give way to repetition] is inevitable, the accusation it incurs [of lapse into non-sense, nihilism] need not be limited to the apophatic moment of negative theology. It may be extended to all language, and even to all manifestation in general. This risk is inscribed in the structure of the mark.[129] (537; 5)

But since the structure of the trace is in general the very possibility of an experience of finitude, I dare to say that the distinction between a finite and an infinite cause of the trace seems secondary here. It is itself an effect of trace or differance, which does not mean that the trace or differance (of which I have tried to show elsewhere that it is finite, insofar as it is infinite) have a cause or an origin. (561;29)

Mais le plus d'Un, c'est sans retard plus de deux.
            —Derrida, "Foi et Savoir" (85)[130]

*AVANT-COURRIER*: Seek out a qualified instructor in the psycho-physical skills of
    Oriental meditation[131]—
        (1) The lotus-position (or your best approximation thereof);
        (2) Breathing techniques;
        (3) 'Walking meditation' (used in Zen at intervals);
        (4) Chant techniques (mantra).
'Sit' with a group, if possible. When you have progressed *technically* to the point that you can 'sit' for half-hour periods at a stint without physical or psychic tumult, you can try Crosshatch. (Remember,—regular physical exercise, when possible, and a healthy food regimen

---

[129] In the structure of the Mark Taylor, too, of course. Who is re-tailored (cf. Thomas Carlyle), de-tailored. But they know that.
[130] In Jacques Derrida, Gianni Vattimo, et al., *La Religion: Séminaire de Capri* (Paris: Seuil, 1996), pp. 9-86.
[131] Though an instructor is necessary, and an instruction-manual is not enough, consulting some of the latter can be of ancillary help. Philip Kapleau's *The Three Pillars of Zen* (N.Y.: Doubleday, 1965) has precise directives and diagrams. I also recommend—for those who can get it—the even more detailed *Zazen* manual of the International Zen Dojo—Chozenji, New York City Branch (134 W. 72nd St). Christians can supplement these with the instructions found in Dom John Main's *Word into Silence* (London: Darton, Longman, and Todd, 1980), or in any other of the growing number of books reviving Hesychastic and other Christian forms leading to deep meditation. [At the time 'Crosshatch' and the foregoing Note were written, I had not yet practiced Theravada meditation-forms, which differ somewhat from the Mahayana's.]

with little or no meat, when possible, do much to *dispose* the mind/body
to meditation.)

*COURRIER*:  Tag your 'own' condition of double-bind, its intellective
and emotive burden, to a geometric figure of line/transverse-line. Let
the figure run through some permutations. For example,—the Greek
*chi*, the Roman X, the Christian crosses, the Buddhist *sauvastika*, the
Buddhist 'cross-thunderbolt',[132] the logico-mathematical X (the 'unknown'),
the chromosomic X, the logico-mathematical + ('plus'),... (Jews and
others might well notice that the Star of David is a rotary of overlapping X's,—palpate it as it spins, and zigzags off the page; Hindus
and others might well note that some geometric yantras involve a
*mise-en-abyme* of X's,—track them, track them...)
......................

The line/transverse-line will tend to disseminate hither-thither. "*X
sans X*." X-ray. "X-man Comics." X-rated. Into history, for example.
"The Knights Hospitaller"... "Red Cross Knight"... The American "Red
Cross"... The Cross of Lorraine[133]... Malcolm X... the "Green Cross," for
example. Then becoming the mark of poison, perhaps... 'Cross-bones'.
Of death,... 'a rifle-sight's cross hairs'. Or the monstrous... 'twisted
Nazi cross, swastika', and its verb, 'to double-cross'.

Sometimes the figure will either drift, or 'spontaneously' mutate, into
other-than-line/transverse-line. The splayed ends of the Greek X may
loop back and attach, forming a chiasmic figure-8 (doubly-bound,
still!). The graphic and phonic and/or graphic and semantic may be
doubly-garbled into each other, and reversed, or scrambled: e.g.,-
'Greek X... *chi*... Chinese *ch'i* (Taoism's energy-stream) ...ich ...*isch*
(H., "man") ...Chimera ...Malachi ...*khairō* (Gk., "I rejoice")' ...Ivan
Ilyich (see Tolstoy). The graphic/phonemic/phonetic/semantic may be
garbled: as in 'Christian +, ...cross ...to cross ...to cross-over ...to
transfer ...Transubstantiate ...translate, ...tr- ....' And the *tr-* may
begin to free-float. *WHEN* you sense connection to a geometric figure
of two intersecting straight lines is *lost*, gently lead (*tr*ansfer) your

---

[132] Two stylized thunderbolts crossing each other: an emblem of Buddha's obdurate
doctrine, which can smash all obstacles.
[133] See Paul Claudel, "... c'est croix accrochée à la croix...," *Oeuvre poétique*
(Paris: Gallimard, 1967), pp. 595-6.

mind/heart back to the meander of line/transverse-line. (You are *not* doing a diagnosis of 'free-association', though some so-called free-association is *bound* to occur; nor are you doing an 'experiment' in dissemination, though dissemination is *necessarily* happening.)

Continue to tag your burden of double-bind to each instance of line/transverse-line. After two half-hour periods, or even earlier, you will notice that the 'same' few particularized versions of line/ transverse-line shall have begun to recur sporadically. Recur situationally, with a difference. Recur-with-a-difference. That is, reinscribe themselves.[134]

You are now at an important crossroad. 'Read' these recurrent nodes (Lt. *nodus*, knot) of reinscription which neither you nor not-you have/has (mentally) 'written'. They are the braille-marks *for you*: they are 'your' mandalas (Skt. *maṇḍala* = 'circle', but cross-hatch writes-over this etymology[135]). Normally you shall be choosing one from out of these your mandalas for each of your future sittings: choose, each time, the mandala that seems inviting to you at the time. If the abstract garble of graphic/phonetic or phonetic/semantic or even of noetic/noematic (or noetic/grammatical, or any of many others) has become your line/transverse-line, your double-bind, make *it* your mandala. (Or one of your mandalas.) This more abstract kind of (decentered) cathexis—though always double-bound into the most concrete—will gradually happen in any case, once you have begun meditation and continued in the practice for many months/years (depending). Also, gradually, your number of (line/transverse-line) mandalas will *either* decrease, *or* (in rare cases) expand astronomically, into myriads you cannot sense now (at this juncture, these possibilities should not concern you). Having chosen your 'initial' mandalas, you are now ready to begin meditation (begin at the *next* session).

---

[134] Derrida has concluded to nodes of reinscription *philosophically*. We shall be attempting, during meditation, *not* to cognize them but to *frequent* them.

[135] In Tibetan Buddhism the mandala represents the Universe and its powers. More broadly, the term mandala has come to mean any noematic object which is designed to abet, structure, meditative focus. Differential mysticism in its own way breaks the circle.

xxx

*POSTE RESTANTE: MEDITATION*[136]: In standing position, pray to the benign Other-Power(s) of your community tradition or 'individual' belief. (Among Buddhists, Mahayanists invoke Buddhas and Bodhisattvas, Theravadins call to mind the historical Shakyamuni and take him as a model.) Ask for help in the meditation about to begin. If you are *not* a believer in benign Other-Power(s), I urge that you open your mind/heart to the *possibility* of such Power(s), and that such Power(s) can help you. That from absolutely *off-the-page* but still somehow folded into you, the Power(s) can help you. (If you find such an opening-up unacceptable, just stand with the others and await the meditation-sitting which shall follow shortly.) Consider the following constatation of Carl Jung: The discipline of psychology/psychiatry, limiting itself to the empirical research which defines it, has established that the structure of belief (ectypes of archetypes) is necessary for the unconscious, and thus usually necessary for mental health. In short, you can be assured that, 'experientially', prayer-before-meditation *can help*. This does *not* mean that it suffices for the non-believer to 'not believe but just go through the motions'. *Rather*, it means that the non-believer really opens mind/heart to the possibility of Other-Power(s), and on the strength of this Hope which-can-never-be-foreclosed, behaves during prayer in a believing way.[137]

If there is a mixed meditation-group of theists and non-theists,[138] they should sit in respective lines at right-angles to each other. During the beginning prayer (silent), the two rows of meditators should each face

---

[136] From L. deponent vb. (= passive in form, active in meaning) *meditari*: compare Germanic cognate *metan*, 'to measure'. 'Meditation' has become the standard English translation for Buddhist-style *zazen*. The usage is confusing in that 'meditation' in the Christian tradition has for quite some time meant 'discursive mental prayer'. 'Contemplation' has been the standard Christian term for deep non-discursive prayer. I prefer not to use the term 'contemplation' because its Latin root *contemplari* ('to observe carefully') restores the subject-object dichotomy which mystic non-rational/off-rational prayer, whether it be Eastern or Western, disowns.

[137] In anthropomorphic terms,—"Are you here/there? I'll not give up asking for help, in the hope that you are here/there!"

[138] For example, Mahayanists are free to invoke Buddhas and Bodhisattvas, but these are not God or gods.

the wall opposite them, their gazes (and energies) thus constituting a giant X or fertile Bind:—

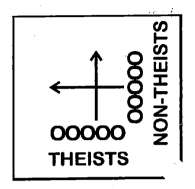

[Aside:—In the above format there can be two more rows, each ranged along one of the unoccupied sides of the *quadrature*. Perhaps these rows can accommodate practitioners who take themselves to be in a third lemma (both ... and) or fourth lemma (neither ... nor). Then the X becomes a sign of Bind/Double-Bind. Not that the quadrature is exhaustive. No matter where one 'sits', no format can capture such an X. The quad*rature* is broken, after all (look at the above diagram again).

In your beginning prayer, you must commit yourself to the daily practice of loving-kindness, and to the rejection of malice. (The specifics of *how* to reject malice differ somewhat according to the tradition one invokes, of course; in the detail, even *what* exactly defines malice differs.) In what turns out to be his version of Nietzschean 'eternal return', Derrida shows how 'history' is sporadically but repeatedly marked by nodes of meaning which reinscribe malice, indeed, which reinscribe Evil. The implication is—for example—that the Nazi Swastika (in all its horror) is an inevitable moment programmed (by chance) into the *limited* but *possible* permutations of the Cross.[139] All signs, and afortiori all texts, are in this sense foredoomed to unleash—according to the 'range of play' in their limited but *disparate* possible meanings—waves of recurrence which activate these meanings. Those verses in the New Testament, for example,

---

[139] This is so, of course, even though the historical origins of Europe's swastika may be in ancient India, and even though the swastika is also found among many aboriginal peoples.

which lend themselves to (semantically) *possible* anti-Semitic readings,[140] will sooner or later come round to be activated as such, just as their other possible moments of meaning will sooner or later be activated. And these disparate 'nodes' of interpretation will repeat, in staggered *waves*, down through the centuries.

Derrida's treatment of evil can be accommodated, with some adjustments, by a Buddhist theory of karma, and of *saṃsāra*. Perhaps to a lesser extent it can be accommodated as well by a Christian doctrine of Original Sin and the effects thereof. In any case, Derrida—in his philosophy of *how* interpretations reinscribe themselves—is aiming for dispassionate description: he is not aiming to take an ethical stand (though he does do so elsewhere). Your purpose when meditating is *not* description, but an increase in serenity, love, and off/rational wisdom, so you can better cope with binds/double-binds. When you are in the meditative darkness of the *tan-t'ien* (q.v., below), non-clinging will preclude malicious intent, but malice can arise if you are a beginner, and also when you are entering/exiting the sacred darkness. Thus, you cannot allow your mandala(s) free rein: if your mandala somehow permutates into/towards malice, gently return it to the good, or at least to what is sensed as neutrality.

Assume your meditation-posture, and begin. Fix attention on your mandala. Breathe slowly, very deeply.[141] For the first few sessions, I would recommend either the mode of Breath-Alone (sense that you are wrapping each exhalation around the mandala); or the mode of Breath-with-Mantra (sense that with each exhalation you are wrapping the mantra[142] around the mandala). Continue for thirty minutes.

---

[140] That the Christian churches have in some centuries condemned an anti-Semitic reading of these passages as incorrect is beside the point.

[141] In Zen, the time ratio of inhalation, hold-full, exhalation, and hold-empty is usually 2:2:4:2. In yogic and Tibetan systems it is sometimes 2:8:4:2 (more difficult). Consult a meditation-manual for specifics, or better—if one is to be found—a qualified instructor.

[142] Choose a mantra from your own tradition, in the vernacular or in a foreign language. In the Christian tradition, Hebrew, Greek, and Latin aspirations make remarkable mantra. Buddhists sometimes project individual Sanskrit letters into their mandala, mixing graph/grapheme/phonemes in intriguing ways. Other mantras intentionally garble phonemes. A salubrious garble. The *décalage* in the Tara Mantra survives Romanization readily: OM TARE TURARE TURE SWA HA.

> The blind one found the jewel;
> The one without fingers picked it up;
> The one with no neck put it on;
> And the one with no voice praised it.
> —*Taittirīya Āraṇyaka*[143]

For several sessions, maybe many sessions, your consciousness will be cluttered, distracted by ideas and images. Ideas will demand to connect with ideas, images with images, ideas with images: do *not* let them build a string. Rather, gently ignore them. Do not hold onto them. Calmly, without becoming flustered, let them pass. Likewise with emotions. Do not fix attention on them: let them pass. Even consolation,—do not rebut it but do not hold onto it either. Gradually, intact movements of your intellect, imagination, and emotion will subside. Spontaneously 'you' will sense that you/not-you are reading/ writing the braille-marks of your mandala. In the zone of your body about two inches below the navel (the zone called *tan-t'ien / dan tian* in Chinese, *tanden* in Japanese), you/not-you are reading/writing the mandala in the sacred darkness. If you are a woman, and if you prefer, name this zone your Womb. Either way, the mandala will begin to negatively[144] double-bind into you/not you. A frequenting of double-bind(s). Salubrious double-binds. Eventually, perhaps after years, 'you/not you' will become 'neither you nor not-you' (in the undistributed sense[145]).

[Aside]   In this kind of meditation, 'differential meditation', the meditative-condition is not centric:—
   (1)  The line/transverse-line act(s) out obverse tensions which pull away from each other, which *decenter*.
   (2)  Even for the advanced, the mandala remains a double-bind, a trauma (Gk.'wound'), though Joyous, and double-bound (by pure negative reference) into the meditator.
   (3)  The 'experience' of Joy is joyously *marked*, i.e., ever-differs: 'it' (*ça*) frequents (cf. 'frequentative verb': in grammar, a verb form or meaning denoting repeated or recurring action).

---

[143] As cited by R. H. Blyth in his *Zen and Zen Classics* (Tokyo: Hokuseido, 1960), Vol. I, p. 28.
[144] That is, by way of absolute negative reference. Consult Magliola, *Derrida on the Mend*, pp. 21-26, 112-3; and Part Two of this book.
[145] This formula is just a 'pointer', of course. A trace. What Madhyamika Buddhists mean by a *prajñapti* (in its more specialized sense).

(4) The eventual meditative condition is not 'non-thinking', but off-thinking: in the experience of meditation, the *debris* of cognition, imagination, and even emotion remain, and continue on as *traces*.

(5) The eventual meditative condition is not 'oneness', and is not a void, nor is it a *plenum*. 'Neither you nor not-you' in the undistributed sense means that Other remains Other ('neither you' = not you), but Other is also somehow entrammeled in you ('nor not-you' = *not* not-you). And nonetheless this 'oscillating' version (cf. Derrida's use of *osciller*[146]) of the fourth lemma is not a reduction to the third lemma (= 'both Other and non-Other'): it is less closed, framed, *totalistic*, than the third lemma, whether the third lemma itself be distributed or undistributed,[147] and thus does not reduce to it.

Nota Bene: I am not suggesting that—for months or years on end—the line/transverse-line meditation be the *only* meditation you practice. You may need other meditations, which you can also practice for shorter or prolonged periods.

After thirty minutes, gradually come out of meditation. Normally you will feel refreshed, strengthened, able to change what can/should be changed, and accepting of what cannot be. Make what traditional western philosophy has called 'acts of the will',—acts of appreciation for what you do have, and repentance for how you have hurt people. (Sometimes, eventually, 'your' will may feel more 'acted upon' than 'acting':—'neither you nor not-you' will be gently, lovingly, moving the will,—a great consolation.) Make, for sure, concrete plans to improve your practice of loving-kindness over the next 24 hours. Do not make

---

[146] In terms of 4th lemma discussion, Derrida in "Dénégations" (564;32) does not favor the distributed version (as in the case of Plato's *hyper*, the *sur-* which absolutely transcends, escapes, the X of 'neither X nor non-X'); rather, Derrida favors that which *oscillates* between escape-from-X and some open-ended entrammelment in X (so that 'neither X' means non-X but 'nor non-X' means some entanglement in X). Consult also Derrida's treatment of *ni...ni* ('neither...nor') in "Dénégations," pp. 593-4; 61-2.

[147] In the distributed version of the third lemma, 'both X and non-X' means 'both *totally* X and *totally* non-X', so that X and non-X come together into a mystical (sometimes called 'paradoxical') unity, a closure. In the undistributed version of the third lemma, 'both X and non-X' means 'partly X and partly Non-X', so that these two parts come together into a mathematical/logical unity, a closure. Thus—for a Derridean—the two versions of the third lemma, distributed and undistributed, are logocentric (though in different ways).

the mistake of thinking that—for coping with double-binds—meditation is itself *enough*; also, realize that for many people meditation cannot be the *most* important practice.

After the volitive acts, assume a comfortable position congenial to logical thought, and cogitate your *philosophy* of double-bind. What do the line/transverse-line mean *philosophically* to you? Work out—either in your own terms or according to your chosen tradition—a rationale for coping. Of course, 'to cope' is also another verb, 'to cover with a cope' (from ML *capa*, ecclesiastical mantle, from LL *cappa*, mantle, head-covering, perhaps from L. *caput*, head[148]: see also Derrida on *cap*). Philosophy is necessary and useful.[149] Then during meditation 'neither you nor not-you' will do the work of dismantling.[150] You are not only 'one': you are double(d), double-bind, and more.

Of philosophizing binds/double-binds: here are some (very few) examples. I am not suggesting they adequate to each other. I do not supply a 'Buddhist' example because western Buddhists—most of them highly-committed recent converts in a hostile environment—would be well-along in these matters already. And most eastern Buddhists, even merely 'cultural' ones, would feel—perhaps rightly—that any 'pointers' from a westerner in these matters would be out of place. Oriental Buddhists will read this book and use its 'crosshatch' as and when it suits them. And I have reason to believe it will suit them. (I see them, ranged along at least three walls of the quadrature; others are in the open doorway and/or ranged ōutside; some are ranged, but in neither place.)

*ROUTAGES*......

xxxxxxxxxxxxxxxxxxxxxxxxxxxxxxxxxxxxxxxxxxxxxxxxxxxxxxxxx

---

[148] All from *Webster's Unabridged*.
[149] In Buddhism, it belongs to *saṃvṛti*, the first of Nagarjuna's 'two truths' (see *Derrida on the Mend* and Part Two of this book).
[150] Which leads to *paramārtha*, Nagarjuna's 'second truth'.

OF A (PHILOSOPHICAL) MATERIALIST—

> I don't believe life has a *purpose*. Life is a lot of
> protoplasm with an urge to reproduce and continue in
> being.
>           —Joseph Campbell[151]

> "...the body on the rocks under the crossroads."
> "...a long crevice running perpendicular to the shoreline."
> "...the general plan of his itinerary: a kind of figure eight..."
>                    —Alain Robbe-Grillet, *The Voyeur*[152]

> -"Isn't it possible in the same way that the values we cherish in the
> world can only exist in combination with evil?"
> -"It's an ingenious notion, Larry. I don't think it's very satisfactory."
> -"Neither do I," he smiled. "The best to be said for it is that when
> you've come to the conclusion that something is inevitable all you
> can do is to make the best of it."
>                    —W. Somerset Maugham, *The Razor's Edge*[153]

I read the above epigraphs slowly. Though not necessarily penned by
materialists, these excerpts set some markers along my route. Then I
reason as follows.

(1)   There are billions of people alive this moment. Some live quite
happy, 'fulfilled' lives. Perhaps their genetic make-up pitched them
towards a healthy body, or intelligence, or a serene temperament; and
they were born into nurturing circumstances in a functional society.
Or into a religion 'functional' for them, so they can ride through the
direst of crises. Or perhaps they went on to find such a religion or
philosophy, and it now serves efficiently enough. Or perhaps no ugly
accident has (or will) intervene, breaking their general happiness. AT
THE OTHER END OF THE SCALE, some are very unhappy. Perhaps
they were born to abusive parents in a dysfunctional society; perhaps
they are mutilated in body and mind, and chronically depressive;
perhaps they have never known love and cannot love. Or perhaps a
disaster 'from without' has preempted all their promise. (I think of the

---

[151] As quoted in Wes Nisker's "More Crazy Wisdom" in *Inquiring Mind*, Vol. 6,
No. 1, p. 32.
[152] Engl. trans. R. Howard (N.Y.: Grove, 1958), pp. 149, 204, 212, respectively.
[153] N.Y.: Doubleday pbk. ed., 1946, p. 312.

millions of Jewish infants and teenagers, under the sign of the Swastika, gassed and thrown into ovens: not that among them the intellectually gifted are more important but as a scholar I am bound to think of them—How many geniuses-about-to-bud were deprived of their spring, decapitated before they could even begin? I think of other victims of other holocausts... American Indians, African Blacks, Chinese, Japanese, Armenians, Ukranians, Poles,...).

I am despondent over the binds/double-binds which make my life a torture. Along the scale of probabilities—a scale along which even this moment billions of persons are ranged—I may very well fall towards the negative end: 'Things don't come together right in me/for me,—I am ill-sorted'. INSOFAR as my lot is unchangeable, I NOW ACCEPT it as the luck of the draw. I SHALL NOT TAKE MYSELF AS SERIOUSLY AS I HAVE in the past. Scientists have dated our galaxy alone at billions of years; the universe is aswarm with countless galaxies. Time and space, time/space,... far, far, far beyond our ken. Despite misery, I SHALL ENJOY WHAT I CAN in the world: the 'now' moment, the 'murmuring of the spring as the night deepens, the coloring of the hills as the sun goes down'.[154] Confronting my IRREDUCIBLE UNIMPORTANCE in the 'grand scheme of things', and in 'the eyes of the world' (human society tends to be very *ocular*), I shall accept and even affirm this my unimportance. When I personally feel sad, and am mired in 'is' and 'is-not', I shall try to use this stance at least to my advantage,—by ignoring my *subject*-hood and celebrating the *object*-world as it passes to-and-fro before me. If I am a beginner, and cannot allay my desire to unite with the concrete Beautiful, I shall imaginatively abstract/extract its so-called Form, and celebrate this *Form* ......

> ...the images, disembodied, are not broken.
> They have, or they may have, their glittering crown,
> Sound-soothing pearl and omni-diamond,
>
> Of the most beautiful, the most beautiful maid
> And mother...
> —Wallace Stevens[155]

---

[154] A famous Zen capping-phrase.
[155] Lines quoted from his "Golden Woman in a Silver Mirror," and appropriated to our purposes.

If I am a beginner, I can abstract Jung's 'ectypal forms' from the 'reality' in/around me, and contemplate them. Celebrate them.

I can celebrate them, and celebrate 'concrete reality' if/when I can, but I shall bit-by-bit learn *not to cling*. 'Be like flowing water', the Chinese say, 'not like honey: honey *sticks*'. [Compare Derrida passim, on *glu/gluant/gluau*, and 'proto*col*': in fact, later on you will learn, perhaps, that water is *gluant*, too, and that even negative traces stick, but you are not at this point now, nor need you be.] That I am driven by a need for justice yet cannot make any sense of my misery, and the misery of (many) others, shows that the world is in these terms *absurd*. Not so much displaced as *misplaced*. I appropriate for my own ends the 'ten singing images' of the great Japanese monk Kukei (founder of Japanese Shingon), who derives them from the *Mahāvairocana sūtra*—

> The world is like-
> > a phantasma,
> > a convection current that distorts,
> > a dream,[156]
> > a shadow-image in/on a mirror,
> > a mirage,
> > an echo-without-origin,
> > a reflection in water,
> > a drop of foam on water,
> > a disturbance floating the (eye's) cornea,
> > a vacuous circle formed by whirling fire.[157]

(2) When meditation-time comes, I shall again *let go* of ideas, images, emotions. Scientists have shown that the brain-waves generated during habitual meditation are unique to the meditative-state. If the human race has stumbled upon this remedy for despair, why shouldn't I use it? Even if Freudians were right to say meditation is a *regressio* to the non-intelligent state, to the womb or death, *even if this were the case*, so what? I shall let the meditation work. And rather than spin the wheels of ideology (ortho*doxies*), I shall

---

[156] Compare Calderón's *La vida es sueño*.
[157] *Tantric Poetry of Kukai*, English version by Morgan Gibson and Hiroshi Murakami (Bangkok: Mahachulalongkorn Buddhist University, 1982). Our appropriation is more like I-Hsing's 'first' and 'second' purpose for the 'ten images' rather than the 'third' (ibid., p. 45), though we are not here retaining their Buddhist doctrinal context.

devote myself to ortho*praxis* (regular meditation-sitting, disciplined posture, disciplined breathing, etc.). I shall let the meditation work.

(3) No matter how futile it may seem, I will act according to compassion. I commit myself—insofar as I can—to the disinterested service of others. Doing injury is a practice humanity shares with the non-human animals (though our harm-doing, unlike theirs, is often *willed*). The disinterested willing and doing of loving-kindness is uniquely human; concomitantly, it is the greatest fulfillment of our specific *humanity*. (An ethic of watered-down and warmed-over Kant-ianism, perhaps, but true nonetheless.)

(4) Though I find no convincing evidence of benevolent Other-Power(s) that transcend(s) nature-as-science-knows-it, I shall be humble enough to leave the possibility open. Thus I pray—If there (*là*) You,... let 'me' know.

xxxxxxxxxxxxxxxxxxxxxxxxxxxxxxxxxxxxxxxxxxxxxxxxxxxxxx

OF A DUAL-PRACTITIONER[158]—

> I have come to realize that I am equally convinced by the truth of the Christian world-view (and the necessity of the existence of God) and the Buddhist world-view (and the necessity of the non-existence of God). I do not know what this means, but it appears to make me a Buddhist-Christian dialogue within myself... Please note that I do not propose in any way to blend Buddhism and Christianity, to have resolved their differences, or even to know if a resolution is either possible or desirable. All I am doing, like the planet earth itself, is sitting in the midst of the confusion which I have discovered. Perhaps this confusion is a koan or, like a crucified (and therefore dead) God, a sign of contradiction.
> —Roger J. Corless[159]

---

[158] See the earlier endnote, on 'dual-practice'.
[159] In the *Newsletter of the Society for Buddhist-Christian Studies*, No. 4 (Fall, 1989), p. 3. Professor Corless (Religion Dept., Duke University), a widely known and respected specialist in Buddhist-Christian dialogue, is a founder of the SBCS.

There is thus no (personal) God in Zen (Buddhism); that is the defect of Zen. There is a God in (Christian) mysticism; that is the defect of Christianity.
　　　　　　　　　—R. H. Blyth[160]

One could sketch a singular *chiasmus.*
The anguished experience of the Nothing
discloses Being. Here, the dimension of
Being discloses the experience of God, who is not
or whose Being is neither the essence nor
the foundation.
　　　　　　　—Derrida, on Heidegger, in "Dénégations"[161]

Sein Sinn ist Zwiespalt. An der Kreuzung Zwei
Herzwege steht kein Tempel für Apoll.
　　　　　　　　　—Rainer Maria Rilke, *Die Sonette an Orpheus,* I:3

Tortuous [winding, twisting] paths are preferred
by beneficent influences......
　　　　　　　　　—Chinese 'Feng-Shui"[162]

　　　　I read the above epigraphs slowly. Detached from their authors, the ideas in these passages may in their own right(s) help me. Raymond Smullyan in his *The Tao is Silent* cites a famous story:—"A Zen-Master was worshipping at a statue of the Buddha. A novice came by and asked, 'Why do you worship the Buddha? I thought Zen teaches us not to. Do not some Zen-Masters spit at the Buddha?' The Master replied, 'Some spit at the Buddha. I prefer to worship the Buddha'."[163] I do not take this story as a lesson in relativism. Rather, I take it to mean that for necessarily unknown reasons different seekers can follow different tracks and off/tracks, and still find liberation, salvation. At this point all we need do is further adjust the rabbi's famous reply to a question on contradiction. 'Why did the Lord supply us with two (sometimes *contradictory*) Talmuds, the Palestinian and the Babylonian?', the rabbi is asked. He answers, 'To teach us there is *not* only *one*'.

---

[160] In *Zen and Zen Classics,* Vol. 2 (Tokyo: Hokuseido Press, 1969), p. 177.
[161] P. 591; 59. See also p. 592;60: "With and without the word being, he [Heidegger] wrote a theology with and without God."
[162] See Williams, *Chinese Symbolism,* p. 178.
[163] *The Tao is Silent* (N.Y., Taipei: Harper and Row authorized Taiwan edition, Caves Bks., 2nd prt., 1982), p. 47.

Perhaps, if here/there... the 'Other which neither is nor is-not', the 'Other which neither is nor is-not' is constituted in/by two registers, *contradictory* registers. And, somehow, (many) more than two.

As a dual-practitioner, I shall take—*as my kung-an/koan*[164]—the contradiction between Buddhism and Christianity. During meditation, its problematic—fixed to/as the 'line/transverse-line'—will become 'my' precious Double-Bind.

xxxxxxxxxxxxxxxxxxxxxxxxxxxxxxxxxxxxxxxxxxxxxxxxxxxxxxx

OF A CHRISTIAN—

"... in the cross of our lord Jesus Christ, through whom

the world has been crucified to me 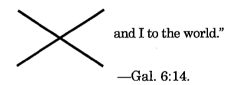 and I to the world."

—Gal. 6:14.

"...for I bear in my body the marks [*ta stigmata*]
of the Lord Jesus."
—Ibid. :17[165]

And Jesus "went, as was his custom, to the Mount of Olives (*elaiōn*);
......and knelt down and prayed,- Father, if thou art willing,
remove this cup from me; ..."
—Luke 22: 39,42

"...mysteries of theology lie hidden in the darkness beyond light of the

---

[164] Chinese *kung-an* (Jap., *koan*) literally means "a *dossier*, or case-record; a cause, public laws, regulations; case-law." In Ch'an/Zen it became a technical term for a problem set by a Master for a disciple; the disciple concentrates on this problem, seeking the solution which shall help him/her towards liberation. See *Ch'an and Zen Teaching*, First Series, pp. 11, 23; and, for more detailed treatment, Miura and Sasaki, *The Zen Koan*.
[165] Jay P. Green, Sr., *The Interlinear Bible*, Vol. 4 (Lafayette: Assoc. Pub. and Authors, 1979).

hidden mystical silence, there, in the greatest darkness,..."
                              —Pseudo-Dionysius the Areopagite,
                                    *Mystical Theology*[166]

"¡Oh noche, que guiaste!          /          ("Oh, night that guided!
  ¡Oh noche amable más que el alborada!"   /    Oh, night more lovable
                                                  than the dawn!")
                                              —John of the Cross,
                                                "Noche oscura"

            "Crux fidelis, inter omnes Arbor una nobilis:
            Nulla silva talem profert, fronde, flore, germine.
            Dulce lignum, dulces clavos, Dulce pondus sustinet."
                              —From the hymn, "Crux Fidelis,"
                                    Good Friday Liturgy.

"And He went out bearing His cross, to (the) place called Of a Skull,
which is called in Hebrew Golgotha, where they crucified Him,..."
                                              —John 19: 17,18[167]

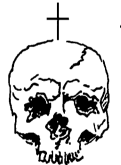
                              "... one can stop at an altar dedicated
                                    to Adam [sic] at the bottom of the rock of Calvary.
                                    Here can also be seen a crack in the rock."[168]

        ......The Cross planted in the Skull has long been
an emblem for me, the *nous* (mind) drawn and quartered, double-bound.

---

[166] See Derrida's discussion in "Dénégations" (579;47). Compare Jean-Luc Marion's treatment of the Pseudo-Dionysius in *L'Idole et la distance* (Paris: Grasset, 1977), and Derrida's response in "Dénégations" (572-4; 66-7). Consult also Jean-Luc Marion's *Dieu sans l'être* (Paris: Fayard, 1982), which treats God inscribed with the Cross, and Derrida's response ("Dénégations," 589;70).

[167] Green's *Interlinear*.

[168] From essay on the Church of the Holy Sepulchre in the *Criterion*, Indianapolis (April 9, 1993); for detailed treatment, see C. Hollis and R. Brownrigg, *Holy Places* (N.Y.: Praeger, 1969), p. 163. See also *Chinese Symbols and Art Motives*, p. 418: "Vulture Peak... It is also called 'The Hill of the Vulture Cavern', because Buddha, by his supernatural power, made a cleft in the rock,..."

"And through a Riddle at the last- / Sagacity, must go-," says Emily Dickinson.[169] I now read the epigraphs slowly. Perhaps, more than once in my life, my skull has melted down and blotted out. The epigraphs involve the Cross, and the promise of double-binds which—through Christ's power—comport liberation. (The Resurrected Christ still bears His wounds, but they are turned All-Glorious.) "For the wisdom of this world is foolishness with God," says St. Paul, "for it has been written, 'He catches the wise in their own craftiness'" (1 Cor 3:19).[170] I take this to mean that God again and again reduces our logical interpretations to irreducible binds/double-binds. To irreducible binds/double-binds that are clues, somehow, to the very constitution of God. To this extent, what (Derrida's) Edmond Jabès says of the Mosaic God applies as well to the God of the New Testament: "...God himself is, and appears as what he is, within difference, that is to say, as difference and within dissimulation."[171] And what 'Derrida' says of the Mosaic God also applies:

> And if this *double bind* is firstly that of YHVH, if each
> time there is this *double bind* in the structure of the
> proper name, there is 'God', the name of God, well then,
> I let you follow [*suivre*], you can forward it [*faire suivre*,
> the postal term]...[172]

Perhaps the *mysterium* of God-as-Chiasm is nowhere better adumbrated than in Flannery O'Connor's darksome story, "A Temple of the Holy Ghost." I now read again the description of the hermaphrodite, and realize again—in all its garish shock—how this 'unnaturally' cross-gendered figure, exhibited in a backwoods 'Freakshow', becomes the very emblem of God's Divine out-and-indwelling:

> The tent where it was had been divided into two parts by a black
> curtain, one side for men and one side for women. The freak went
> from one side to the other, talking first to the men and then to the
> women, but everyone could hear. The stage ran all the way across
> the front. The girls heard the freak say to the men, "I'm going to
> show you this and if you laugh, God may strike you the same
> way."... "God made me this away and if you laugh He may strike
> you the same way. This is the way He wanted me to be and I ain't

---

[169] In her "This world is not Conclusion."
[170] See Green's *Interlinear*, and the *R.S.V. Interlinear Greek-English New Testament* (Grand Rapids: Zondervan, 1970).
[171] *Writing and Difference*, p. 74. Derrida is here paraphrasing Edmond Jabès.
[172] *The Post Card*, p. 165.

disputing His way.".... "I never done it to myself nor had a thing to
do with it but I'm making the best of it.".... Then there was a long
silence on the other side of the tent and finally the freak left the
men and came over onto the women's side and said the same thing.

The child felt every muscle strained as if she were hearing the
answer to a riddle that was more puzzling than the riddle itself.
"You mean it had two heads?" she said.

"No," Susan said, "it was a man and woman both. It pulled up its
dress and showed us. It had on a blue dress."

—Flannery O'Connor, "A Temple of the Holy Ghost"[173]

For the discerning, the scriptural references are unmistakable—to the
Old Covenant's Temple, and to Christ the New Temple (Rev. 21:22).
Allusions to the *shechinah*, the Divine Presence 'showing' in the Holy
of Holies, are super-imposed upon New Testament allusions,—to the
Christ (the 'only Temple' of the New Covenant), to the (Holy) Spirit,
and to the 'other Christs', the disciples who take up their Cross.
Marked with Christ's Chiasm, they are outcasts, 'freaks', monsters
(from L. *monstrare,* to show). In the dream which follows the Freak-
exhibit, the hermaphrodite proclaims—"I am a temple of the Holy
Ghost."[174] The connection to Christ and the Spirit is clinched by the
rite of sacramental Benediction—which is evoked near the story's
start, when the girls sing the *Tantum ergo* hymn; and is fulfilled at the
story's end, with the ceremony itself. In the Benediction rite, the 'host'
or consecrated Bread (through which form God dissimulates)—the
*shechinah* of the New Covenant—is 'exposed' and 'exhibited' in a
golden receptacle (called the 'monstrance', from L. *monstrare,* to
show). That is, Christ is concealed/revealed: He is self-concealed under
the form of Bread, and thus *dissimulates*, yet He is really the Bread,
and thus self-reveals. Raising the monstrance on high, the priest
moves the host in a giant 'sign of the Cross' over the adoring faithful,
blessing them, *marking* them, in and into God's Chiasm. The girl's
subconscious at once identifies the cross-gendered monster and the
Divinity-in-the-monstrance: "...when the priest raised the monstrance
with the Host shining ivory-colored in the center of it, she was
thinking of the tent at the fair that had the freak in it."[175]

---

[173] In O'Connor's *A Good Man Is Hard To Find: Ten Memorable Short Stories*
(Garden City: Doubleday, Image pbk., 1970), pp. 93-4.
[174] P. 95.
[175] P. 96.

(1)   The religious kinesthetics of meditation shall sense—for me—our chiasmic God. I shall become, God-willing, a true CHIROPRACTOR (homonym, CHI-RHO/PRACTOR). Criss-crossing the comic and tragic, not without reason is Flannery O'Connor's work laced with like puns,- chiropodist/CHI-RHO-podist; palmist/chiromancer/CHI-RHO-mancer; and so on. Christ is our healing and orthodox Divining.

I am called to Christ's differential way. Christ in the scripture prays "that they may all be one, even as thou, Father, art in me, and I in thee, that they also may be in us,..." (John 17:21). Differential theology would argue that the Father and Son (and Holy Spirit) constitute their 'oneness' precisely by their negative reference to each other.[176] Thus, for the faithful to "all be one" *AS* the Father and Son are 'one', the faithful must build their unity by way of 'difference', not 'sameness'. Though 'centering prayer' is designed to empty out the ego, and let God be our true 'center', for my personality-type the opposite can easily happen: the meditation practice of 'centering' can—in devious ways—bolster the ego without the ego knowing it. Taking the good advice of St. Ignatius of Loyola to *agere contra*,[177] I shall continue the line/transverse-line meditation—which for me as a Christian is Christ-Cross meditation—because this kind of meditation *decenters*. (Another differential meditation I can practice is to give myself entirely away to/for other sentient beings[178]; ...to give myself, body and psyche, to be consumed by all the sentient beings around me,—picked clean, even by black crows and by vultures, their bald heads reddened by the sun, *picked clean*... until 'nothing' is left: consider the case of Jesus consumed in Communion.)

The cleft in the side, the four punctures, the back hatched-in-blood, the hatched xxx-crownlet on the brow,—forgetting myself I shall read their holy braille in the darkness. Eventually, God-willing, neither I nor not-I shall read/write.

(2)   Flannery O'Connor's hermaphrodite incises three signs. The first pertains to Faith. Being that there really are biological androgynes

---

[176] See Part Two, ahead.

[177] Lit., 'to act against': a code-word in Ignatian spirituality meaning that when the soul naturally inclines in a detrimental direction, one should spiritually militate in the opposite direction.

[178] I would argue that this is an action of the Feminine archetype, though of course either biological gender can perform it. Maleness, which controls society much more than it should, prefers 'centering' and the 'drive to oneness'.

born into the world, their torture and self-torture must be mind-shattering (and even when corrective surgery intervenes). What is more,—How can a good God 'will' such a birth-in-the-world?[179] O'Connor's hermaphrodite affirms and does not "dispute." The second sign pertains to Wisdom. O'Connor's allegory is such that the hermaphrodite is the *shechinah*: God is a Bind/Double-Bind. The third sign pertains to .Love. "Jesus thrown everything off balance" (O'Connor: 27). I must take the preferential option for 'displaced persons', the Old South's "artificial Negroes" (O'Connor's Christ-figures: 121; 232). That is, I must always choose in the best interest of the world's suffering Displaced,[180]—no matter how or where they suffer. Eventually, as Mother Teresa of Calcutta shows, I may be called to suffer grievous Displacement, in order to better join the all-and-everything which is truly chiasmic, truly *displaced*.

(3) I shall read/pray the Scriptures prayerfully, deconstructively, differentially, so I can sift more of God's displacements. Religion is primarily a matter of right (hemisphere of the) brain/left hand activity. For me, scientific/historical research functions to abet differential readings of Scripture, and not to 'validate' Scripture. Scriptures bear two negatively entangled truths. The logocentric truths of Scriptures are born of and confirmed by 'both-the-inside-and-not-inside' of human beings, not the 'outside'. Scriptures' differential truths, which deconstruct the logocentric truths, are read/written by 'neither-the-inside-nor-the-not-inside'. (This does not mean logocentric truths are '*un*-true'.) Because there is not only one,

there is not only one,

there is not only one,

there is not only one.

There is not and there is only one.

---

[179] It is clear in O'Connor's story that she does not mean androgyny in the positive Jungian (and Taoist) sense, viz., the *yin* and *yang* of every human being regardless of sex (and the *yin* and *yang* of God too). She would of course affirm androgyny, though I think she, like me, would read *yin* and *yang* chiasmically: in every human being *yin* and *yang* are not only displaced into each other, but even unbalanced in unpredictable ways. The emphasis in the story "The Temple of the Holy Ghost" is on 'out-of-placeness'. In this sense, we are all literally *litter*, refuse. Logocentrism, in which all-and-everything is proper, is 'in place', is not by itself our script (or God's script).

[180] *Not* my nation's 'national interest', or the institutional Church's worldly interest.

There is not and there is only one.
There is not and there is only one.
There is not and there is only one.

...somebody was hammering nails into a coffin in the passage.
Suddenly the dead priest winked at him—an unmistakable blink
of the eyelid, just like that.
He woke and there was the crack, crack of the knocker on
the outer door.
—Graham Greene, *The Power and the Glory*[181]

There/here ...

neither not-only-one nor only-one.
neither not-only-one nor only-one,

. . . . . . . . . . . . . . . . .

neither not-only-one nor only-one.

"......... quanta è la larghezza
di questa rosa ne l'estreme foglie!"
—Dante, *Divina commedia*, Paradiso xxx: 116-17

*di questa rosa*

"St. Rose* of Lima*: Isabel De Flores Y Del Oliva,*
called Rose by her mother because of her red
cheeks and confirmed with that name by St
Turibius of Mogrovejo, was the first person in
the Americas* to be canonized as a saint."
Sancta Rosa, ora pro nobis.

---

[181] New York: Time special editions, 1962, p. 267.

**PART TWO**


**CURRICULA VITARUM:**
**PHILOSOPHY/RELIGION IN SALTIRE**

Telle fleur porte toujours son double en elle-même, que ce soit
la graine ou le type, le hasard de son programme ou la nécessité
de son diagramme. L'héliotrope peut toujours se relever. Et il
peut toujours devenir une fleur séchée dans un livre. Il y a
toujours, absente de tout jardin, une fleur séchée dans un
livre; et en raison de la répétition où elle s'abîme sans fin,
aucun langage ne peut réduire en soi la structure d'une
anthologie.[1]
                                       —Jacques Derrida, "La Mythologie Blanche"[2]

> The lotus... its *fruits* are said to be ripe
> when the *flower* blooms,...
>                     —Masaharu Anesaki[3]

> ...exelexato ho theos kai ta mē onta hina ta
> onta katargēsēi,...
> ["... and (God chose) what are-not[4] in order that
> he might cancel (nullify, negate) what are,..."]
>                     —1 Cor 1:28

Part Two—it can be said—is hooked on the graphics of the three
epigrams above,—as these three crochet, double-bind, and evade each
other.

The first epigram above evokes a convention: the heliotrope,
because its face follows the diurnal course of the sun, is a metaphor

---

[1] Literal English trans.: Such a flower always carries its double in itself, whether
it be the seed or the type, the chance of its program or the necessity of its
diagram. The heliotrope can always raise/right itself again [*se relever*]. And it can
always become a dried flower in a book. There is always [or 'always *ago*'], absent
from every garden, a dried flower in a book, and by reason of the repetition in
which it is endlessly spoiled/collapsed [*s'abîme*: etymologically, 'no-bottoms itself ']
no language can reduce down into itself [or, 'reduce to itself ', *réduire en soi*] the
structure of an anthology [*anthologie*: from Greek, *anthos* + *logeia*, 'flower-
gathering'].

[2] *Poétique* 5 (1971), p.52. There is an available English translation, smoother and
thus necessarily less literal and analytic than suits our purposes: "White
Mythology," trans. F. C. T. Moore, in *New Literary History*, 6, 1 (1974), p. 74.

[3] *Buddhist Art in Relation to Its Buddhist Ideals* (Boston: 1923; rpt. N.Y.:
Hacker, 1978), pp. 15, 16 (emphases mine).

[4] Or: "and (God chose) things 'not-being' in order that he might cancel [nullify,
negate] things 'being'." About half the early Greek mss. include the *kai* ("and"),
but even if "ta mē onta" is in apposition with the previous predicate object, the
notion of 'not-being' still survives. For mss. evidence I have used K. Aland, M.
Black, et al., eds., *The New Testament: Greek and English* (N.Y.: American Bible
Society, 2nd ed., 1966, 68), p. 580.

for 'effect',[5] and ultimately for the 'logocentric'[6] closing of meaning into a circle, into identity, into the self-same. Derrida's emblematic flower deconstructs the convention because in the procreative order its "double," its 'seed', cannot come around in a circle of perfect duplication. Instead, the seed (=effect) shifts forward in what can be called 'differential' repetition: each flower/seed is the intersection of the "chance" of its individual fate ("program") and the genetic code ("diagram") of its species. The theory of logocentric cause-and-effect— that is, of effect mirroring cause in the 'self-same'—is displaced by way of the 'differential same', the 'sameness which is not identity'. The second epigram above, drawn from the Buddhist tradition, also deconstructs the self-same, i.e., logocentric cause-and-effect.[7] In the Buddhist case, the lotus is taken as an emblem of 'effects-only' (or conversely, 'causes-only').[8] Flower is supposed to precede fruit (thereby suggesting linear cause-and-effect), but the lotus, bearing flower and fruit at the same time, can be taken to represent the real state-of-affairs: life is repetition, but of the same, not the self-same. Buddhism rejects entitative causality and affirms *pratītya-samutpāda* ('dependent co-arising'): in particular, the Madhyamikan-Prasangikan tradition,[9] by

---

[5] It is also specifically a metaphor for metaphor, in this very complex passage.

[6] Thus also, by implication, Christ the Logos too. I maintain that 'differential' theology—if it takes its cue from how Derridean deconstruction works elsewhere—can claim that Christ is Logos *and* Logos-deconstructed (which would be also an adaptation of Nagarjuna's 'two-truths-at-once').

[7] Note however that it can also be appropriated by 'centric' forms of Buddhism: since the lotus opens and closes with the rising and setting of the sun, it—like the heliotrope—can be affiliated to logocentric 'sun myths'. Centric traditions within Buddhism, while of course accepting *anitya* (impermanence), recuperate holism by way of a formulaic unity of some kind. For an excellent discussion of these often disguised and unrecognized formulae, see Hsueh-li Cheng, "Emptiness: Exoteric and Esoteric Buddhism," in *World Sutric and Tantric Buddhist Conference Report* (Kaohsiung, Taiwan: Fo Kuang Pub., 1988), pp. 107-24, especially pp. 120-22.

[8] The point either way is that entitative causality, the bond of cause-and-effect, is rejected. This is a Madhyamikan approach (in Chinese Buddhism, one looks to the San-Lun tradition for this). The Madhyamika is most 'differential' of the Buddhisms, though some *Ch'an*/Zen is also 'differential'. The motif of the lotus's simultaneous fruit-and-flower constitutes a rich motif throughout Chinese and Japanese Buddhism, of course, and is interpreted to suit sect and occasion. *Ching-t'u* and *Chen-yen* often take it to mean that the Teaching (flower) carries Enlightenment (fruit) at the same time; *T'ien-t'ai* and *Hua-yen* sometimes take it to represent the interpenetration of all things.

[9] Unlike the Yogacara.

far the most deconstructive form of Buddhism, refuses to recuperate *pratītya-samutpāda* into a formulaic circle of any kind.[10]

Section One of this Part Two treats the 'earlier Derrida' and the Madhyamika Buddhist tradition; and Section Two treats the 'later Derrida', of the essay "Dénégations" wherein 'he' is said to address anew the problematic of 'negative theology'.

The epigram from 1st Corinthians, above, betides the oncoming repetition of another 'same', a Christian 'same',—again not at all a 'self-same'. The Jewish and Christian Scriptures, in their differing and indeed unique ways, are already crosshatched through and through with *ta mē onta*, as are Jewish and Christian theologies. For Christianity to intersect (which is *not at all* to duplicate) the Buddhism of Asia, it must first cross deconstruction-West. Section Three hooks onto a 'keynote text' in the current Buddhist-Christian Dialogue, and tries to show how easily, perhaps, deconstruction-East can be confounded with logocentrism-East. Finally, Section Four, crossing deconstruction-West and Christian theology, gives an instance of how differential theology has always been there. Read past, glossed over, erased. But always there.

---

[10] Effect-only is very much like Derrida's version of 'signifier-only' ('pure signifier').

(i)

(Derrida's) Double-Binds and the Prasangika-Madhyamika

—For Edith Wyschogrod, John D. *Caput*o and John Dominic *Cross*an

A moins que l'antho*logie* ne soit
aussi une litho*graphie*. L'héliotrope est encore une pierre:
pierre précieuse, verdâtre et
rayée de veines rouges, espèce de
jaspe *oriental*.
                —Derrida, "La Mythologie Blanche"[11]

In this section I begin with a stenographic review, a very brief one, of the theses in my *Derrida on the Mend* which show how Nagarjunist and Derridean thought intersect. I then elaborate further by playing out this argumentation against the claims of Harold Coward, who in his recent book *Derrida and Indian Philosophy*,[12] broaches a contrary version of this intersection. Lastly, I extend my argumentation by discussing in more detail the pertinence of the Prasangika-Madhyamika tradition, both Indian and Tibetan.

The procedural sequence (*prāsaṅgika*, the procedure reducing adversaries to absurd *consequence*) followed by Nagarjuna in his *Mūlamādhyamakakārikās* (abbreviation henceforth: MK) is first to reduce all entitative thought (what Derrida calls 'logocentric' thought) to dilemma. In the pivotal MK 1:6, for example, Nagarjuna concludes "Neither non-Ens nor Ens can have a cause."[13] So what is the cause for? On the other hand, if there is no entity at all (i.e., no 'effect'), what's the use of postulating a cause of any kind? The next step is *not* to eliminate the debris of this negation, but to regard the 'fall-out' as a

---

[11] P. 52. Italicization mine.
[12] Albany: S.U.N.Y. Press, 1990.
[13] From Th. Stcherbatsky's trans. of MK 1 in "Madhyamaka Sastra of Nagarjuna," in Stcherbatsky, *The Conception of Buddhist Nirvana* (Leningrad: Acad. of Sciences of the U.S.S.R., 1927).

'conductal thread' (*prajñapti* in its second sense[14]) leading to a potentially 'wiser' state-of-affairs. The 'debris' from the above deconstruction of entitative causality, for example, is that 'everything is pure cause' or alternatively 'everything is pure effect'. Both conclusions are nonsensical within the very logic which Nagarjuna here limits himself to using (he uses this logic because his adversaries use it, and he wants to show that the adversaries contradict themselves). Nagarjuna chooses to work with 'pure effect' (i.e., 'effect alone') as his *prajñapti* because the Buddhist tradition had already given the clue. The tradition had said the 'true' state-of-affairs is 'dependent co-arising' (*pratītya samutpāda*). This is to say, the 'true' state-of-affairs is that happenings devolve forever as if each happening were a pure dependency, a 'pure effect'. Indeed, B.K. Matilal even renders *pratītya samutpāda* as 'dependence only'.[15] Nowhere is there an entitative cause, neither within the happening nor outside the happening. Happenings are devoid (*śūnya*) of self-nature, and—as Nagarjuna also shows—devoid of entitative transfer or continuance. 'Whatever is dependent co-arising is *śūnyatā*', asserts Nagarjuna, but even *śūnyatā* is a 'provisional name' (*prajñapti* again, here rendered in its first sense, though here too it should be taken in both senses). The term and concept *śūnyatā* come 'under erasure', i.e., they can be helpful but they are not to be equated with how *śūnyatā* actually 'works'. Somehow, *śūnyatā* is involved with 'traces', is 'marked': happenings still *happen* yet not within closure, not even intuitive or centric mystical closure. Happenings are not a question of plenum nor of void. Happenings are marked but empty: they are *devoid*.

Nagarjuna's other pertinent entry into the problematic of *śūnyatā* comes by way of 'pure negative reference'. The Buddhist tradition taught that (1) all happenings are utterly impermanent (*anitya*), and that (2) all happenings are *related* but in a *non-entitative* way (this is sometimes called 'Buddhist causality'). Nagarjuna, working with these doctrinal 'givens', brings them together in a new way that initiates the Madhyamika School. He interprets 'impermanence' to mean that so-called 'identity' and 'time' are actually born totally anew at every moment. Then comes his stroke of genius. If one

---

[14] See Mervyn Sprung, "Being and the Middle Way," in *The Question of Being*, ed. Mervyn Sprung (Univ. Pk. and London: Penn. State UP, 1978), pp. 133-34. Recall that *prajñapti* in its first sense means 'provisional name'.
[15] In his *Epistemology, Logic, and Grammar in Indian Philosophical Analysis* (Hague and Paris: Mouton, 1971), p. 150.

combines 'impermanence' in this utterly pure sense with the doctrine of 'relatedness' (Buddhist causality), the only relatedness possible is *pure negative reference*. Any happening is purely, totally *not* (like) any other, but therefore, necessarily, this *difference*, this relation which is pure *is not*, is *constitutive* of (i.e., establishes, appoints, raises) the happening.

Jacques Derrida, extending in a more sustained and analytic fashion a project of Nietzsche, has demonstrated how logical discourse necessarily leads—*in its own terms*—to the disenfranchisement of logic. This is to say, logic at bottom undoes its own founding premises, such as the 'principle of identity' ('whatever is, is'). And Derrida shows that this 'same' undoing extends to the most current and non-traditional of theories, such as those associated with the Anglo-American Analytic School, with Wittgensteinian game-theory, etc., which camouflage, cosmeticize their own holism ('logocentrism') and are really no more than an 'essentialism' displaced. Like Nagarjuna, Derrida inserts himself into whatever logical system he is deconstructing, and turns its own premises against its classic conclusions— which have usually been forced by wishful thinking. Thus, for example, he deconstructs entitative causality and ends up with a debris-thesis of 'pure effect' ('pure signifier'). He deconstructs 'definition by negative reference' (Sartre, Saussure, etc.) and ends up with a debris-thesis of 'pure negative reference'. These debris-theses, nonsensical within a larger frame of reference, he therefore necessarily brings 'under erasure'. From under the scratch-lines of the erasure, however, they somehow work as better *indices* ('pointers', 'clues') to how happenings 'go on' than the old classical formulae did. What is more, in his cross-inscriptions of inside and outside, Derrida leaves open the wherewithal to deconstruct even so-called 'practical reality'. That is, even our so-called personhood's common-sense 'experience' of what is outside itself (or inside itself) becomes problematic. And thus does 'personhood'. (Another way of explaining this is to say that Derrida shows how in fact the distinction between epistemology and ontology is garbled, all tangled up.)

According to the 'clue' of 'pure signifier' (i.e., 'signifier alone', 'effect alone'), happenings 'go on' as an erratic stream of 'pure effects' (they 'appear' erratic because they violate the expectations of entitative causality). According to the 'clue' of 'pure negative reference' (i.e., 'negative-reference alone'), the 'going on' is entitatively *empty.*

Happenings devolve as empty 'effects only', and necessarily happenings purely *differ*. Nevertheless, each happening is somehow 'there': the flux of happenings is not a monistic void; rather, the flux is purely marked by pure difference. Thus the flux of happenings is better called *devoid* than 'void'. That which is constituted (appointed, raised) by 'pure negative reference', that which is 'empty' but 'there', Derrida calls *trace*. Because 'pure difference' is more easily detectable in 'writing' and 'texts' (that is, in how they devolve) than in 'speaking' (though it constitutes *both*), Derrida treats 'writing' and 'texts' as *prajñapti* for 'how happenings devolve' (which he calls, emblematically, Writing or Textuality). In my own work, I argue that the way happenings devoidly 'go on' in Derrida and the way Buddhist 'dependent co-arising' goes on, intersect at several points: the two notions s'entre*croisent*.

Nagarjuna in the *Mūlamādhyamakakārikās* elaborates the famous doctrine of the Two Truths. MK 24:8 says the teaching of the *Dharma* (here meaning the Buddhist 'teaching') is based on two truths, *saṃvṛti-satya* (the 'concealing', the world-ensconced truth) and *paramārtha-satya* (the supreme truth). And MK 25:20 says that the limits of *nirvāṇa* (Buddhist bliss, etc.) are the limits of *saṃsāra* (the 'life-and-death cycle'), and that "between the two, also, there is not the slightest difference whatsoever."[16] How to negotiate the problematic generated by the juxtaposition of MK 24:8 and MK 25:20 becomes one of the most contested topics of subsequent Buddhist literature. In my own work I have opted for the tradition detected (through historical research) by, and nowadays represented by, B. K. Matilal, R.S. Misra, Mervyn Sprung, Frederick Streng, and a large group of other very respectable scholars. These scholars distinguish between the historical Nagarjuna's teaching in the *Mūlamādhyamakakārikās*, and many subsequent developments, be they later Madhyamikan or Yogacaric (though in general these scholars adhere to the formulations of the Prasangika-Madhyamika). Matilal and the others in this group argue that *saṃvṛti-satya* is not a contrivance in the sense of an unconditional falsehood. *Saṃvṛti-satya* is *not* categorically invalid. For them, Nagarjuna's purpose was to assert that the 'two truths' both frequent the same 'going-on': *saṃvṛti-satya* frequents the 'going-on' as *phenomenal*, and *paramārtha-satya* frequents the 'going-on' as *devoid*. Concurring

---

[16] Trans. from Kenneth K. Inada, *Nagarjuna: A Translation of his Mūlamādhyamakakārikā with an Introductory Essay* (Tokyo: Hokuseido, 1970).

with this interpretation, my claim in its regard has been that Derrida's 'logocentrism' approximates the Nagarjunist notion of *saṃvṛti-satya*, and Derrida's 'differentialism' ('pure effect', 'pure negative reference', etc.) approximates—at least conceptually—the Nagarjunist notion of *paramārtha-satya*. That there is for Nagarjuna only one 'going-on' (see MK 25:20) ensures the notion of Derridean *trace*, since the world—ever differing and deferring—is thereby *marked*. What Derrida's texts lack, I have maintained, are indications of the utter 'frequenting' which can only come from *prajñā* (a wisdom which is 'other-than-from-reason-alone'). This wisdom can only come from (1) non-clinging and (2) meditative practice.

In his book *Derrida and Indian Philosophy*,[17] Harold Coward argues (1) that the 'silence' which is used to describe *paramartha* puts Nagarjuna at variance with the Derridean claim that the human condition is always entangled with/in language (135-36,153,155-6). And Coward rejects, at least tentatively, my notion (2) that Nagarjuna's *saṃvṛti-satya*, the 'concealing' truth, deploys logocentrism as 'valid' for everyday experience (see 126,157), though it seems Coward misconstrues what my claim actually is.[18] At least it is clear that Coward rejects the consequence so important for my thesis, namely, that Nagarjuna's adroit adjudication of the Buddhist 'two truths' can help Derrida towards an even better appreciation of logocentrism (to be taken as *saṃvṛti*) and logocentrism-as-deconstructed (to be taken as *paramārtha*). Derrida of course has always necessarily granted that human action depends in the everyday world on logocentrism, and that his deconstructive analysis—operative as it is within the Western rational tradition—wields a logocentric tool, viz., *logic*, in order to deconstruct logocentrism.[19] Indeed, the ongoing alterity which is

---

[17] I supply page references parenthetically, ahead.

[18] Surely it is a distortion to attribute to me the claim that Derrida's "spiritual realization" is in "needing" of "logocentric completion" (157). My claim rather is that Buddhist spiritual realization (though I would name it otherwise) justifies logocentrism as 'valid' or 'effective' for the mundane world. Buddhism can help Derrida 'work out' a better justification for retaining the logocentric while still continuing deconstruction.

[19] For the beneficent role of logical teaching in the Madhyamika, see David Ross Komito, *Nagarjuna's 'Seventy Stanzas' [the Śūnyatāsaptati]: a Buddhist Psychology of Emptiness*, [dGe-lugs-pa] commentary by Geshe Sonam Rinchen, trans. and commentary by Tenzin Dorjee and D. R. Komito (Ithaca: Snow Lion, 1987), pp. 95, 181. And Hsueh-li Cheng, *Nagarjuna's 'Twelve Gate Treatise' [Shih-erh-men-lun]* (Dordrecht: Reidel, 1982), [San-Lun School], p. 24.

Writing includes the double-bind of 'logic-deconstructing-itself'. Derridean 'happenings' are an ever fraying bundle of double-binds, inextricably singular yet doubling/doubled, ever differing yet repeating as the 'same' which is not the 'self-same'.

As to Coward's first point above, I maintain he poses a spurious opposition because he misunderstands Derrida. When Derrida says there is no *hors-texte*, he means that all human going-on is 'textuality', is Writing, in the sense I have just described. The going-on is Writing because it is always a bearer of *traces*, always marked, and it is traced, marked because each 'moment' is purely *different*. To *constitute by difference* involves necessarily a preemption of an entitative *same*: it is to deny an unmarked field, a unitary or totalitarian field, be it spatial or temporal; to defer and differ is to mark time, mark space. And in this Derridean sense, Nagarjuna's *śūnyatā* is also marked, *traced*, because—as explained above—if it is to be true to Buddhist *anitya* and 'relatedness' both, it must be a going-on of pure negative reference, of *pure difference*. For Derrida, 'literal' silence belongs to textuality as much as speaking does, and writing does. Regarding the privileged Buddhist silence of the enlightenment experience and of *paramārtha*, the fact it is privileged would make it no less marked: on the contrary, enlightenment would be to 'frequent' Writing. Wise to pure difference, the silently Wise adept would be pure difference and its trace, a 'marked silence', a silence 'marking (serene) time'.

As to Harold Coward's second point, what is most at issue between us is our sources—that is, the various interpretive traditions we draw upon. The scholarship past and present on the Two Truths is so intricate and vast that even the several computerized data-banks in Buddhist Studies already established cannot keep abreast of it. But this situation surely exists to serve us, not deter us. In short, I am suggesting that Dr. Coward has made several historical and methodological errors. He cites Vasubandhu's definition of *vikalpa* and supplies Yogacaric definitions of "convention," as if these prove I misunderstand the Madhyamika's Two Truths. But Vasubandhu's *Trisvabhāvanirdeśa* (which Coward cites), in contradistinction to Nagarjuna's *Mūla-*, sets forth a three-fold model of intrinsic nature,[20]

---

[20] For concise descriptions of the three-fold model, see *Crystal Mirror*, V (1977), p. 85; and John P. Keenan, "Asanga's Understanding of Madhyamika: Notes on the *Shung-chung-lun*," *Journal of the International Association of Buddhist Studies*, 12.1 (1989), pp. 102-3. John P. Keenan's scholarship in Mahayana Buddhism has been focused on the Yogacaric tradition, and his recent book, *The Meaning of*

and becomes, of course, a key text of the Yogacara. And the Yogacara is, of course, the most important concurrent Buddhist school *opposing* the Madhyamika. More disconcerting still, what Coward does overtly some other critics of mine do more subtly. Their interpretations of the Two Truths, while purporting to be faithful to the Madhyamika, assume—even without saying so—a one *dharmadhātu* which is entirely dissociated from conventional experience. And these interpretations refer to a nondual unity which dispels the (categorical? unconditional?) *illusion* of the subject-object dichotomy. (The *cittamātra* or Mind-only motif in some Ch'an/Zen induces a like perspective at times, in part because of Ch'an's predilection for the *Laṅkāvatāra-sūtra*, its Tathatagarbha and *ālaya-vijñāna*.) These formulations are Yogacaric rather than Madhyamikan in sympathy.[21] The Madhyamikans, instead, struggle in various and divergent ways to remain true to Nagarjuna's "The limits of *nirvāṇa* are the limits of *saṃsāra*. Between the two, also, there is *not the slightest difference.*"

What I have tried to do is draw from those scholars who aim to understand the Sanskrit so-called 'Ur-version' of the *Mūlamādhya-makakārikās* (which must be extracted from Candrakirti's 6th-7th cent. commentary). As best they can, these scholars have aimed to 'catch' the *Mūla-* before its formulations were embellished by later sectarian developments (many of them 'synthesizing' in nature). In order to build a more global view of the *Mūla-*, some scholars also compare other texts which *in all probability* came from Nagarjuna's hand, though the range of this canon is disputed, being that the texts are in large part available only in Tibetan and Chinese translations. This is not at all to deny the helpfulness of living traditions, as long as one cautiously notes—again, as best one can—*how* these traditions have developed, or added to, or changed (different, these three) the meaning of the earlier text, the so-called Ur-text.

What enormously complicates matters is that even the Madhyamikan interpretations of the *Mūla-* diverge significantly, with Candrakirti figuring as the foremost representative of the Prasangika-

---

*Christ: A Mahayana Theology* (N.Y.: Orbis, 1989), assimilates mainly from the Yogacara. No one denies that the dialogue between centric Buddhism and centric Christianity retains import, and for those called to this (form of the) dialogue I highly recommend Keenan's interesting book.

[21] For a good discussion of this problematic, see C. W. Huntington, with Geshe Namgyal Wangchen, *The Emptiness of Emptiness: An Introduction to Early Indian Mādhyamika* (Honolulu: Univ. of Hawaii Press, 1989), p. 64.

Madhyamika and Bhavaviveka (6th cent.), his rival, representing
Svatantrika-Madhyamika. The Tibetans, from the 8th century, further
evolved both schools, so that their two most important 'philosophical'
systems become the Prasangika ('Consequential School') on the one
hand and the Yogacara-Madhyamika-Svatantrika ('Autonomy School')
on the other. In relation to these two traditions, the rNying-ma-pa,
Sa-skya-pa, bKa'brgyud-pa, and dGe-lugs-pa each stand to these two
traditions in a different way, with the dGe-lugs-pa representing a very
erudite/scholastic Prasangika.

Harold Coward indicates the vein of modern scholarship he
mines—he lists T. Stcherbatsky, T. R. V. Murti, Mervyn Sprung, and
Gadjin M. Nagao (132). Of course Stcherbatsky, publishing in the
1920s, was active at a more primitive stage in the West's perception of
the *Mūlamādhyamakakārikās*, and of Indian Buddhism in general.
Though a brilliant philologist and good logician, his absolutist
interpretations of *śūnyatā*, intended at the time to off-set Vallée de
Poussin's nihilistic simplification is now—in the view of every
Buddhologist I know—superseded. Most present-day Buddhologists
would also rate T. R. V. Murti's interpretation of Madhyamika as
much too Vedantic on its Eastern side and much too Kantian on its
Western side.[22] If one is opting to work within a logocentric frame,
there is nothing historically wrong with *comparatio positiva* between
East and West, but this procedure requires that one demonstrate a
plausible congruence so that the features of neither *comparatum* are
violated. It is generally conceded that Murti fails in this respect. From
Gadjin M. Nagao, the eminent Japanese scholar, I of course learn very
much, but for Coward to measure Derrida against Nagao's openly
Yogacaric reading of Nagarjuna is completely off the point. As Paul
Griffiths puts it in a recent review of Nagao's *Mādhyamika and
Yogācāra*, Nagao "is not afraid... of presenting Madhyamika as an
incomplete version of Buddhist thought, a version properly completed
by the Yogacara of Asanga and Vasubandhu." For example, "in his
discussion of subjectivity," Ngao "presents Nagarjuna's denial of
essences as incomplete precisely because it does not fully elucidate the
meaning of human existence as Yogacara does."[23] My point here is

---

[22] Huntington builds a good case showing this, p. 27.
[23] Paul J. Griffiths, review of *Mādhyamika and Yogācāra*, ed., trans., and coll. by
L. S. Kawamura (Albany: S.U.N.Y. Press, 1991), in the *Journal of the
International Association of Buddhist Studies*, 14.2 (1991), p. 346.

that if there be any meaningful intersection of Derrida and Nagar-juna, its likelihood is less if the terms are set by an actively pro-Yogacaric figure.

Lastly, there is Coward's appeal to Mervyn Sprung. What he cites from Sprung involves "the utter emptiness [*śūnya*] of all ontological statements" (134), and does not touch upon the matters of difference between Coward and me. Indeed, I find Sprung supportive of what I am trying to demonstrate, viz., that conventional language has validity for *saṃvṛti*. Coward passes from Sprung to Nagao, saying language's *vikalpa*-formations (cogitation, false discriminations) "play over the surface of the real without giving us access to it" (135). Surely Sprung would not agree here, because for him Nagarjuna's *paramārtha* does not have a "surface of the real," nor is it a 'substratum' over which *vikalpa* can "play." Rather, the yogi "takes things in their truth... the 'way things really are' (*tattvam*) is the way of the wise man."[24] And "It will surely occur to one that seeming things, which neither exist nor do not exist, must be chimeras; but it is not so. Their nature is as they give themselves to the wise man or as he takes them."[25] Sprung's explanation of Nagarjuna's *saṃvṛti* ascribes to logocentrism the value I would assign to it: "Existence and non-existence are quite *legitimate* terms in the realm of cause and effect, action and consequence, explanation and proof [*saṃvṛti*], but are not to be used in the realm where causes, actions, and explanations have come to an end [*paramārtha*]" (emphasis mine).[26]

In my work, I have found the Prasangika-Madhyamika tradition most helpful, largely because it so well intersects with Derridean deconstruction. The motivation in my East-West work, after all, is to develop—at least as long as my ongoing meditation-and-research continue to confirm it—the following conjoined thesis. Namely, (1) a

---

[24] Sprung, p. 136.

[25] Sprung, p. 134.

[26] 26 Sprung, pp. 135-6. And please here permit me a (relevant) aside. Though Sprung and Huntington are both serviceable to me, in that I am concerned with expert support for the validity of logocentrism within *saṃvṛti*, the exactitudes of these two specialists do disagree with each other. I do not want to collapse critical differences among my sources. Sprung and Huntington, for example, disagree on the precise definition of 'logocentric validity' in Nagarjuna. For Huntington, the 'valid role for language' has the status of a Wittgensteinian language-game, and he would consider Sprung's evaluation of language too 'Kantian'.

Derridean version of post-modernism,[27] with its radical deconstruction of holism, had best come to prevail among Western philosophers; (2) that Buddhism—especially of the Madhyamikan sort—already shall have (future perfect tense) tracked-with-a-difference these deconstructions; and (3) that Christian theology, coming across deconstruction-East and deconstruction-West, shall have, in due time, re-found itself as deconstructive/differential.

The Madhyamika makes for a better intersection with Derrida than does the Yogacara (and by 'intersection' here I mean only intellectual intersection, *nor* do I mean congruence) because the Yogacaric philosophers posit a 'mind-basis-of-all' (which carries karmic seeds, etc.). Theories of 'consciousness', no matter of what kind, are so suspect to a Western deconstructionist, that my use of Yogacara is strategically precluded. On the other hand, the *Mūlamādhyamakakārikās*, key text of the Madhyamikan schools, and some of the (possibly) authentic other Nagarjunist texts we can add to it, present a programme which on its intellectual side remarkably resembles the Derridean protocols ('protocols': fr. GK *prōt-*, first- + *kollan*, to glue,—as Derrida well knows). In general, I find that as the centuries of Madhyamikan post-Nagarjunist polemic unfolded, the ever multiplying swell of commentaries (and controversies) bore the *Mūlamādhyamakakārikās* further and further away from what have become Derridean concerns. Several centuries intervene, of course, even between Nagarjuna and Candrakirti, and figures such as Aryadeva (Nagarjuna's 'disciple'), Kumarajiva (whose Chinese translations initiate Chinese textual lineages), Buddhapalita (founder, Prasangika), and Bhavaviveka (founder, Svatantrika), differ quite significantly from each other. In *Derrida on the Mend* I followed the Prasangika, and especially Candrakirti, because his reduction of adversaries to *prasanga* (absurd 'consequence' which is dilemma) seems to work the most like Derrida's negation of entitative formulae.

---

[27] By postmodernism I here mean no more than the deconstruction—musical, architectural, literary, artistic, philosophical, etc.—of holisms (not only of 'modernist' holisms but of the many 'traditional' period-styles). Derrida himself takes great care to distance his work from the terms/concepts/movements labeled 'postmodernism', largely because the label has become polymorphous and often represents projects to which Derrida's work has no affinity. For an excellent account of Derrida's attitude towards 'postmodernism', consult Christopher Norris, *What's Wrong with Postmodernism: Critical Theory and the Ends of Philosophy* (Baltimore: Johns Hopkins, 1990).

Here I tentatively track the Prasangika again, even though there are some ways in which the Svatantrika also resembles Derrida.

Please permit that I here attend a little more closely to the thorny controversy over the Two Truths, since it is relevant to our present concerns. There are many Prasangikan versions of Nagarjuna's Two Truths, but in general the Prasangikans hold that the 'conventions' of *samvrti*, though not having inherent existence, can 'validly work', i.e., be *effective*.[28] The Svatantrikans go further than this, saying that the conventions of *samvrti-satya* inherently exist[29] (Prasangika and Svatantrika agree, of course, that *śūnyatā* is the *paramārtha-satya*). The Svatantrikans claim that the Prasangikan insistence on the 'unreal' status of *samvrti* is dangerous: it can lead—*de facto* if not in name—to the cryptic restoration of a traditional Indian model Shakyamuni originally rejected, viz., the model of illusory appearance and transcendental absolute.[30] Since the Svatantrikans in general accept the traditional Indian tripartite syllogism (*trairūpya*) as inherent to the structure of logical inference, the Prasangikans counter by charging the Svatantrika can too easily backslide into elaborate, hyperspeculative rationalism.[31] (It is this tendency in Svatantrika that deters me also.)

Candrakirti attributes to *samvrti-satya* a conventional effectiveness which is imputed and unreal ('unreal' to him means *not* inherently existent). Imputed and unreal (in this sense), but—it is important for us to recognize—still *logocentric* in Derridean terms. Knowing conventional existence is not inherently existent (i.e., knowing objects, subjects, etc., are 'designated' as such only on their bodily and mental

---

[28] See Jeffrey Hopkins, *Emptiness: The Middle Way Consequence School* (Ithaca: Snow Lion, 1987), pp. 95-107 (which address the question of 'validity' in great detail, and the 'effectiveness' of *samvrti-satya*). See also Huntington, pp. 66-67.

[29] See Notes 2 and 3 in Tsong-ka-pa's "Guide to the Stanzas" (of Nagarjuna's *Mūlamādhyamakakārikās*, and chapter two of Candrakirti's commentary thereon, called "Analysis of Going and Coming"), in Jeffrey Hopkins, trans., in accordance with instruction from Kensur Nawang Lengden, *Analysis of Going and Coming* (Dharmasala: Library of Tibetan Works and Archives, 1974; 76), pp. 24, 25.

[30] Consult discussion in Huntington, pp. 34-36.

[31] Apropos of the *trairūpya*, for the famous debate between Bhavaviveka (Svatantrika) and Candrakirti (Prasangika), see José Ignacio Cabezón's review of Huntington's *Emptiness*, in *Journal of the International Association of Buddhist Studies*, 13.2 (1990), p. 158. Cabezón and Huntington disagree in their interpretations of the Prasangika, but agree that the *trairūpya* is one of the cruxes of the debate between Prasangika and Svatantrika.

'bases of designation'[32]), the 'non-defective awareness' can effectively use what Derrida would call 'logocentric' phenomena. Derrida's definition of logocentrism is wider than Candrikirti's, so that the 'match' of an unreal designation and its unreal 'collection of parts'—even when recognized as a mere imputation—is still *holistic*. As an unreal holistic formulation, it can still be deconstructed. But that it is logocentric and *can still function* as an effective convention for Candrakirti is precisely—from my point of view—what makes the Prasangika valuable to my project. For Candrakirti's version of *samvrti-satya* shows how Buddhism can help Derrida: how it can *validate* logocentrism while pointing to *paramārtha-satya*. Of course, as I have repeatedly noted, further advances in awareness require meditative practice, the supplement Derrida has (perhaps) yet to try.

In the Tibetan translation of the *Śūnyatāsaptatikārikānāma*, Nagarjuna declares "Those who have faith in the teaching of emptiness will strive for it through *a number of different kinds of reasoning.* Whatever they have understood about it in terms of non-existent existence, they clarify this for others, which helps others to attain nirvana by abandoning grasping at the apparently true existence of cyclic existence and non-cyclic existence."[33] José Ignacio Cabezón and others remind us of the importance of 'reasoning' for the Tibetan dGe-lugs-pa Prasangikan tradition,[34] and Hsueh-li Cheng reminds us of its importance for the Chinese Madhyamikan *San-Lun* (Three-Treatise) School.[35] These primary and secondary testimonials stand over and against C.W. Huntington, Jr.'s reading of the Prasangika-Madhyamika, and especially of Candrakirti, for Huntington makes a strict distinction between contextual (and non-mystical) 'seeing' whereby one recognizes 'things' are mere fictions (though 'necessary fictions'),[36] and—on the other hand—logical analysis. Thus Huntington declares: "...in order to know and accept the world as it is both in its

---

[32] See Hopkins, *Emptiness*, whose explanation comes via a Mongolian scholar who writes in Tibetan and is a proponent of the Prasangika, pp. 86-89, 96, and 469. Very good for contrasts with the Autonomy School. Also, see Sprung, pp. 132, 133; and Komito, *Seventy Stanzas* (which comes by way of Tibetan trans. and commentary on the *Śūnyatāsaptatikārikānāma* attributed to Nagarjuna), p. 178.

[33] Komito, *Seventy Stanzas*, p. 95 (Engl. trans.) and pp. 180-81 (commentary by Geshe Sonam Rinchen).

[34] *Journal of the International Association of Buddhist Studies*, 13.2, pp. 154, 161.

[35] See Note 19, above.

[36] See Huntington, pp. 55, 56, 110; also pp. 50, 111, et passim.

everyday appearance and in the paradox and mystery of this appearance, he [the Madhyamikan] *steps entirely outside* the language game that can be played only by holding onto propositions (*pratijñās*) and views (*dṛṣṭis*). In taking this step he makes the *first critical move* away from a form of life caught up in the anxious and generally manipulative attitude associated with this way of thinking and acting"[37] (emphasis mine).

In other words, Huntington argues that Candrakirti's affiliation with *no-view* means the jettisoning of logic, whereas most interpreters regard *no-view* as the use of logic against ideology, and against higher-order logical formulations. The majority position is more congenial to my project, since Derrida uses logic to deconstruct logic. A Derridean would find Huntington's distinction between *seeing* devoid phenomena (albeit via a non-mystical but 'careful attending') and *logical thinking about* phenomena a naive distinction. For much of language itself is logical in structure, and—at least when we are in a non-mystical mode—logic and ideas pervade our 'perception' and 'cognition'. Huntington draws upon Wittgenstein to explain his distinction between conceptualizing and attending. A trained Madhyamikan, seeing that phenomena are simply part of a conceptual *language-game*, can use this game at will, and without falling into the trap of ratiocinating it. All very well, a Derridean would say, *except* that language-games are *also* logocentric, and all Wittgensteinian 'forms-of-life' are cryptic displacements of system, of closure, of—indeed—the being/non-being dialectic. For my part, I would argue it is more honest to grant that logic and other-than-logic, necessarily entangled as they are, must deconstruct themselves and each other.

Finally, it may be objected that Nagarjuna's 'dependent co-arising' is not at all 'marked', 'traced', in the Derridean sense because the *Mūlamādhyamakakārikās* says categorically:

> "When the domain of thought has been dissipated,
> 'that which can be stated' is dissipated.
> Those things which are unoriginated and not terminated,
> like *nirvāṇa*, constitute the Truth (*dharmatā*)." [MK 18:7[38]]

---

[37] Huntington, pp. 58, 59.
[38] Trans. by Frederick Streng, in the Appendix to his *Emptiness* (Nashville: Abingdon, 1987).

and:

> " ' Not caused by something else', 'peaceful', 'not elaborated
> by discursive thought',
> 'indeterminate', 'undifferentiated': such are the character-
> istics of true reality (*tattva*)." [MK 18:9]

To regard these stanzas as necessarily precluding Derridean 'marks', 'traces', etc., is to misunderstand how/what 'marks', 'traces' indicate. Permit me two preliminary observations. First, the technical Sanskrit term *lakṣaṇa*, sometimes translated 'mark', refers—in the context of Nagarjunist debate—to what Derrida would reject as *ontic* qualities, viz., the 'states' or 'phases' through which entities pass. For Buddhism, these characteristics are 'origination, duration, change, and destruction', and Nagarjuna, like, Derrida, rejects them. (But let me add parenthetically here that for Nagarjuna *lakṣaṇa* can also just mean 'distinguishing descriptor', as in MK 18:9, above—"characteristics (*lakṣaṇam*) of true reality (*tattva*).") (My second observation—) The technical Sanskrit term *bīja* (seed, impression), associated with Yogacaric theory, sometimes is translated 'trace', but insofar as the *bīja* moves from potency in the repository-consciousness to maturity (forming as 'apprehender' and 'apprehended'), and then, reducing, returns to the repository-consciousness again, 'some*thing*' stays the same in this process. *Bīja* is to this extent *entitative*, and Candrakirti rejects it on this count. Derrida would do likewise.

   In the *Derridean* sense, 'mark' and 'trace' (or any of many other words) serve as empty descriptors which designate whatever happens to be the *ad hoc* 'necessary but impossible remainder' of pure difference (a logocentric term, 'remainder' cannot as such survive pure difference). Derridean trace, mark, etc., is perhaps the closest a Western thinker has yet come to the Buddhist notion of *tattva*—the 'thisness/thatness' broached by the Madhyamika as the intersection of spontaneity (i.e., pure impermanence) and Buddhist 'relationality' (i.e., pure dependency). That 'thisness/thatness' is *impermanent* as well as devoid requires that each thisness, each devoid 'moment', differ completely from all others—that it be, we say in our Derridean provisional language—'uniquely' *marked*. These unique moments are the 'same' not because they share an entitative substratum or any other ontic or ontological continuity, but rather because they are *all* purely *devoid* of being (or any of the displacements or dialectical spin-offs from being, such as positive Nothingness, etc.). Candrakirti, in his *Mādhyamakāvatārabhāsya*, tries to clarify by means of a metaphor drawn from logocentric absence-and-presence:

> "For example, even though jugs, bowls, and other such
> vessels are different, still they are equivalent insofar
> as they are (all) hollow, and the space inside them is not
> different. Similarly, even though form, feeling, and the
> other psychophysical aggregates are different (from each
> other), they are real [tattvic] in that each possesses the
> distinguishing characteristic of nonproduction. In this
> way they are without difference and should be understood
> as identical."[39]

Candrakirti asserts that the aggregates are different ('purely different', in our Derridean terms,—i.e., not sharing a common essence) but that the aggregates are "without difference" in that "each possesses the distinguishing characteristic of non-production" ('the sameness which is not self-same', in our Derridean terms). Candrakirti is *not* taking "nonproduction" as the opposite of 'production' (and Derrida does *not* treat devoidness, trace, as the opposite of 'being'). "Nonproduction" for Candrakirti and Nagarjuna means, rather, that the dialectic of 'produced-and-not-produced' *does not apply* (and Derrida claims both poles of a dialectic are equally specious).

Recall, after all, that in Nagarjuna's MK 18:7 that we cited, it is the dialectic of 'originated-and-terminated' (*utpāda* and *niruddhā*) which Nirvana *eludes*. Likewise, as MK 18:7 and MK 18:9 both tell us, *logocentric* thought and language do not apply: verse 7—'the domain of thought' (*cittagocare*) and its logocentric formulae (-*abhidhātavyaṃ*) *dissipate*; verse 9—'discursive thought' (*prapañca*), its 'determinations' (*vikalpa*) and 'differentiations' (*artha*) are rejected.

Note that the stanzas do not say that logocentrism-as-*deconstructed* cannot act as a *clue*. The 'not caused by something else' (*aparapratyayaṃ*) of verse 9 is part and parcel of Nagarjuna's rejection of 'produced-and-not-produced'. The dGe-lugs-pa Prasangikan tradition, for example, emphasizes that "going and coming in general are not

---

[39] Huntington, p. 265. (Note: Only a through-and-through-awakened Buddha can thoroughly frequent this 'sameness'.)

being refuted but inherently existent going and coming."[40] The dissipating (*nivṛttam-... nivṛtte*, verse 7) of logocentric thought and language, and the attaining of 'peacefulness' (*...śāntaṃ*, verse 9) do not mean literal *cessation* but logocentric cessation. (Aside: of course logocentrism can remain as 'effective' deployment in *saṃsāra*.) During silent, calm meditation the adept may indeed be silent and calm in terms of *words*, but she/he 'frequents' what is in a Derridean sense devoid and *marked*.

I make the above observations so the reader avoids the snare of equating Madhyamikan deconstruction of movement, production, etc., with (what I call) *centric* Buddhism. For in Section iii (two sections ahead) this book shall discuss Masao Abe's Kyoto School notions of 'paradox' and 'openness' (a 'closed openness' of 'infinity', a Derridean would say),—notions which I maintain are centric, and Yogacaric in sympathy. In that Nagarjuna's verses involving 'cessation' and 'peace', etc., would seem in a naive first reading to bolster notions of centrism, let us delve further. I argue that—though of course the Yogacaric tradition and much of the Yogacara-Madhyamika-Svatantrika affirm 'dependent co-arising' according to their own lights, the privileged *prajñapti* of these schools seems really to be 'cessation' in the sense of both (1) Stillness and (2) extinction of desire. On the other hand, the privileged *prajñapti* of the Prasangika-Madhyamika, I argue, remains 'dependent co-arising', *pratītya-samutpāda*,[41] and thus this school can be more instructive to us.

A *prajñapti* is always just provisional, but this being the case, its *efficacy*-as-conductal must somehow involve its denotations (or rather, the traces thereof),—though of course its success in the long run depends on the dispositions of the meditator. There has been from the beginnings much controversy over the exact meaning of *pratītya* in *pratītya-samutpāda* (whether *pratītya* be a continuative or a noun-in-compound or, as *prati-*, a distributive[42]). Nonetheless, all agree that its meaning somehow involves 'change', 'movement'. Since *pratītya-samutpāda*, as the Dalai Lama says, is *The* slogan of the Buddha[43] (we

---

[40] Hopkins, *Analysis of Going and Coming*, p. 24.

[41] It should be clear we are not discussing meditative *posture* here. Prasangika-Madhyamika meditation is often 'still', and the meditator's passions, etc., are—s/he hopes—stilled, extinguished.

[42] Hopkins, *Emptiness*, pp. 307-310.

[43] Hopkins, *Emptiness*, p. 307.

find versions of it in all three Yanas), *movement*—it seems to me—must be the Buddha's paramount clue.

Since provisional language in Buddhism is *au bout* just soteriological anyway, I opt for the Prasangika-Madhyamika because its 'clues' to *śūnyatā* bespeak *movement X'd over*. Specifically, its clues bespeak movement which, lacking substantial continuity, appears—at least amid deconstructive analysis—as *discontinuous, erratic*. But again, please gauge that the 'discontinuous' and 'errant' are *also* X'd over: they cannot operate in their normal entitative sense, since 'discontinuity' normally belongs to the dialectic of End and 'erratic' to the dialectics of Truth and End.[44] Below the X, they remain—for Nagarjuna and Derrida alike—the 'discontinuous' and 'erratic' as movements which are *elsewise*, but then this floating clue must undergo erasure in turn. The elsewise is elsewise.........

---

[44] In short, the Madhyamika deconstructs both 'cessation' and 'movement' as dialectical opposites, but tends to take 'movement-under-erasure' as its clue. The Yogacara, on the other hand, tends to take 'cessation' (and sometimes, a Yogacaric version of 'cessation-under-erasure') as its clue. The Madhyamikan's movement-under-erasure, like the Derridean's, appears—in the process of deconstruction—as discontinuous and errant, but insofar as these terms/concepts recuperate the language of teleology, logocentrism, they must submit to erasure in turn. The elsewise is elsewise.

(ii)

## Double-Binds and (Derrida's) "Dénégations"

—For the dear Black Robe in question:
    Did I just hear "braille" (thank God!)
    when the revenant was writing "braile"?
       "Braile" of
            *Beliar* [GK] (*Belial* in L., of course)
            El-Biar
            Braile?
    And then there's *Khōra*/Korah and the rest.
    *Kappōreth!*
    *Adōnay hu ha-elōhim*, for sure, and the Lord God
    of Israel loves thee and awaits thee.

                    The Lord God "will be like the dew to Israel...
                    (Israel's) beauty shall be like the
                    Olive-tree."
                              —Hosea 14:6,7

In 1986, in Jerusalem, there unfolded a conference on Absence and Negativity. At this conference Jacques Derrida delivered a lecture, in English, entitled "How to Avoid Speaking." In 1987, he published a longer French version named "Comment ne pas parler—Dénégations."[1] The etymology of the noun *dénégation* equivocates. In Derrida it 'means' 'denial', but, athwart this 'first sense', it means 'backing off from denial'. Hence, in Derrida 'to denegate' means 'to mark' (i.e., to inscribe with the Derridean notion of 'to mark'). Two years later, an English translation of the French text appeared, rendering the French title as "How to Avoid Speaking: Denials."[2] Considered Derrida's most direct engagement yet with 'negative theology', the aforesaid 'Jerusalem texts' have solicited much attention, including publications and conference-papers.[3] It is widely argued that the Jerusalem texts

---

[1] In Derrida, *Psyché: inventions de l'autre* (Paris: Galilée, 1987), pp. 535-95.
[2] Trans. by Ken Frieden in *Languages of the Unsayable*, eds. S. Budick and W. Iser (N.Y.: Columbia UP, 1989), pp. 2-70.
[3] Apropos, one of the first of the book-anthologies to see print in English is H. Coward and T. Foshay, *Derrida and Negative theology* (N.Y.: S.U.N.Y. Press, 1992). It comprises several important essays, and a reprint of Frieden's English

signal a Derridean *Kehre,* a turn testifying to a newly found belief in God, at least the God of negative theology and apophatic mysticism. Working from the published French version (henceforth, "Dénégations"), my point in this section is that 'Derrida' has not 'changed' all that much nor so simplistically.

Be warned that because of its vertiginous com*pli*cation, "Dénégations" can easily become, in its own way, what Nagarjuna (who is quoting already a long tradition) calls "a snake wrongly grasped" (see MK 24:11). Recall what 'Derrida' says of his naive readers—that, like fishes for the bait, they head straight for the lure.[4] I concur that Derrida, who does 'alter' and has been 'altering' all along—indeed he tells us as much—does differ today from twenty years ago. But I maintain that these and other differences, as they are at work in "Dénégations," are both more elaborate and less stable than simple *conversio.* And Derrida continues to reinscribe the 'necessary but impossible' moments he 'always' has—albeit always with the necessary but impossible *décalages.* Left-handedly, perforce, I here note how Derrida has most clearly changed.—

(1) His early texts were categorically pejorative of negative theology, a discipline he saw necessarily committed in advance to a philosophy of logocentric closedness: that is, when negation is saturated, 'God' is supposed to be what *is left,* what remains *within* the implied field or metaphoric space. 'God' is the *reserve* in this theological economy. Derrida also took negative theology to be involved in study of logocentric Void, i.e., Void as the dialectical antithesis of Plenum and thus just as invalid (the subtext of Plenum or Void is *hyperessence*). "Dénégations" takes great care to *retain* these criticisms (7-12)[5] but adds that many negative theologies more or less escape them.

(2) Whereas Derrida's early texts did not develop at length the comparison between *différance originaire* (the 'prior' difference enabling *no* and *not-no* talk in language, and thus enabling language) *and* 'God'

---

translation of "Dénégations." Derrida's own new contribution, "Post Scriptum: Aporias, Ways and Voices," bears the 'same' differences as "Dénégations": I plan to treat it at another venue.

[4] See *The Truth in Painting,* p. 173.

[5] For the reader's convenience, I parenthesize page references to the published English translation of "Dénégations." When it is *especially* important (it is always important) to consult the French text, I supply the French pagination also: in this case, it appears first, and the English pagination follows the semicolon. Occasionally, in order to provide a more literal rendering, I have modified quotations from the published English translation.

as pure differance (the 'prior' difference making possible the 'naming' of beings and their negations), "Dénégations" strongly poses this comparison (4,6). From his earliest writing, Derrida has argued that what is called negation and affirmation in language, in thought, in metaphysics, were possible only because 'always already' there is a difference between *no* and *not-no*, and this differance (the *différance originaire*, spelled with an *a* in French and English because it is not 'mere difference' dialectically spun off from identity) is itself a *pure no*: 'not-no' and 'no' are *purely not* the same. Derrida's genius in "Dénégations" is to show how *différance originaire* is mixed into all *ad-hoc* differences by the very fact it is constitutive of them: *différance originaire* enables and thereby 'marks' a vast range of 'actualities', from grammar on the one hand all the way over to negative theologies on the other. Negative theologies, within the protocols of their discipline, provisionally name the *différance originaire* by the name of 'God'.

(3)   In his early texts Derrida emphasized how permutations level ethical systems based on a hierarchy of value,—though from early on he was engaged in active political deconstruction which surely had a positive ethical intent. Perhaps prompted by both the Heidegger and Paul de Man affairs, he has of late addressed ethics more affirmatively. In "Dénégations," he argues that the prior condition which enables humanity's *no* and *not-no* comports necessarily a hidden injunction: humanity *must* deploy (the 'il faut') that which is rendered possible. In short, humans *must* speak. And this injunction passes inevitably into a second: one must speak *well*, i.e., speak ethically (otherwise, how is communication possible?). Here Derrida is appropriating from J. L. Austin, who asserts that speech-acts require a covenant, a 'promise to the other' that the protocols of veracity will be observed. Simultaneously, of course, Derrida is working a parallel allusion: the Torah's concatenation of 'Divine Injunction'— 'Promise from/to the Other and others'—and 'Ethic' (11-16, 48, 49).

(4)   'Dissemination' in Derrida's first texts is more the ever retreating rhyzogeny of inverse semination (the *dis-* here = 'away from') and less (but also) the 'law of aberrant reinscription'. The later texts prefer the 'law of aberrant reinscription': 'dissemination' becomes the dissipating of decidability (the *dis-* here = 'in several directions'), so that—like the case of a teletype machine out of whack—the aberrancy introduced within the limits of the machine brings about a random but inevitable return of several 'possibles', and these 'possibles' are asymmetric to each other. In the 'history' of any

text, the unleashed forces of signification—blind and aberrant but limited—inevitably criss-cross again and again at *several* disparate nodes, and these nodes are, each of them, *double-binds* (or at least involved in double-binds). In Nietzsche's writing about women, for example, Derrida finds the arhythmical but interminable return of at least three nodes: "He [Nietzsche] was, and he dreaded, such a castrated woman. He was, and he dreaded, such a castrating woman. He was, and he loved, such an affirmative woman."[6]

In "Dénégations" (as always) the swathe of nodes one meets is dependent upon the *tranche* ('cut' in playing cards, etc.) one makes in the text. The question of Derrida's 'intention' is doubly problematic because 'his' texts have for so long argued (a) that the 'law' of writing overwhelms authorial intention (the spider is always unequal to the web it has 'produced'), and (b) that an 'author' appears *in* a text by way of *unintended* dissociated 'effects'. What is more, in so far as the preceding sentence seems to reinstate Derrida's 'intention' positing 'non-intention' (or better, 'off-intention'), the sentence—as 'he' himself would be the first to grant—is itself a double-bind.

In terms of the Buddhist two truths, double-binds 'in one stroke'[7] both utterly empty themselves (*paramārtha-satya*) and survive (*saṃvṛti-satya*), as does the entire text of "Dénégations". In "Dénégations," there are interminable ways in which Derrida's affiliation with negative theology is confounded. Left-handedly/right-handedly, perforce, I herewith list and annotate at least six of them.—

(1) 'Derrida' as narrator represents 'his' voice sometimes by first person singular (*je*), sometimes by first person plural (*nous*), sometimes by the impersonal (*on*), and so on: this is common practice, of course, 'dictated' (it is said) by rhetorical/stylistic factors rather than semantic ones, but 'Derrida' even within "Dénégations" makes much of the inevitable breaks and shifts in narrative identity forced by (what are traditionally said to be) these *semantically unjustified* dislocations. Furthermore, the voice quotes other voices (often quoting yet other voices), and often incorporates them in a patchwork. When

---

[6] From Derrida, "The Question of Style" [excerpted from Derrida, *Eperons*, Venice: 1976], in *The New Nietzsche*, ed. David B. Allison (Albany: S.U.N.Y. Press, 1977), pp. 186-7.
[7] 'In a single stroke/gulp', *d'un seul trait*; 'at a stroke, at one stretch', *tout d'un trait*. Derrida predilects *trait*: 'stroke', 'trace', 'thunderbolt', 'prime move' [in chess], as well as a linear 'dash' (*trait d'union*, 'hyphen') which connects but thereby necessarily postpones, defers.

are these, in J. L. Austin's sense, 'mere mention', and when are these 'use'? For example, who is the speaker in the following sentence decked out with brackets and parenthesis?— "As for those theologians who have 'praised' its inaccessibility and penetrated its 'secret infinity', they have left no 'trace' (*ikhnous*) [ibid.; I underline]" (581;50). See also the 'representation' of Meister Eckhart: "Here the voice of an utterance can conceal another, which it then appears to quote without quoting it,..." (44).

(2) The 'Derrida' of the footnotes in "Dénégations" sometimes subverts the 'Derrida' of the text's body; and then these footnotes— behaving as supplements do—'subvert' the boundary between themselves and the body by making cryptic 'appearances' above the line, in the body itself. For example, a sequence in the main text explains that Dionysius's 'beyond Being' exceeds the opposition between affirmation and negation (as *différance originaire* does). The main text goes on to explain that Dionysius transfers by analogy the relation between 'beyond Being' and 'below Being' to *society*: mystic masters, High Priests, etc., claim a hierarchical supremacy over the uninitiated. The main text seems to encourage this analogy, offering as examples of the 'initiated' such figures as Dionysius himself, and Moses, and the Gileadites (who used the *shibbōleth*). The pertaining footnote (553,54; rendered as #9, p. 65 in the Engl. trans.) addresses the problematic of hierarchy, challenging Jean-Luc Marion's distinction between hierarchy as a "sacred ordinance" and the "vulgar concept of hierarchy." 'Derrida' reduces Marion to dilemma: either give up analogical transfer as an argument, or grant that the 'vulgar concept of hierarchy' must be included in the analogy. The consequences for what is devolving in the main text are enormous: the first horn of the dilemma undoes Dionysius's thesis, which depends on the analogy; the second horn implies that 'beyond Being' must be at least as perverse as history shows religio-social hierarchies to often have been. Then, at the end of the footnote, 'Derrida' lets float 'his' notions of "an-economy (*an-économie*)" and the "anarchy of the gift (*anarchie de don*)," which implies a 'beyond Being' which is reckless, senseless. Float they do, up into the main text, where they 'appear' unexpectedly at several points, for example, as "...atopics of God; I say *atopics*, hardly even playing: *atopos* is the senseless, the absurd, the extravagant, the mad" (26). Shades of Herman Melville! Gratuitous gifts.

(3) 'Derrida' 's assertions and practices in parts of the essay double-bind with 'his' assertions and practices in other parts. For

example, 'Derrida' itemizes severe accusations directed against 'deconstruction' by his adversaries (552;18,19), calling their inquisition an *instruction* but also a *procès* (trial), and implying 'without saying', that their *réquisitoire* (indictment) is a grave misrepresentation. Then he goes on, seemingly, to indulge these very perfidies. Thus he lists as an indictment: "Some of them [deconstructionists] appear 'Greek', others 'Christian': they have recourse to many languages at once, and one knows some who resemble Talmudists" (ibid.). 'Derrida' of course appears 'Greek' in this very essay, 'representing' Plato's *Khōra* in several ways that evoke deconstruction positively (on Plato: 31-38; on *Khōra*, 34-38). 'Derrida' likewise 'represents' the Christian apophatic theologian, Dionysius the Areopagite (*Denys l'Aréopagite*[8]), in several ways that 'appear' deconstructionist (on Dionysius: 40-43,47-51; deconstructionist: on the 'promise', 49, the 'seal', 50). And throughout "Dénégations," 'Derrida' indulges the Midrashic style of a Talmudist.

Citing Dionysius via *indirekte Rede*, 'Derrida' says the theologian "evokes a double tradition, a double mode of transmission..., on the one hand unsayable, secret,...; on the other hand, philosophic,..." (556;24). Derrida holds that everyone does this at least unknowingly, but the Talmudist does at least part of this knowingly. And when 'Derrida' recourses, as he tells us, to the use Lacan makes of the word *mathème* (ibid.), he is playing a Talmudist indeed. 'Derrida' tells us, "This non-matheme [Lacan's term for how a signifier works in an analysand's discourse] can and must become a matheme [Lacan's term for a formula, usually algebraic, signifying natural laws]." But 'Derrida' doesn't inform us that the Greek root of matheme, *mathēma* (science) connects to *manthanein* (to learn) and that *mathētēs*, in Dionysius' Greek, means 'disciple'. So the esoteric off-reading of 'Derrida' 's sentence is, "This non-disciple can and must become a disciple." Which is what Derrida in the broader context has been discussing in relation to Dionysius (how Dionysius keeps the 'secret' of Divinity from the profane), and which is what the text of "Dénégations" is largely about (i.e., is 'Derrida' keeping/not-keeping a

---

[8] *Denys (pseudo-Denys*, the 'false' Dionysius the Areopagite, as he is known) runs a gamut of perfect and off-perfect homonyms in French: *dénie*, 'he/she/it denies'; (*St*) *Denis*, 'St. Denis' (patron saint of France); and more. Plus 'allusions' to *denier* (n.), 'cash', 'money put in Church poor-box'. And more. But I must curtail.

secret? How not to say?[9]). Very like a Talmudist, which is the aforesaid indictment of the accusers. And "Dénégations," almost every phrase and sentence, works in this 'Talmudic' way. And more.

(4) And more, because in "Dénégations" the double-bind saturates the text—applying to the 'God' of negative theology, too; and even to the *différance originaire* of which this 'God' may be an (aberrant) reinscription. And the double-bind applies as well to 'Derrida' 's Talmudic-like reading. Indeed, 'Derrida' had immediately preceded 'his' reference to Dionysius and Dionysian "double tradition, double mode of transmission" by saying via *indirekte Rede* "the theologian must practice not a double language, but the double inscription of his knowledge" (ibid.). If the text of "Dénégations" double-binds (-itself), it is by a 'law of aberrant reinscription' rather than straightforward subversion (which mere 'double language' implies). For example, take the mode of the esoteric ("unsayable, secret") and the mode of the exoteric ("philosophic"): they double-bind each other (double-bind Θ, say). Then take the discourse of 'Derrida' and the discourse of Dionysius (or, one ratchet-click away, of a Talmudist): they double-bind each other (double-bind Σ, say). Double-bind Σ, it can be said, *aberrantly reinscribes* double-bind Θ, or it can be said *vice versa*.

'Derrida', when 'reporting on' the two modes of transmission, the esoteric and the exoteric, 'reports' Dionysius to recognize "that these two modes 'intersect' ['s'entrecroisent']" (ibid). Then 'Derrida' develops further:

> "To what mode does this discourse belong, then, both
> that of Dionysius and that which I held about him/his
> subject ['à son sujet']? Must it not necessarily keep
> to the place, which cannot be an indivisible point,
> where the two modes cross—such that, properly speaking,
> the crossing itself, or the *symplokē*, belongs to neither
> of the two modes and doubtless even precedes their
> distribution? At the intersection of the secret and of
> the nonsecret, what is the secret?" (557; 24,25)

---

[9] *Comment ne pas dire?*, 'How not to say?', can be asking the question, 'How to be silent in general? How to avoid speaking?' But it can also be asking the question (as in English too), 'How to hold back such a predicate? How to hold back saying X?' See "Dénégations," p. 548;15.

Note that the "crossing itself," belonging to neither of the two modes, "even *precedes* their distribution." That is, even the *différance originaire* which is *prior* to and in excess of differences, is a double-bind.

(5) 'Derrida' throughout "Dénégations" resorts to trace-words and trace-phrases which neither mean nor do not mean what they mean in his other texts. This problem re-opens the question of teacher, disciple, and secrecy. It constitutes less a problem for the readers of "Dénégations" who are not 'familiar' with his *oeuvre*. To those readers who know his work well, it is clear that 'Derrida' in "Dénégations" is invoking and *miming* his own past terminology 'purposively': the 'allusions' come in almost every sentence, and are not innocent. Here are just some of the many so-called trace-words and trace-phrases which can be lifted directly from the French text— *laisse, sceau, apparence, torture, oeil, synoptique, filtre, crible, fiction, fable, pas d'écriture, plus d'être,* (L.) *copula, propre, sans, trait, traduction, il s' écrit, position* (Gk., *thesis*), *prétend, le ça, seuil, il y a là cendre.* Moreover, off the margin of "Dénégations" are figures in the history of thought, past and present, whose *effets* are crypted in(to) the text (thus Derrida's deconstructive version of 'inter-textuality'). It is crucial for "Dénégations" that these prior 'influences' from off the margin be recognized and read. Some examples of these thinkers: Kant, Nietzsche, Kierkegaard, Freud, Levinas, Lacan. Also off the margin and deconstructed, by reason of how their *effets* off-work in the text, are the Hebraic and Islamic traditions, and the contemporary politics of the Mideast, and 'Derrida' 's auto/otobiography. And more.

To take the 'allusions' as *Rosetta* stones, to be deciphered faithfully by members of a cult, would be precisely to miss Derrida's larger claim—that repetition is always repetition-with-a-difference, and to this extent a necessary mimicry. (Even the repetition necessary to language necessarily dislocates the intention supposedly commanding it.) In that the latter assertions are themselves repetitions-with-a-difference, they involve the 'informed' reader in yet another double-bind. Perhaps this is just what is to be learned. According to Buddhism, we can say that this 'infinite retreat' of double-binds is what is to be learned. It can be a *prajñapti* for *pratītya samutpāda.* Examination would show that the trace-terms appearing in "Dénégations" play a crucial (X) role in arbitrating the text's interpretative possibilities: the history of Derrida's terms should not be ignored. Neither should they be interpreted so as to prevent Derrida's differing from 'his' past. I have tried in my treatment of "Dénégations," above, to negotiate the 'neither... nor' of the *fourth* lemma (recall the tetralemma of Oriental logic: X is; X is-not; X both is and is-not; X neither is nor is-not). Of the fourth lemma understood in what logicians call the *undistributed* way (in the *distributed* mode, the fourth lemma takes X to absolutely escape and transcend 'X both is and is-not', the third lemma). It so happens that 'Derrida' in "Dénéga-tions" probes, though necessarily with a difference, the equivocating status of the fourth lemma (e.g., see pp. 61, 62). And in 'his' decon-struction of the *sur*, seems to side with the undistributed version, which can be said to "oscillate [*oscille*] between the 'neither this - nor that' [*ni ceci - ni cela*]" (32). Oscillation. Between neither this - nor that. Oscillation. Buddhism, for its part, has been invoking the fourth lemma for a long, long time.

(iii)

## Differentialism and the Buddhist-Christian Dialogue

"...and finally applying the method of Ch'an
to dissolve the unified state."
—Ch'an Master Sheng-Yen[1]

Given that the dialogue between Buddhism and Christianity (and increasingly, Judaism too) has much potential for good (it has), the *good effect* of Buddhism depends on two factors: (1) Buddhism's radical difference from traditional Christianity/Judaism, and (2) Buddhism's situational 'pertinence' (which must be exploited by/as *upāya*, 'skillful means'). In this section I aim to show that the current Buddhist dialogian most active among Western intellectuals, the scholarly and kind Masao Abe (of whom I am personally very fond), is perhaps not attending to these two factors. That is, he is advancing a version of Yogacara too *commodious* of the logocentric 'Absolute' and of 'oneness', both of which values are already indigenous to traditional Christianity/ Judaism; and this duplication is *untimely*, in that western history is entering a deconstructive moment. What Buddhism must needs exhibit is *how* to achieve *liberation* while carrying on deconstruction. In my opinion, only the Madhyamikan tradition, and the 'differential' (as I call it) strain in Zen and several other Buddhist schools, can do this.

Masao Abe's approach is best represented, I think, by his recent essay, "Kenotic God and Dynamic Sunyata,"[2] which clearly confirms his affiliation to the thought of the Kyoto School. The Kyoto School, founded by the famous Buddhist philosopher Kitaro Nishida (1870-1940), initiated the modern involvement of Buddhism in dialogue. The School came to the fore at a time when German Idealism (and often, scientism) still dominated European philosophy/theology. In "Kenotic God and Dynamic Sunyata," Abe argues that the notion of Absolute Nothingness in Nishida's Zen Buddhism can contribute to a necessary re-working of Christian theology. To wit, the *kenōsis* (Gk., 'emptying out') which St. Paul attributes to the Son of God makes better

---

[1] In his *Getting the Buddha Mind*, p. 28.
[2] In *The Emptying God: A Buddhist-Jewish-Christian Conversation*, eds. John B. Cobb and Christopher Ives (Maryknoll, N.Y.: Orbis, 1990), pp. 3-65. I supply page references parenthetically.

theological sense if it is taken to apply to the total God, both
'immanent' (relations within God) and 'emanant' (the relation of God
to 'creation'). Masao Abe formulates *śūnyatā* as follows:

> "Sunyata is fundamentally non-Sunyata—that is, Sunyata
> with an 'X' through it (Sun-X-yata). That is the true and
> ultimate Sunyata. This means that true Sunyata empties
> not only everything else, but also empties itself.
> Through its self-emptying it makes everything exist as
> it is and work as it does." (33)

Quoting from the *Prajñāpāramitā Sūtra*, he establishes what he
means by the sign of the X:

> "Sunyata is non-Sunyata (*aśūnyatā*): therefore it is
> ultimate Sunyata (*atyanta-Śūnyatā*). Sunyata not only
> is not Being or God, but also not emptiness as
> distinguished from somethingness or fullness. Just
> as the attachment to being must be overcome, the
> attachment to emptiness must also be surmounted.
> Accordingly, however important the notion of Sunyata
> may be in Buddhism, following Martin Heidegger, who
> put a cross mark 'X' on the term *Sein*, thus rendering
> it as *Se*-X-*in*, in order to show the unobjectifiability
> of *Sein*, we should also put a cross mark 'X' on
> Sunyata, and render it Sun-X-yata." (27)

Clearly, we are not dealing with Derridean erasure (which works as a
deconstruction of the Heideggerian X), since the double-bind of Derrida's
X does not/cannot signal the unobjectifiable 'presence' of an "ultimate."
For Derrida, any 'ultimate' would be asymmetrically but doubly bound
into its 'traces' in the 'other-than-ultimate'. That Abe means "ultimate"
in the Absolute logocentric sense is confirmed by many other passages in
his work, of which the following is typical:

> "In this living realization of true Sunyata, self and
> Sunyata are dynamically identical. That is to say, true
> Sunyata is nothing but the true self and the true self
> is nothing but true Sunyata. Apart from the absolute

present—right here, right now—this dynamical identity
of self and Sunyata cannot be fully realized. Again,
apart from the non-objectifiable and pre-representational
standpoint, the absolute present, and the dynamical
identity of self and Sunyata cannot be properly grasped." (28)

If this passage resonates with any formulation in the West, it is with
the Still Point, a concept belonging to (what deconstructionists call)
'displaced holism', and not at all with Derrida's ongoing alterity. (For
this reason, in section i, above, I preferred the differential Buddhism's
*prajñapti* of 'change' rather than the centric Buddhism's *prajñapti* of
'cessation'.) *Différance originaire*, be it discussed in the largely gramma-
tological terms of Derrida's early phase, or the largely apophatic terms of
"Dénégations," is always entrammeled, entangled (1) in an *ad hoc*
situational difference, whichever one happens to be happening at the
time, and even (2) in the empty traces which 'it' (there is no self-
identical 'it', of course) is singularly 'then and there' constituting.
Especially in Derrida's later work, the gesture of the X is enhanced to
mean precisely a double-bind, whatever the double-bind happens to be
in the given situation, but this double-bind writes *under erasure* the
'finite' insubstantiality, the non-totalizing devoidness of the given
situation. This is no less so in terms of *différance originaire* as 'prior'
double-bind, since 'double-bind' precludes a logocentric 'prior' (otherwise we are back to Immanuel Kant again), as well as absolute
logocentric unity, even a 'unity of opposites'. 'Prior' double-bind
*asymmetrically* and *arhythmically* doublebinds with the situational *ad
hoc* double-binds it constitutes (otherwise, how can it be a 'double-
bind'?). Even 'prior' double-bind—doublebound into chance, randomness,
'spottiness' in space and time—*disseminates. (Catch* word—'One never
has it all at once'.) Thus the ever erratic going-on. (*Prajñapti* for
Nagarjunist *pratītya samutpāda*, I say.)

Masao Abe, like most Japanese Zennists and Nishida in par-
ticular, is heavily influenced by the tradition which, flowing from the
Prajnaparamitan literature, undergoes further development in the
Yogacara and more transformation still when it meets Chinese
Taoism. It has been argued by several modern scholars that Nagarjuna,
whom tradition retroactively named the compiler and even 'father' of

the Prajnaparamita canon, was in fact not even familiar with it.[3] Though this position may be too extreme, there surely is a big difference between the Prajnaparamita's Buddhism, which in general treats *śūnyatā* in a 'logocentric' way, and the Nagarjunism of the *Mūlamādhyamakakārikās*, with its radical deconstruction of absolutes and its refusal to replace with a more 'positive' non-rational Absolute. Most of the later Mahayanists (but *not* the Prasangika-Madhyamika), maintained that Nagarjuna's Buddhism was incomplete, and required the formulation of 'positive *śūnyatā*' (understood, of course, as 'transcending' conventional positivity/negativity) as a fulfillment. Thus they proposed an ideological progression in the history of Buddhism, viz., from Hinayana to Madhyamika to Mahayana. Japanese Zen is dominated by this 'progressivist' or 'incrementalist' version. Not without good reason has the Chinese Buddhologist, Hsueh-Li Cheng (U. of Hawaii), gone so far as to decry Japanese Zen's famous 'missionary to the West', D. T. Suzuki, as a 'transcendentalist'. Cheng (disapprovingly) quotes from Suzuki's *Outlines of Mahayana Buddhism*,—"Nagarjuna's famous doctrine of 'the Middle Path of Eight No's' breathes the same (Upanishadic) spirit (Absolute Reality is to be described by No, No!)."[4]

The Yogacaric component of/in the progressivist reading (in which Abe concurs) is very strong, and this is why Abe consistently evokes formulations such as the *nondual unity* of *śūnyatā* (e.g., p. 35), and the unity of opposites realized in *śūnyatā* (31). It is also why the 'Christian' formula he contributes to Buddhist-Christian dialogue is a paradoxical unity in the strict third-lemma sense:

> "God is not God (for God is love and completely self-
> emptying); precisely because God is not a self-

---

[3] See, for example, A. K. Warder, "Is Nagarjuna a Mahayanist?" in *The Problem of Two Truths in Buddhism and Vedanta*, ed. Mervyn Sprung (Dordrecht: Reidel, 1973), pp. 80, 81.

[4] New York: Schocken Bks, 1963, pp. 102-3. Cited in Hsueh-Li Cheng, "Emptiness: Exoteric and Esoteric Buddhism," in *World Sutric and Tantric Buddhist Conference Report* (Kaohsiung, Taiwan: Fo Kuang P, 1988), p. 121. Cheng is pointing out that Suzuki's version of Nagarjuna's 'Eight Negations' makes them behave like a classic negative theology. That is, Suzuki's version assumes an Absolute Reality transcending the human attributions which the Eight Negations negate. Cheng would instead take the Eight Negations as a canceling-out of four dialectical (and therefore logocentric) opposites, such as, for example, 'annihilation' and 'permanence'. For him the Middle Path does not involve the negated pairs, but neither is there an Absolute which transcends them.

> affirmative God, God is truly a God of love (for
> through complete self-abnegation God is totally
> identical with everything including sinful humans)." (16)

Of course Masao Abe would not grant that this is a third lemma formation. No doubt he would argue that his definition of the Christian God, and his definition of (centric) *śūnyatā*, escape even the fourth lemma. My point, however, is that we are dealing in philosophical/theological *discourse* here, and in logical and rhetorical terms Abe's statement above conforms to the third lemma. Surely it is our obligation in philosophical/theological *discourse* to show as best we can 'the way happenings go on'; we should not build unnecessary distractions, obstacles. Appeals to notions of Unity, the Absolute, Nothingness, the Ultimate, the Center, the Circumference, etc., or the negation of these or the synthesis of these, may function for some, but for postmodernists these notions—*posed simply as they are*[5]—bespeak undeconstructed theologies/philosophies.

In that Derrida deconstructs logocentric paradoxes, but sometimes seems to deploy the term favorably, definition(s) of sorts of paradox(es) is/are in order here. There are at least three kinds of paradox, and the first two are logocentric. (1) The first we may name 'the (mere) rhetorical paradox', in that its apparent contradiction can be 'solved' by logical analysis. Example: "A dungeon does not a prison make" can logically become 'A physical prison does not make (necessarily) a spiritual prison'. (2) The second we may call the '(logocentric) mystical paradox'. Example: 'Good = Non-Good', as Naptha is sometimes taken to claim in Thomas Mann's *Der Zauberberg*. Here we take the third lemma in the *distributed* sense, as an absolute identity: 'X (totally and absolutely) both totally is and totally is-not'. This paradox, for a Derridean, is logocentric because it closes into a unity or whole (a non-rational identity, in this case). The form of Masao Abe's thesis belongs to the third lemma, surely: 'God/*śūnyatā* is not God/*śūnyatā*, and therefore is God/*śūnyatā*'. (3) The third paradox we may call the 'paradox of the double-bind', though strictly speaking a double-bind is not a paradox. By 'double-bind', Derrida usually means either a Catch-22 situation ('A necessarily thwarts B and B necessarily thwarts A') or (what I call) a Möbius-strip situation ('the

---

[5] That is, posed before the deconstructive gesture which unconceals them as both deconstituting *and* constituting (compare Nagarjuna's 'two truths').

necessary must perforce drive that which thwarts it').[6] For Derrida, a 'classic' case of the latter is 'intention'. Intention is always already involved in language, and language by a very law of its production (viz., the law of repetition) must necessarily thwart intention.

Double-binds as we find them in Derrida are not logocentric. Why so? The clue is in the word 'thwart', from M.E., *thwert*, 'across, athwart, perverse'. In the case of the Catch-22, for example, A and B thwart each other; they do not annul each other: that is, each necessarily causes the other to *veer from* its objective. For each, a negative interval or differential opens up between target and result. In the case of the Möbius-strip situation, a negative overlap or differential occurs— erratically sliding and 'imprévu'—between the necessary and that which it necessarily drives. Logocentrism, remember, is any concept or even 'experience' taken as 'closed', so that its parts adequate (adequate) to it and/or to each other. Logocentrism bespeaks a frame-concept or frame-experience, and its dialectical transformations (thus, even 'no frame' is a frame).[7] But in the case of the Catch-22, for example, what *really* happens is measured by the negative differential, i.e., by what/how much is *missed*, and what/how much is *missed* by A and B respectively is unpredictable and disproportionate in each instance. And in the case of the Möbius-strip, for example, there is always less or more of necessity, or—conversely—less or more of counter-necessity. In the 'less' or 'more' which is *left out*, happenings really 'go on'. According to the what/how of *lack*, different sorts of double-binds differ. What Derrida sometimes calls *trace* becomes in these terms 'that which does *not* fit', 'that which does *not* match', 'that which is left-out', but which—by virtue of this lack—generates what 'goes on'. Throughout my own work, I argue that Derridean going-on can make an effective *prajñapti* for Buddhist *pratītya-samutpāda*. Already there are, perhaps, deconstructionists who begin to know that in the negative overlap, devoid happenings go-on. So,—

---

[6] What I here call Derridean 'double-binds' are in my own nomenclature in Part One called 'binds' (see Part One). That is, for me, the Catch-22 situation and the Möbius-strip situation are sorts of 'bind'. In order to avoid needless confusion, I retain Derridean 'double-bind' throughout Part Two.

[7] I mean the word 'frame' in its logocentric sense. Derrida of course deconstructs this sense, by showing that the crypted role of 'frame' is to be *both* inside and outside, and to be *neither* inside *nor* outside. See "Parergon" section in Derrida, *La Vérité en peinture* (Paris: Flammarion, 1978).

Centrists, differentialists—Even in differing, let us all each to
each defer, and not contemn. There are those on the way to becoming
Tathagathas (*tathāgatha*: 'thus come/gone').

> "Ça vient de partir.
> Ça revient de partir.
> Ça vient de repartir."
> 　　　　　　—Derrida, *La Vérité en peinture* [8]

"Where the accomplished *Buddhas*
do not appear and the *Śrāvakas*
cease to be, the enlightened
mind of the *Pratyekabuddhas*
comes forth on its own [*jñānaṃ-
pratyekabuddhānāmasaṃsargātpravartate*]."

　　　　　　—(MK 18:12)[9]

---

[8] P. 436.

[9] Inada's translation, modified. The *Mūlamādhyamakakārikās* accompanied by
Romanized Sanskrit text can be found in K. K. Inada, *Nāgārjuna: A Translation
of his Mūlamādhyamakakārikās with an Introductory Essay* (Tokyo: Hokuseido,
1970).

(iv)

## Differentialism and Trinitarian Theology

I have argued for some time already that a Christian deconstruction of logocentric Scripture will find a differential Scripture in the very same (not self-same) Sacred Pages. And that differential readings of logocentric theology can release differential theologies, even 'orthodox' Christian theologies. This section (Lt. *sect-*, cut) stakes such a *program/diagram* by crosshatching some Conciliar definitions of the Most Holy Trinity— Father, Son, and Spirit. Two strokes shall be required of us. First stroke: a 'découpage' from Derrida on Sollers[1] (for 'pure negative reference', II). Cross-stroke: a 'découpage' from Conciliar theology (for 'pure negative reference', I). At the end, the theology of the Blessed Trinity is found to hatch a 'glitch', a Divine Glitch:—This Glitch figures as a Clue to how God and the world go-on.

The first stroke is across pure negative reference, and it deconstructs the Latin *est*, and this *est*'s 'duplications',— copula, the = sign, the self-same (self = same), and many others, and it deconstructs the French *est/Est* ('east/East') too, and many others:

> "On ne peut donc pas se reposer dans la copule.[2] L'accouple-
> ment est le miroir. Le miroir se traverse *de lui-même,*
> autrement dit ne se traverse jamais. La traversée ne sur-
> vient pas accidentellement au miroir—à l'Occident—elle
> est inscrite en sa structure. Autant dire que se produisant
> toujours, elle n'arrive jamais. Comme l'horizon." [392-3;353]
> —*La Dissémination*[3]

For analytic purposes, rather than the published English translation, I supply my more literal translation:

> "One cannot, then, repose in the copula. Coupling is the
> mirror. The mirror is traversed *of/with/by itself* [se

---

[1] See Part II of the title essay of Derrida's *La dissémination*.
[2] Sexual coupling too. Throughout Derrida, there are potential analogies to be drawn to Tibetan Vajrayana in this regard.
[3] Pagination is supplied in brackets, the French before the semicolon, the published English translation after it.

traverse *de lui-même*], which is to say that it is never
traversed. The being-traversed does not come upon [ne sur-
vient pas...à: happen to] the mirror accidentally—in the
West—it [the being-traversed] is inscribed in its
structure. As much as to say, forever producing itself, it
never comes to be (n'arrive jamais: never arrives]. Like
the horizon."

From Derrida's deck I shall here take only one cut, the argument—
like Nagarjuna's—which unconceals dilemma, and then opts for a
debris-thesis X'd over. The formula of copula, A = B, is a fundament of
much western thinking. But literally ('au pied de la lettre'), it is
nonsensical. First horn of the dilemma: The = sign is traversed with
no gain, "The mirror is traversed *of/with/by itself*," of its own accord.
This is to say, if A = B, the A = B actually asserts A = A, a
redundancy. Second horn of the dilemma: But a redundancy is to say
the mirror really "is never traversed." If A = B, this is really to assert
"only A." Two horns of a dilemma, both really asserting no more than
that "A *is not* B," A is *purely* not B. Pure negative reference. As for the
third lemma, A both is and is not B, if posed in the undistributed
sense,[4] it is here reducible to the first two lemmas (the same as in
Nagarjuna's *Mūla-*); and if posed in the distributed sense, it is
considered irrational (the same as in Nagarjuna's *Mūla-*).[5]

In the same chapter, when "dealing" with the 'ontological' *est*,
Derrida reiterates the strategy deployed against the logico-
mathematical *est* (the = sign). "The 'is', which is 'Being' as an
indication of presence, procures this [false] state of calm, this
consciousness of ideal mastery......the column [of numbers, of print,
of architecture, of the Bible's 'column of Fire', etc.] *is* this or that, *is
there*; whether it is obvious or hidden behind the multiplicity of
apparitions, the column *is*. But the column *has* no Being, nor any
being-there, whether here or elsewhere" [391;352]. As much as to say,
the *est* is never really traversed, A *is not* B, is never B. "The column *is
not*, it is nothing but the passage of dissemination." The column is

---

[4] Please permit me to review the distinction:—In what is technically called the
undistributed sense of the third lemma, 'Both A and not-A' means 'partly A and
partly not-A', so that these two parts come together into a mathematical unity. In
the distributed sense, 'Both A and not-A' means 'both *totally* A and *totally* not-A',
so that A and not-A come together into a paradoxical unity.
[5] See *Derrida on the Mend*, pp. 108-09.

hollow, empty, "as transparent as the burning air in which the text carves out its path" [391;351]. The column is an abyssmal square, an open cube with no top to cap it or bottom to hold it unless one *fantasizes* it either flat or a closed cube (whose closing surface can only be 'constructed' imaginatively, i.e., by mathematically 'cubing' the length of the side). The fantasized surface is logocentrism, the "mirror" which is the logical coupling we saw earlier (note that Derrida emphasizes, again, the double-cross of ontology and numbers). Our 'découpage' continues:

> "Et pourtant l'«*e s t*»[8] qui a toujours voulu dire l'au-delà
> du narcissisme se prend dans le miroir. Lu dans l'écart,
> il n'arrive jamais. En tant qu'il est tourné vers
> l'«*e s t*», l'être se tient désormais sous cette rature comme
> quadrature. Il ne s'écrit que sous la grille des quatre
> fourches." [ibid, 393]

Here is my literal translation:

> "And yet the '*est*' ['it is'; the East] which has always meant
>   [voulu dire: Fr. locution from lit. '*wanted* to say']
> what is beyond narcissism is caught in the mirror. Read
> in the fault/gap [écart: difference, deviation, digression,
> mistake, swerve, the 'discard' in cardgame, deviation,
> 'quarter' of a heraldric shield], it never arrives.
> Insofar as it is turned towards the '*est*' [the East; 'it
> is'], being confines itself [se tient: is held, sticks fast,
> contents itself ] henceforth under this erasure [rature] like
> quadrature [quad*rature*: geom./astron. term—configuring of
> a square]. It is written only under the grid/grill/grille
> [grille: grid, grill, cloistered nuns' grille] of the four
> forks."                [bracketed italicization mine]

It should be clear enough that the *grille*, above, or *carrefour* ('crossroads') is not just nullification. In that ongoing doubling/

---

[8] The *st* in French *est*, when *est* means the third person indicative of the verb 'to be', is not pronounced, allowing Derrida several highly instructive puns such as *écart* [*est cart(e)*, *est quart*], etc. And *est* is a French adverb meaning 'east' and noun meaning 'east' or 'East' (with these geographical meanings, the *st* is pronounced).

doubled style so reminiscent of Ch'anist Buddhism's differential *kung-an*, Derrida has at least designed this passage to reveal/conceal that (1) a logocentric X nullifies and establishes, (2) a differential X (pure negative reference, here) negates and constitutes, and that (3) the logocentric and differential X's cut athwart each other, tangling each other up. In holistic terms a 'tangle' is of course read as a most unwelcome snag, a 'glitch'. But one of Derrida's most important contributions to 20th century thought is his showing wherein lies the real fecundity of logic (and here it is worthwhile recalling Derrida's steady commitment to the French rationalist tradition):—logic is at its best when, defense-mechanisms and pseudo-logical sleights of hand swept aside,[7] the thinker confronts logic-under-erasure, i.e., logic self-deconstructing (*not* self-destructing, mind you), and leaving the inevitable trace. A trace which is here a logically inescapable snag or 'glitch'. And what is more/less, this trace is a *clue*: it is on-the-move.

Perforce, I limit myself to one zigzag through this 'passage', to show that the X is 'under erasure' but *conductal*. The traditional 'it is', thinking to escape the narcissism (cause and effect, signified and signifier, etc.), is caught precisely in the mirror of narcissism (the copula). Read in the empty square, it never traverses (i.e., it is in the condition of pure negative reference). Being, insofar as it is turned towards *logocentrism*, is unknowingly erased by its own logical assumptions, its own quadrature, the squaring which carries within itself its own undoing (logic undoing itself). Derrida is ALSO saying that Being, when turned towards the *East* (the Orient, off the east side of the page, etc.) is erased, quartered-up, put under the sign-of-quadrature, the sign of crossroads, the X. Given his celebration—via Sollers and otherwise—of the deconstructive traits of Chinese philosophy (they come from "the *other side* of the mirror,"[8] etc.), Derrida is here marking the not naive—let us say the X-wise—cutting-up of being, this quartering, as ORIENTAL.[9]

So being is also written under the Oriental *grille*, the *grille* of difference, the grille of *is-not*. (But note, even in negating traditional logic, logic must at once erase even this gesture—pure negative

---

[7] At least as much as possible.

[8] *Dissemination*, p. 356.

[9] But conversely, Derrida is also here satirizing anti-Oriental stereotypes, much as Edward Said does. And, obverse to this, he throughout this section deconstructs the *logocentric* tradition in the Orient (for as we have noted, of course the Orient has its 'centrisms', its logocentrisms, too).

reference comes 'under the X' too.) Notwithstanding, the Eastern *grille* purports a sort of LIBERATION from naiveté. [The good-humored off/allusions to food—the Messianic Banquet-Celebration to take place in the (Near-) East, etc., reinforce this note, though the Banquet is *not* treated as an attainable End.] Situational in its operation and plying the 'necessary but impossible' moment, the *est* which "ne s'écrit que sous la grille des quatre fourches" is here a Derridean *prajñapti* (in this Sanskrit term's second sense, 'conductual clue'). Derrida's *prajñapti* is a double-bind, so much so that even 'perversion' and mimicry, twisting in and up and over, subvert the ideal of an absolutely-defined *teleological* hope (e.g., western barbecue grill, the martyr's torture-grill, Chinese *grillade*, and the Eucharistic banquet-sacrifice—these diverse senses here 'level-out' by way of 'mix-up').

The *prajñapti* is a double-bind: the DOUBLE-BIND is the *prajñapti*. It is 'conductal' to a sort of wisdom, and in Derrida not to a fulfillment (*full*-fill-ment) of a logocentric end, be that parousia or void. In the text entitled *La Dissémination*, there is repeated rejection of "the final parousia of a meaning at last deciphered, revealed...," deconstruction of "a truth past or a truth to come, to a meaning whose presence is announced by enigma" [389;350]. Instead, happenings issue as "altogether other" to each other yet as ongoing reinscriptions of "the same" ("Tout autre. La même") [407;366]. Always situational, the Derridean 'return of the same'—his version of Nagarjuna's 'two truths' (*'samvrti* is *paramārtha'*[10]) is well-exemplified in the chapter we have been treating. What Derrida situationally calls the "horizon-value" [390;351], that "pure infinite opening for the presentation of the present and the experience of meaning, here all at once it is framed [la voici tout à coup encadrée—the 'phenomenological moment', cf. *samvrti*]. All at once it is a part [Et voici qu'elle fait partie]. And all at once apart [La voici partie—'the devoid moment'—cf. *paramārtha*]. Thrown back into play [Elle est remise en jeu]."

Remark the "...expérience du sens, la voici encadrée tout à coup. Et voici qu'elle fait partie. La voici partie. Elle est remise en jeu." The "pure infinite [infinie: unfinished, unending, etc.] opening" and its

---

[10] Recall again that *samvrti* is the 'concealing truth', the mundane; that *paramārtha* is the 'supreme truth'; and that Nagarjuna's unexpected and revolutionary move is to indicate the 'limits, realm' of *samvrti* 'are' the 'limits, realm' of *paramārtha*.

perpetual framing and deframing are *on-the-move* ('on-the-move' without 'traversing'). "As soon as a sign emerges, it begins by repeating itself. Without this, it would not be a sign, would not be what it is, ... the non-self-identity which regularly refers to the same. That is to say, to another sign, which itself will be born of having been divided."[11] Presence must "come to terms with [pure negative] relation... ." It eventuates that this problematic "prevents there being *in fact* any difference between grammar and ontology."[12] When Derrida asserts that the ongoing alterity of happenings is "textual," is Writing, his strategy is to deconstruct the traditional notion that happenings are *logoi*, i.e., unities of meaning (analogically 'like' spoken words). Since for Derrida happenings are double-binds which move forward by the pure lack (the *is-not*) which is *negative overlap*,[13] happenings— including of course spoken words—are better understood *not* by a description of language-as-experienced[14] but by an analysis of how written signs really work-off/work. Otherwise put, spoken language better masquerades as self-identical, though such language too is necessarily in the double-bind: all talk is double-talk, and double-talk is double-bind (which is not at all to say, mark you, that all talk is outrightly untrue). Derrida would say that all speaking and writing and thinking and doing are all Writing.

"The form of the chiasmus, the X," interests him, he says, "not as the symbol of the unknown but because there is here a sort of fork [the series *crossroads, quadrifurcum*, grid, grill, key, etc.] which is more-over unequal, one of its points extending its scope further than the other."[15] Further than the other so chiasmus can have a tilt to it, a tilt which necessarily engineers mobility, but a mobility which is somehow *neither* random *nor* purposeful. Both writing and Writing are as artificial as they are conventional, as much a question of free-play as of author's intention, of spatiality as temporality, etc., and such-wise that these moments criss-cross and undo each other, but always—

---

[11] Derrida, *Writing and Difference*, p. 297.

[12] *Dissemination*, p. 166.

[13] See *Dissemination*, p. 304.

[14] In other words, not by *phenomenology*.

[15] Derrida seems to have in mind the calligraphic form of the Greek *chi*, wherein the left-to-right downstroke is normally longer than the right-to-left second stroke. For this quotation (itself a citation from Derrida's *Positions*), see Derrida, *The Truth in Painting*, p. 166. Recall, from my section iii, that Derridean double-bind is necessarily *not* congruent with itself, and therefore *not* logocentric. Constitution is by way of the *negative differential*.

please note—*unequally*. Disproportionately. Thus the *overlap*. And always necessarily by pure *is not*. Thus the *negative* overlap.

In reprise, we can say that writing is a *prajñapti* for Writing, and Writing in Derrida means the ongoing alterity of happenings.[16] It falls to me to rewrite once more the foregoing with a *further*more, the more and no more that Derrida's Writing is a *prajñapti* for Nagarjuna's *pratītya samutpāda*, 'dependent co-arising'. Like the dependent co-arising in the *Mūlamādhyamakakārikās*, remember that Derridean Writing is dependence-only, and thus is never a totality, never a whole (Derrida: "The supplement is always unfolding, but it can never attain the status of a complement [and thus consummate the unity]. The field is never saturated"[17]). Like dependent co-arising, which is *marked, discontinuous* (each 'moment' unique, purely different) yet the 'same' (pure negative relation as constitutive: constitutive of the 'sameness without self-identity'), Derrida's Writing is purely different yet the 'same'.

Mark what Derrida says about the series of marks, what he calls in one situation a series of *traces*, and in another the *tr-* (as in "travail in train, trait, traject, in-trigue," but it could be just as well a *gl-* or an *fr-* or an x[18]: how to act-out, how to *signature*, that which is off-namable, i.e., that which is not a unity?). Derrida says, in a 'reinscribed' figure, 'forever recurring' in his treatment of Adami,[19] that the marks on march, the traces, the *tr-*, whose "so-called whole words are different each time in form and content," the *tr-* which is "not a self-identity, [not] a proper meaning or body,"[20] *are* at once "the *same* mutation."[21] That which "only holds together ... by having nothing to do with"[22] is like "double scale [= *échelle*], double measure, and yet the *same, one* ladder [also = *échelle* in French]."[23] "Thus works, in or outside language, a *tr-*."[24] (Even the theologian David *Tracy*

---

[16] See Derrida, *D'Un ton apocalyptique adopté naguère en philosophie* (Paris: Galilée, 1983), p. 85; and his "Living on: *Border Lines*," pp. 96, 97; *Writing and Difference*, p. 296; and *Dissemination*, pp. 351, 366.

[17] Derrida, "White Mythology," p. 18.

[18] See (or better, palpate) *Truth in Painting*, p. 169.

[19] *Truth in Painting*, pp. 149-182.

[20] Nor a question of a "semantic nucleus" such as *trans-* or *tra-*, of course. Read *Truth in Painting*, p. 171.

[21] *Truth in Painting*, p. 181, my emphasis.

[22] *Truth in Painting*, p. 174.

[23] *Truth in Painting*, p. 166, my emphasis.

[24] *Truth in Painting*, p. 173.

carries the *trace* of it, one might say.) Which I *t*ranscribe, 'THUS works, in or outside writing/speaking, a Writing'. Dependently co-arising. Holding together by having "nothing to do with."

Next comes the cross-stroke, which marks how Christianity's Blessed Trinity is *not* holistic, but goes-on quite *otherwise*. The writing of this 'otherwise' is right here/there in the Christian tradition, though it may take the Oriental 'other' to teach Christians to find it. Christians too often like to self-stroke instead of cross-stroke: they too often inspect other religions just to find what bolsters their own (false) sense of safety. If Christians 'dialogue' with Masao Abe's proposal that 'God' is a Dynamic Nothingness originating identity-and-difference by way of pure *kenōsis*, they are—perhaps unconsciously—targeting in (centric) Buddhism that with which they are *already most comfortable* (so as to make of it 'more of the same'). For, despite the complex doctrinal differences which may render even Abe's thesis 'unorthodox' (in historical Western terms), Christianity has been familiar with its paradoxical model and its rhetoric for a long time.

That God is better served by the formula of 'A is not-A' appears (for example) in one form or another in the work of the Dionysian tradition from Pseudo-Dionysius down through Eckhart, Tauler, Suso, Ruysbroeck, and Boehme. In the final analysis, a Dynamic Nothingness as Abe presents it is still holistic, paradoxically transcendent and immanent, infinite yet within-a-frame. In the final analysis, then, still *safe and comfortable* for traditional Western discourse about God. What I have long contended is that Christianity must learn (and 'test', as St. Paul says[25]) that which is 'uncomfortable'. For example, that 'God'—as Raimundo Panikkar and Karl Rahner remind us[26]—is impersonal as well as personal. Indeed, that 'God' is sometimes frighteningly *impersonal* and that this *impersonality* double-binds into Divine *personality* in erratic, ever-altering ways that *do not* close into logocentric unity. (Which, by the way, is not at all too say that God is not a *loving* God.) That such a God is not encompassed, is not *captured* by either the formula or experience of a

---

[25] 1 Thes. 5:21.
[26] See R. Panikkar, *The Trinity and the Religious Experience of Man* (N.Y.: Orbis, 1973), pp. 50, 64, 68-9; also, pp. 19, 38-9, 52-5. For the Rahnerian school's claim that humanity is united to God precisely because of God's difference from human 'personality' (a 'difference' enabled by the Divine difference within God), see Elmar Klinger, in Karl Rahner, ed., with C. Ernst and K. Smith, *Sacramentum Mundi*, Vol. 4 (Herder and Herder, 1968), p. 95.

'unifying source' *is* unsettling, *is* frightening for most Christians. All the more reason why it is differential Madhyamika Buddhism which can most serviceably witness to Christians in dialogue, as should happen, for example, when a Christian meets the rNying-ma-pa's (Tibetan) Madhyamika critique of the 'mentalist' (Tibetan) Yogacara:

> "The difference between the mentalistic and Madhyamika systems is that the former locates this mistakenness in not recognizing a purely luminous (*gsal*) and cognitive (*rig*) noetic capacity (*shes-pa*) which is beyond the subject-object dichotomy (*gzung, 'dzin*), as the source of experience; while the latter reject even this noetic capacity as as much a postulate as that of a corresponding external object."[27]

No undeconstructed 'source' for these Madhyamikans. Surely we should not expect that Christianity's deconstruction of holism *imitate* Buddhist deconstruction. Indeed, 'pure negative reference', a key thought-motif of this very section, means that the two religions erect their 'samenesses' by way of their very differences. What I have found, rather, is that pure negative reference has been 'crypted' into Christian theology for a long time, perhaps from the beginning. Crypted into Christian theology in ways purely differing from the Buddhist ones. For me the topic of Buddhist-Christian dialogue becomes, then, an intersection of Buddhist devoidness and Christian devoidness, two intersecting lines that necessarily have no 'common ground'.

The cipher to/of 'pure negative reference' is secreted in a place some would deem most unlikely (especially since its results prove to be 'postmodern'), namely, Christian Conciliar theology. Designed for other *ad hoc* reasons, the cipher has never really been decoded in terms of devoidness. And because of its traditional provenance, nowadays it is largely ignored (the word Gk. *kruptos*, 'hidden', makes not only the word 'crypto[gram]' in English, but also 'crypt', after all). But let us all agree, at least provisionally, to try useful ideas when/where we can, whether we believe they come by serendipity or whatever. For prejudice is a most craven craving.

---

[27] Kennard Lipman, "Introduction" to Klong-chen-pa, trans. K. Lipmann, *Yid-bzhin rin-po-che'i mdzod*, in *Crystal Mirror*, Vol. V (1977), pp. 345-6.

It was the Council of Florence (1438-9 C.E.) that affirmed "everything is one" in God, "except where an opposition of relationship [*relationis oppositio*] exists,"[28] so that each of the three Persons *as* a Person is constituted (i.e., defined, established) *only* by oppositional relations among the Persons. Most theologians have always taken *relationis oppositio* in the Thomist sense (though this is by no means strictly necessary for the case I am making), namely—the 'opposition of relation' is *contrariety* rather than *contradiction.*[29] (The relation between black and white, for example, is an opposition of contrariety, whereas the relation between black and non-black is an opposition of contradiction.) The only 'functions' that are applied *uniquely* to the Father, Son, and Holy Spirit *respectively* in Scripture are the following: 'Paternity' to the Father, 'Filiation' (Sonship) to the Son, and 'Passive Spiration' (That which is 'breathed-out') to the Holy Spirit.

That such is the case becomes one of the reasons, apparently, why Karl Rahner rejects the 'psychological' theory of Trinity associated (among his contemporaries) with Bernard Lonergan. Conciliar theologians who define the Father as the Knower, for example, and the Son as the Known (i.e., 'Truth'), seem to ignore that Scripture in one place or another identifies Knowing with (in this case) each of the three Persons all told. Which is to say, according to the *relationis oppositio* clause, that Knowing (in our example) does not define the Persons at all, but the Unity of God *instead.* (Scripture's attribution of Knowing, then, to any one Person at any one time is said to be just 'appropriated' to the Person: it does not *really* belong to that unique Person.)

If one considers this operation carefully, it is mind- bending in a very wonderful and 'postmodern' way. *All* that the Persons would share is sacrificed, is preempted, is always already 'gutted out' of them, so that it belongs to the Unity. This 'syncopation' in the midst of God is *kenōsis*, certainly, but—since the Personal contrarieties 'remain'—it is 'devoid' *kenōsis* (and not the 'void' *kenōsis* of Abe's model). Furthermore, we should speak of *kenōses* (plural) rather than

---

[28] Karl Rahner's adroit translation, in Rahner, "Divine Trinity," *Sacramentum Mundi*, Vol. 6, ed. Karl Rahner, with C. Ernst and K. Smith (N.Y.: Herder and Herder, 1968), p. 298.

[29] See Edmund Fortman, *The Triune God: A Historical Study of the Doctrine of the Trinity* (London and Philadelphia: Hutchinson/Westminster, 1972), pp. 222-23. In this matter, for a more finessed treatment of contrariety and contradictory than I supply here, see *Derrida on the Mend*, pp. 146-7.

*kenōsis*, since the 'opposition of relation' between Paternity and Filiation, say, is not the same as that between Active Spiration and Passive Spiration, and thus what is preempted out of them is not the same. (As for the special problematic of Spiration, we shall address it in a moment.) Finally, apropos of the Personal contraries, there is at least one other point to be noted here. Namely, while it is the case the *kenōses* are devoid, Persons relate in terms of *pure negative reference*. Somehow the Father (for example) *is purely not* the Son (recall that what they 'would' share has instead gone over to the Unity).

In the model of the Triune God Masao Abe proposes for Christians, the "oneness of the one God must possess the characteristic of zero" (absolute *kenōsis*: here in fact Abe uses the traditional German term *Ungrund*) in order that "Trinity be fully and dynamically realized... three distinctive beings—Father, Son, and Spirit—are then clearly and thoroughly realized in their distinctiveness... ."[30] The originating unity of God is absolute emptying-out (*Ungrund*, or '-A'), and thus paradoxically concretizes the three Persons (Persons, or '+A'). The model of the Triune God proposed by Conciliar theology stands in sharp contrast. Its *relationis oppositio* clause limns a Trinity that works converse to Abe's model, in that the three Persons raise the 'sameness' of the Unity by way of *their* emptyings-out; and crosswise to Abe's model in that the 'lateral' contraries (of the Persons) constitute the Unity *indirectly*, that is, by default, and the contrary relations are themselves 'pure negative references'. The *kenōses* raising the Divine Unity are devoid, and the Unity and the Three Persons are *not* interchangeable. Masao Abe's model, on the other hand, is strictly holistic: it postulates an absolute and direct *kenōsis*, and the interchangeability of Unity and Trinity (-A = +A). This is a paradoxical formulation, and—as Richard H. Robinson well pointed out in his groundbreaking *Early Madhyamika in India and China*[31]—paradox is nowhere found in Nagarjuna's *Mūlamādhya-makakārikās* itself. Derrida has demonstrated how paradox 'properly' speaking is a logocentrism.[32] Nor does it suffice, according to a radical

---

[30] Abe, p. 24.
[31] Madison: U of Wisconsin, 1967, p. 57. Nor in this matter does the *Mūlamādhya-makakārikās* choose the way of synthesis.
[32] Derrida's analysis of paradox and other higher-order holisms (as distinguished from straightforward monism, say), belongs for the most part to his early phase. See, for example, "The Double Session" in his *Dissemination*, and "Differance" in his *Speech and Phenomena*, pp. 134-5, 148-9.

point of view, to synthesize *śūnyatā* and image/concept (as some Buddhist schools do), so that 'empty image/concept' issues forth as the 'solution' (and the 'escape' from the fallacy of paradox). Such a solution, according to a radically deconstructive point of view, is simply too facile and neat:—it is a sleight-of-hand actually functioning to restore holism. Somehow, instead, the operation of images/concepts must be fractured, twisted, unsettled.

As promised, I now turn to the problematic of the Holy Spirit and its 'procession' (*Processio*) from the Father and/through[33] the Son. The Holy Spirit is said to proceed from the Father/Son "*as from one principle.*"[34] Given that even in (what is called) the Eastern Church's formula (i.e., "through the Son") it is not a question of the Father *transferring* Himself or a part of Himself to or through the Son (this would vitiate the *relationis oppositio* clause), the question opens up,— How does the 'one principle' work? I have argued elsewhere that the Derridean deconstruction of Signifier-Signified dyads can supply us with a clue in this regard.[35] The relevant citation from Derrida is the following:

> "In this play of representation, the point of origin becomes ungraspable. There are things like reflecting pools, and images, an infinite reference from one to the other, but no longer a source/spring [*source*]. There is no longer simple origin. For what is reflected is split *in itself* and not only as an addition to itself of its image. The reflection, the image, the double, splits what it doubles [*le double dédouble ce qu'il redouble*]... and the law of addition of the origin to its representation, of the thing to its image, is that one plus one make at least three."[36]

The representation, or Signifier, boomerangs back as *different* from the Signified, and therefore as *its* cause (while the Signified *also* remains as cause), so the model of simple dyad breaks down. Or, to

---

[33] At the Council of Florence, both the formula of the Western Church ("from the Father and the Son") and the Eastern Church ("from the Father through the Son") are confirmed.

[34] Second Council of Lyons (1271-6 C.E.).

[35] See *Derrida on the Mend*, pp. 134-44; also, 9-20.

[36] Derrida, trans. G. Spivak, *Of Grammatology* (Baltimore: Johns Hopkins, 1976), p. 36. French edition, *De la Grammatologie* (Paris: Minuit, 1967), pp. 54-5.

conceive of this action from the other end, as Derrida did for us earlier in this section, the Signified is "caught in the mirror" and "never arrives." Instead, it is split there in the mirror.

Either way, the "addition" of the Third requires the interaction of what we called the 'initial' Signified and Signifier; and requires that the interaction involve infringement. I use the word 'initial' advisedly, because what we are doing is, after all, a *deconstruction*. That is to say, we are learning/showing 'sequentially' where the traditional logic of Signification *really* must lead, if one doesn't flinch and fudge. I use the word 'infringement' advisedly, because the Signifier usurps the causality of the Signified. What we learn from the deconstruction is that the Signified-Signifier dyad is *'always already'* three, and that the Third of these three proceeds perpetually from a transgressive yet singular interaction of the other two. And we learn finally that this 'alternative solution', the workings of the two that are three, must also necessarily come *sous rature*, "under the grid of the *four* forks."

I argue that this Signified-Signifier dyad Which-is-always-already-Three operates as the best clue (towards understanding the *Processio*) that 20th century philosophy has hatched. The Derridean account would indicate how the Father and Son infringe each other and still 'as one principle' spirate the Holy Spirit. As we have just seen, Derrida's Signified and Signifier so split as to make a Third, and a split is of course disruption. 'Disruption' in the sense that the Signifier does not at all close around into the Signified (does not do so even though this 'circle' is conventionally expected, indeed, *most* expected). In short, the Signifier does not somehow *mediate* the Signified. And in Conciliar theology it turns out that a like 'disruption' is necessarily in effect.

The theology strictly distinguishes between the 'one principle' that spirates the Holy Spirit and the Father's *Generatio* that begets the Son. The *Generatio* is unilateral (the Son cannot beget the Father in turn) but the 'aspiration from one principle' involves the Father and Son in a kind of mutual *transgression*,[37] in a kind of *disruption*. Which is to say, in short, that there is no *mediation* between them. The Holy Spirit proceeds "from the Father and *at once* from the Son, and *from*

---

[37] In the literal sense, i.e., the Father and Son 'cross' each other's (logocentrically expected) 'defining borders'. By 'infringement', 'transgression', 'disruption', etc., I do not imply hostile action, but rather—working with the literal Latin etymology as I am—I mean a breaking across logocentric definitions.

*both* eternally as from one principle" ("...... ex Patre *simul et* Filio, et *ex utroque* aeternaliter tamquam ab uno principio"). Even in what is called the Eastern formula, "ex Patre per Filium," "from the Father through the Son," any 'mediation' as such is excluded: "the Son, also, is according to the Greeks indeed the cause, according to the Latins indeed the principle" of the Procession, "and the Father is too" ("Filius quoque esse secundum Graecos quidem causam, secundum Latinos vero principium... sicut et Patrem"). All the while remaining 'one cause/principle', the Son is considered the cause/principle and the Father is considered the cause/principle.

Next, there is a wonderfully Divine *'glitch'* in the Conciliar theology of the Triune God. Given that the 'one principle' of Father and/with Son is in 'oppositional relation' to the Holy Spirit it establishes, the 'one principle' would appear to be a *fourth* Person. But a fourth Person is deemed Biblically impossible. Thus theology has long insisted that this Active Spiration (of Father and/with Son) which 'breathes out' the Holy Spirit (Who is the Passive Spiration) is *virtual*, not real.[38] ('Virtual' is taken to mean 'of only functional validity'.) But the Councils have long said the Passive Spiration, on its side, is *real*. Otherwise, the Holy Spirit would not be real, and thus not a Person. The equivocating status of the Active Spiration has long exercised the problem-solving temper of speculative theologians. I think, however, that the equivocating status works more like a Derridean double-bind,[39] and is very fruitful when taken as such. Written "under the grid of the four forks," it becomes Divine trace, and conductal towards the *mystērion* of the Triune God.

The Active Spiration as Double-Bind. To wit:—(1) The Active Spiration *overlaps* with the definition of a Divine Person because it is in oppositional relation (*relationis oppositio*) to the Third Person, the Holy Spirit, and thus would be a Person too, but (First Bind) this is *negative overlap* because the Active Spiration is virtual, not real, and thus *not* a Person. (2) The Active Spiration *overlaps* with the definition of the Divine Unity because 'as one principle' the Father and/with the Son are transgressive of each other but are not oppositional to each

---

[38] See Karl Rahner, *The Trinity*, trans. J. Donceel (N.Y.: Seabury, 1974), pp. 77-8, and Edmund J. Fortman, *The Triune God: A Historical Study of the Doctrine of the Trinity* (London and Philadelphia: Hutchinson/Westminster, 1972), pp. 293-4.

[39] That Derridean double-binds are not paradoxical should be clear: the binds are not congruent with each other, nor do they somehow compose a whole. See Derrida's commentary/demonstration in *The Truth in Painting*, p. 162.

other, and "everything is one in God except where *relationis oppositio* exists," but (Second Bind) this is *negative overlap* because the 'one principle' *cannot* belong to the Unity: it is locked instead into a singular *oppositional* relation with the Holy Spirit, who is a real Person. (X) The Active Spiration, as *neither* Personhood *nor* Divine Unity, is thus a privileged clue to the Difference between them. That is, to the Difference 'within' the Triune God. Somehow, in negative overlaps and non-holistically does the happening of God perpetually go-on.

Karl Rahner and Raimundo Panikkar remind us that Christians still need a theology of the 'impersonal' in God. The problem is compounded when we remember that even the term 'Person' in trinitarian theology does not mean 'person' in the human sense of the word. The Greek term *hypostasis* was meant by the Council theologians to avoid twin fallacies: that the Trinity involved a 'modal variation of the Divine Unity' on the one hand, or an 'anthropomorphic personhood' on the other.[40] If we go on to distinguish between the terms 'Person' (as in the Trinity) and 'person' (as in human personhood), differential theology can assert (1) the Divine Unity is devoid and imPersonal, (2) the Trinity—because of its internal voiding oppositions—is Personal, and (3) the Triune God is 'impersonal' (except for the Son, insofar as the Son is incarnate in Jesus Christ, who in His human nature has 'personal consciousness'). What is more/less, this formulation of the Triune God undergoes dislocation by way of the Divine Glitch addressed earlier, so that God becomes—for those demanding a God of 'stable definition'—quite frightening indeed. (All the more so, still, if one recalls that this Glitch is just a paltry clue—it too comes under erasure, and, 'needless to say', the swish of God's own erasure: for God, like the Plains Indians, counts coups.)

The semantic pair 'personal-impersonal' opens up a third sense as well, wherein 'impersonal' means 'not-caring', 'not-loving', etc. The Biblical tradition reveals almighty God to be Lover of humanity and performer of Loving deeds (culminating with Love on the cross), and thereby teaches Christians that God is radically *not* 'impersonal' in the human pejorative sense. But my point here is that God is 'personal' *and* 'impersonal', and this latter, this 'more-than-personal', can easily appear to humans as non-Loving. What differential theology does is confirm what many Christian mystics (and other mystics) have attested, that God—while still imbricated into us—is

---

[40] Nor is it supposed to involve human *gender*.

nonetheless radically *otherwise* ("neither are your ways my ways," Isa.
55:8; "how inscrutable his ways," Rom. 11:33).

No doubt the reports of mystics belonging to the 'centric' tradition
later recast this Otherwise into familiar logocentric formulae, but others
most certainly do not.[41] For the differential mystics, the Burning Bush,
unquenchable, is all afire for sure, but all atangle at the same time. In
particular these mystics report how God has to shock them into the
divine Otherwise. Differential theology, for its part, suggests that the
'unchanging God' is the God of Same, not the Self-Same. And that God
is better served by the notion of alterity than stasis. The Same of the
Divine Unity then becomes more like an ever-roaming (MF *errant*)
Sameness, an infinite Repetition-with-a-drift. And this Divine
Unity is raised by Personal (trinitarian) *kenōses* which ever differ,
forever. Like a truly Infinite Retreat of emptyings-out. And this
Triune God would seem to loop forever from the elegant double-bind at
its (unwedged) core.

Healing becomes, then, not a question of holism but of sameness
established by difference. In Christianity, even when Christ prays "that
all may be one, as you Father in me, and I in you" (John 17:21), the
point would be that as the Father and Son purely differ and so
establish their oneness, *so* (by differing) shall "all be one." And in
Madhyamikan Buddhism too (as we saw), where the explanation of
difference differs so dramatically from the Christian explanation, the
constituted sameness works all the more by way of negative reference,
indeed—in the Madhyamikan Buddhist case—a purely negative reference without exception.

.XXXXXXXXXXXXXXXXXXXXXXXXXXXXXXXXXXXXXX

---

[41] For an example of a Christian mystic who is not centric, read Derrida on
Angelus Silesius in Derrida, "Post-Scriptum: Aporias, Ways and Voices," in H.
Coward and T. Foshay, *Derrida and Negative Theology*, 282-323.

> One group at times reacts to another
> with total negation... The proper
> unity results only from this separation.
> —Rav Kook, *Orot Hakōdesh* [42]

Intersections are lines-crossing-each-other. Lines have no 'width', so when crossing each other they cannot have ground 'in common'. Let us calmly agree upon disagreeing. The devoidnesses of Buddhism, and Christianity, and Judaism, and other religions, and the devoid consequences of Derrida's deconstructions too—while/as intersecting—are by this very fact *apart*. The 'samenesses' that these INTER-SECTIONS constitute can help to heal the world.

The Christ-like figure again, of the 'who?'['qui?'], of the X. of *L'arrêt de mort*, over whom 'it's about time we raised a cross', says the doctor who condemns him. . . . ?

Hai!—Swoosh!

—CROSS-STROKE

of the two-edged sword

. . . . . . . . . . . . . . . . . . .

---

[42] In *Rabbi Abraham Isaac Kook* [Classics of Western Spirituality Series], trans. and intro. Ben Zion Bokser (N.Y.: Paulist Press, 1978), pp. 203-4. Though this citation may sound like 18th-19th cent. German Idealism, there was too much of the mystic and Cabbalist in Rabbi Kook for that. Nor did he mean hostile separation, since he defended the 'Jewish Liberalism' of his day, and a loving cooperation with all religions.

*For*

        Christ was *transfor*med not on the Cross
                           but in the Tomb

                                     (It took B.
                                     PASCAL to remind us[43]).

                                               Selah.

"Suddenly the dead priest winked at him—an unmistakable blink of the eyelid, just like that."

The Buddha on the mantle was smiling.

---

[43] See Blaise Pascal, *Pensées*, trans. A. Denomy, in Anton Pegis, *The Wisdom of Catholicism* (London: Michael Joseph, 1950), p. 598: "The Tomb of Jesus Christ.— ...It is there, not on the Cross, that Jesus Christ assumes a new life."

# INDEX

This index may seem arcane, and for so short a book, at points too detailed. But the book is short because perhaps more than most it is contrived to be read up, down, backwards and at diagonals as well as across. And the index is designed in particular to signal/mime some of the text's disseminations,-- graphic, phonetic, phonemic, and semantic traits and the inevitable garblings of these. With or without you and me, disseminations go on, of course. Criss-crossings that are neither random nor not-random, and that can be clues to Clues. Index fingers get tired, though, so after most entries below, the page references are not exhaustive (alas there may be errors besides); and the headings themselves are more indicative than comprehensive. Some notable omissions are the 'bell/ clock' disseminations, the 'thirst' disseminations, and the 'crypt/tomb/Divine womb, crucible' and 'mixed male/female' disseminations. Plus all the ones that are in the text but that I don't know about. The index doesn't have many of what are technically called 'blind entries', but if you are at all like me you'll still find it best to feel your way. These index fingers don't point at the moon.

[Given even Buddhism can be Centric, leave it to the more centric of the Buddhist traditions to have a whole* empty page for itself... ... ... ]
... ...

*Any good Prasangikan knows this empty page is marked, though.